from
BLOOD
to
VERDICT

from BLOOD *to* VERDICT

THREE WOMEN ON TRIAL

Deborah Homsher

McBooks Press
Ithaca, New York

Permission to reprint photographs which first appeared in *The Ithaca Journal* has been received and is hereby gratefully acknowledged.

Cover photo: Cascadilla Photography
Book/cover design/production: Paperwork

Library of Congress Cataloging-in-Publication Data

Homsher, Deborah, 1952–
    From blood to verdict: three women on trial/Deborah Homsher.
        p. cm.
    Includes index
    ISBN 0-935526-20-X (paperbound): $12.95
      1. Trials (Homocide)—New York (State)—Ithaca.   2.Trials (Murder)—New York (State)—Ithaca.   3. Female offenders—New York (State)   4. Homocide investigation —New York (State)—Ithaca.
I. Title.
KF221.M8H66   1993
345.747'710252—dc20   93-9996
[347.477105252]   CIP

This book is distributed to the book trade by Atrium Publishers Group, 11270 Clayton Creek Road, P.O. Box 108, Lower Lake, CA 95457. Booksellers may write for their most recent catalog which includes all McBooks Press titles. Individuals may order this book through bookstores or directly from McBooks Press, 908 Steam Mill Road, Ithaca, NY 14850. Please include $1.50 postage and handling with mail orders. New York State residents must add 8% sales tax.

Printed in the United States of America

9 8 7 6 5 4 3 2 1

contents

acknowledgments

I WOULD LIKE to thank the New York Foundation for the Arts for the grant in nonfiction writing which enabled me to begin this project. Thanks also to my husband, Hugh Egan, for the time and patience he spent reading the manuscript, to S.K. List, editor, Diane Bruns, advisor, and Alex Skutt of McBooks Press, publisher. Thanks to Pat Kain and Kevin Murphy for their readings of the first chapter, and to Bill Kehoe, proofreader. And I would like to express my deep gratitude to every person who agreed to be interviewed. Some of the interviews were hard. Special thanks to Tom Schneider, Gordon Gabaree, Caroline Brown, Nancy Falconer, Diane and David LaBar, Judge William Barrett, Tompkins County District Attorney George Dentes, New York State Police Investigators David Harding, Don Vredenburgh and Robert Lishansky, New York State Police Major Robert Farrand, Wesley McDermott, William Sullivan, Richard Stumbar, Humphrey Germaniuk, volunteer members of the Lansing Fire Department and a number of anonymous, thoughtful jurors.

introduction

ITHACA is a small city located in Tompkins County, in the central Finger Lakes region of New York State. Drive northeast from Ithaca for about five hours, and you will find yourself among the heavily forested Adirondack Mountains. Drive southeast approximately the same distance, and you can cross over into Manhattan, a shadowed landscape of a different kind. Northwest of Ithaca is Niagara Falls. To the southwest run the arteries that move out into Ohio, Indiana, Illinois. Transports heading from central New York westward carry wine, car timing chains, road salt, grain, gravel and apples.

But Ithaca, New York, never identifies itself as an industrial or farming town. It's mainly a college town, rich in expensive backpacks and soft, crushable briefcases, Democrats and decaf coffees and articulate citizens' committees that make life hell for administrators. Strong-arm tactics are met with public disapproval in Ithaca, though one often hears residents mutter wistfully that it would be nice if the city government could settle a few questions with less community input, more dispatch: less talk, more action.

People who have heard of Ithaca usually know it as the home of Cornell University. The university's various buildings stand up among the trees and can be seen clearly from a number of vantage points because the local landscape is hilly. From the valley, the town has grown up the sides of three big hills. Cornell's Italianate clock tower and distinctive, blocky art museum dominate East Hill. The twin towers of two high-rise dormitories on the campus of Ithaca College, a private undergraduate institution, dominate South Hill. West Hill is strictly residential. Between these three hills run thin, settled valleys and a network of precipitous gorges; some of the most spectacular residences in Ithaca sit propped on the edge of this or that abyss. Traffic descending the hills, trying to reach the downtown "flats" or cross over to one of the colleges, regularly backs up at a few notorious intersections. Creek waters spilling down through the gorges empty into the central flats and pass through the reinforced ditches of downtown Ithaca before mixing with the deep water in Cayuga Lake.

This lake, which is narrow and approximately forty miles long, fills the landscape to the north of the city. It constitutes one of the two longest "fingers" of the Finger Lakes, the glacial handprint that defines the region on a map. Summer cottages clinging to its steep west shore face the hulking salt mine and gravel pits on the east shore. Children attending summer day camp at Cayuga Nature Center on the west shore join together by hooting at the old, bleak industrial buildings they see across the water.

When Ithaca's colleges are in session, its population is 29,541, but when the students leave, the number of regular residents in the city shrinks to just over 11,000. In all of Tompkins County, the total population is 94,097.

Visitors generally consider Ithaca picturesque. Parents of graduates recall the impression of compact repose and youthful industry that fulfilled their expectations of a college town. Ithaca is always hosting visitors—the fluid swell and ebb of an international student population marks the seasons. As a result, even many legal residents feel like sightseers, like visitors. They expect their neighbors to have arrived in central New York from other, distant places and they suspect that eventually many of those neighbors will move again. Ithaca's professors and their students are known to travel frequently. They've moved through a number of cities, harvesting academic degrees before arriving at Cornell or Ithaca College. The professor spends her sabbatical leaves in France, Kenya or China. Her best student comes from Thailand. She plans to meet her husband when their conferences collide in February in Utrecht. Their summers are spent in England. Her home town is Omaha.

It's common courtesy in any university town to utter a surprised exclamation when an acquaintance reveals that he or she was actually *born* there. Nobody expects to die in Ithaca.

So the Tompkins County homicides were a shock. They came from all directions and never connected. Many of them happened in 1990 or just before. The number of cases was too small to be statistically indicative. They really didn't *prove* anything. So Tompkins County residents trying to study them, arrange them or find patterns in the overlapping local news stories about violent deaths, and the subsequent criminal trials that spanned 1989 to 1991, ended up feeling haunted and uncertain.

In the fall of 1989, an Ithaca College student beat up a Cornell student and killed him (assailant convicted). Just before Christmas in 1989, all four members of a popular local family were murdered in their home (assailant killed by police; mother of murderer convicted of burglary and arson). In February, 1990, a two-year-old girl was reported missing; weeks later the mother confessed she had hidden the child's body in the woods (mother convicted). And there was the case involving a drunken kid who swerved his car off the road to hit a lady bicycling to work in the fog; she died (driver convicted). And the shooting of a wealthy local lawyer by his estranged wife, the veterinarian (wife acquitted). And there was the murder of the woman who had gone out drinking after her friend's funeral; she was found in a clearing with her shoes neatly set off to one side and her brain pan smashed by a carpenter's tool (carpenter convicted). And the strangling of the boy from Pittsfield, Massachusetts, who was found tied to a tree in the woods (this one, among all the deaths, did not result in a trial since no suspect has yet been apprehended). Then the killing of one local bookie, allegedly by another. (Surviving bookie and one accomplice convicted; second accomplice plea-bargained.)

I live in Ithaca. We moved here about seven years ago when my husband got a job as an assistant professor at Ithaca College. I began visiting the courthouse and watching criminal trials first because the topic—this eerie string of violent events—came up at a dinner party. I went also because we have children and a few of these true, encroaching stories, which told about the deaths of children, frightened me. And I went because I was tired of feeling like an onlooker, a visitor in town. My husband and I are hill dwellers; our children attend school on East Hill, we both teach college students on South Hill and we live on West Hill. If there was bedrock under Ithaca, a bed of salt or hard judgment, I wanted to come down off the hill, find it and stomp on it until the land around me quit shivering.

I was able to attend two of the trials that dominated local news in 1990; it was impossible to sit through every hour of both, since by October they were running simultaneously, like performances in a bleak circus. First was the trial of Shirley Kinge, 55, who was ultimately convicted of helping her 33-year-old son, Michael Kinge, attempt to burn down the house of the family he had murdered. Shirley Kinge was also convicted of subsequently accompanying her son to a few shopping malls where they used the victims' credit cards to purchase Christmas gifts. (Michael Kinge himself died in a police raid on February 7, 1990.) The second trial ended with the conviction of Christine Lane, 23, a single mother who had phoned police in early February 1990, to report that her toddler Aliza was missing. Trying to find the child, hundreds of citizens participated in a useless winter search. Two weeks later, under pressure from investigators, Lane confessed and led a small band of men to the spot where the body of her daughter was hidden. Lane said she had found Aliza dead in her crib and panicked, but the jury was not convinced; they convicted her of manslaughter.

In late September 1990, while Kinge's trial was going on, just before Lane's trial began, a third local woman suddenly appeared in the area newspapers. *The Ithaca Journal* reported that Debra Dennett, 37, had killed her husband, Nat Knappen, 39, a prominent Ithaca lawyer, with a shotgun blast to the head when he came at her with a knife in the bedroom of their large cliffside house. The trial of Debra Dennett would begin in late summer, 1991, and end with her acquittal on all counts.

I attended these trials as often as I could and began interviewing men and women who had been involved in the criminal investigations and the legal proceedings. It very soon became clear that I had been naïve to think the courthouse stood on bedrock and that a few weeks spent sitting on a hard courtroom pew would settle my nervous terrors. It also became clear that actual criminal trials were fascinating dramas to watch, in part because they differed so much from the sleek, dramatic contests usually represented on television and film. Our Anglo-American criminal trials are cultural rituals which have evolved, like sophisticated threshing machines, to process loads of physical evidence and self-interested, contradictory personal testimony. What interested me was this machine's habit of fragmenting the emotional testimony of witnesses and stifling passionate responses to tragedy. The attorneys' direct exams and cross-exams efficiently transformed most personal testimony to rubble, and witnesses or jurors who showed emotion were often reminded to "keep to the facts." We aim for dispassionate judgments. At the same time, this trial machinery was obviously fueled by sporting passions, the passions of two antagonistic attorneys each playing the game to win. It is much more proper in a courtroom to argue than to mourn.

It seemed to me that this whole system appeared extraordinarily civil and dignified at first glance but, from a slightly different angle, looked quarrelsome, childish and myopic. Once a trial has begun, our legal professionals rely very little on mediation or generosity. The tendency of our trials, especially those involving domestic disputes, to magnify a quarrel in order to conclude it, is odd, very possibly destructive. Most thoughtful attorneys concede the irony, then move on to insist that it is all part of the "best system in the world." But certainly we can conclude that American citizens would be ill-advised to trust this noisy legal machine to help quiet, help reduce our nation's endemic violence.

An actual criminal trial is designed to reach judgment and decide punishment by reshaping—into *words*—an irretrievable, often violent event so that it can become part of a legal, historic, documented network. It is also designed, I think, to *conclude* a tragedy. A number of legal professionals have remarked on the fact that trials are oddly forgettable. It may be that a primary objective of any trial is to dissect a tragedy into a heap of chill, pathetic scraps so that at last it can be easily discarded by citizens who would like to forget and move on.

The following chapters tell about the criminal investigations and jury trials of three women—Kinge, Lane and Dennett—who faced Tompkins County judges and juries in 1990 and 1991. Many of the men and women interviewed for this book strongly disagree with one another about whether the verdicts in each of these trials were right or wrong. Hearing their voices, we can begin to understand why the task the courts have been assigned to accomplish— the task of deciding guilt after a wrongful death has taken place— is so awful that it requires a fairly rigid, cool/hot mechanism to accomplish the work. We can also begin to contemplate how these civic rituals, these jury trials, relate to tragedy.

In part because the defendants in these three cases were women, all three trials involved physical evidence that had to be dug out of homes, out of private houses. Baby cribs and carpet remnants were displayed in the courtroom. The ironies grow painful when we begin to feel that a legal investigation necessarily invades, for a second time, private sanctuaries that have already been ravaged once. And the stories of the three female defendants were entangled with family. Children stood in the shadows behind all of these proceedings. Three of them were dead, the others silent. We are reminded by them that tragedies do not conclude with legal verdicts.

Some people quoted in the following chapters searched either for the attacker or for the victim in a particular case. Others searched for answers, comfort or decision. The crossed trails these people followed, the uncertain territories they explored, do not lead directly to reassuring bedrock. They tell us much more about flux, about wishes and nightmares, and about the difficulties people encounter when trying to face death, which alters its appearance constantly, looking hard as iron one minute, soft as air the next. The dead remain dead and two women went to New York State prison; those plain facts are solid salt. But we can't understand the meaning of those hard facts unless we investigate the terrain that surrounds them. Elusive shapes inhabit that terrain. They lead us a terrible chase and continue to haunt us even after judgment is rendered.

■ ■ ■

THIS BOOK was completed before the summer of 1992. But the persistence of uncertainties, even after a verdict has been reached, was dramatically illustrated in July 1992, when State Police Investigator David Harding, 34, a prosecution witness whose testimony concerning fingerprints had been crucial in Shirley Kinge's conviction, was himself indicted for perjury and evidence-tampering in a separate case. According to news reports, Harding allegedly confessed during an interview for a CIA job that he had once lifted a defendant's fingerprint from a discarded beer bottle and then testified falsely that the print had come from inside the victim's house. By the time this news was made public, Shirley Kinge had been incarcerated, in county jail and then state prison, for over two years.

By November 1992, David Harding had admitted testifying falsely for the prosecution in four cases, including the case against Shirley Kinge. He confessed that he did not find her fingerprints on a gas can in the murdered family's house; the prints were a hoax. Pleading guilty to four counts of first-degree perjury, Harding faced a sentence of at least four, but not more than twelve years in prison.

■ ■ ■

Except where noted, this text, including a long interview with David Harding, stands as it was composed before the news of the investigator's beer bottle trick came to light, before his indictment, before the renewed study of the fingerprint evidence that convicted Shirley Kinge.

But mysteries persist. What exactly happened in December 1989? What will we learn tomorrow? What will we never know?

BUT it may be fancied, that from the naked skeleton of the stranded whale, accurate hints may be derived touching his true form. Not at all. For it is one of the more curious things about this Leviathan, that his skeleton gives very little idea of his general shape. . . .

For all these reasons, then, any way you may look at it, you must needs conclude that the great Leviathan is that one creature in the world which must remain unpainted to the last. True, one portrait may hit the mark much nearer than another, but none can hit it with any very considerable degree of exactness. So there is no earthly way of finding out precisely what the whale really looks like. And the only mode in which you can derive even a tolerable idea of his living contour, is by going a whaling yourself; but by so doing, you run no small risk of being eternally stove and sunk by him.

— Herman Melville, *Moby-Dick*

▌▌▌

PART 1 Shirley

1

prints

MICHAEL KINGE'S face appeared many times in *The Ithaca Journal* after his death. An old grey mug shot showed him with his eyes lowered, his hair (1970s' high Afro) nearly filling the top of the frame. His mouth was tucked up at the side and his brow furrowed, giving him a look at once sarcastic, pained, weary; the photo seemed to have been taken through thick glass pressed against his forehead. He had a narrow jaw, like his mother's.

Michael Kinge was killed by the New York State police early in the morning of February 7, 1990, while sitting on his bed, armed with a shotgun, in a rented duplex apartment (520B) just north of Ithaca. That same morning his mother, Shirley Kinge, was awakened in the adjacent apartment (520A) by an armed, helmeted policeman wearing a Second Chance Bullet-Proof vest. She screamed, "Don't kill my grandbaby!" Other members of the assault team had already discovered Mrs. Kinge's two-year-old grandson and Mrs. Kinge's own mother asleep in nearby rooms. No one in 520A was harmed. The volley of gunshots erupted in 520B. Shirley

Kinge's grandson and mother would be released from police custody by the end of the day.

Shirley Kinge remained under arrest. Before the year was out, she would be convicted of burglary, arson, hindering prosecution, criminal possession of stolen property and forgery, as an accomplice in her son's crime.

Her son's guilt was not in question during her trial; defense essentially conceded that Michael Kinge had murdered the four members of a well-to-do Ithaca family three days before Christmas, stolen the adult victims' gold VISA cards, attempted to incinerate their large grey house, then used the stolen credit cards the next day with his mother, to go shopping in the Fingerlakes [sic] and Camillus malls up around Syracuse.

According to the prosecution's version of events, Michael Kinge was driven in a truck, by his girlfriend, to a spot near the victims' house. He removed a stolen mountain bicycle from the truck and rode that bicycle to the Harris family residence, in the freezing weather of the late afternoon. Armed with a shortened .22 caliber Charter Arms semi-automatic rifle, Kinge entered the house and terrorized, then murdered, the family. He drove the family's van to the lot of a nearby bowling alley and parked it there. At some point that night, he contacted his mother and she allegedly came to the victims' house, where she helped her son first clean the premises (the police said the residence was strangely free of fingerprints), then spread gasoline throughout the rooms. The gasoline was ignited. A smoke alarm went off, startling the suspects, who fled the premises at approximately 7:00 a.m. in the family's van. Eventually, that van was abandoned in the bowling alley lot. Michael Kinge rode his bicycle to the nursing home where his girlfriend worked and replaced the bike on their truck. On the morning of December 23, Michael Kinge tried three times to remove money from local ATM machines using the male victim's access card. Later the same day, he and his mother went Christmas shopping together with the VISA cards stolen from the victims.

Some part of Mrs. Kinge's guilt was also conceded during the trial. Defense never challenged the state's assertion that Shirley Kinge had forged Dolores Harris's name on the unsigned gold VISA çard which she then used in the malls to buy Reebok tennis shoes, Christmas sweaters for her own mother and a pair of diamond earrings. Defense counsel did insist, however, that when Shirley Kinge used the stolen VISA card she had no idea this Dolores Harris was dead, murdered by Michael Kinge just a few hours earlier, or that this woman's family was also dead. Defense insisted that Shirley Kinge had never set foot in the Harris house, never doused their rooms with gasoline and never ignited that gas in an attempt to help destroy evidence of her son's guilt.

But the jury accepted state testimony that two fingerprints discovered on a rectangular gas can in the victims' living room had been left there by Shirley Kinge. Her trial, a prolonged, repetitive, swollen drama, balanced on the prints of two fingertips.

Mrs. Kinge wore a wig throughout her trial because she didn't have enough money to post bail, and hair dryers and electric hair curlers are not allowed in the Tompkins County jail, where she resided for approximately one year. It was a good-looking dark brown wig. Slim, impenetrable, her bones delicate as a wren's, Shirley Kinge withstood scrutiny. It did no good for jurors, courtroom visitors or people at home (the trial was broadcast live for three and a half months on Channel 7, normally the local weather channel) to stare at this defendant's face in an attempt to comprehend her. She remained encased in a shell, not only the stoic shell she'd chosen as a defense against her predominantly white audience, but also a shell of baroque American clichés that make an imaginative comprehension of this whole story nearly impossible.

Luckily, our courts do not require jury members to comprehend whole stories. The law knows how to deal with unimaginable tales dragged out of private homes into the public courthouse. First, it cools and fragments personal testimony. It forcefully hampers the voices of witnesses who would like to testify to their own memories, some of these dreadfully passionate memories of lost friends, permanently hurt children, pain. Our courts require that legal testimony be stripped of "irrelevant" elements such as a witness's passions and conclusions, a witness's ambiguous memories and lingering, unanswerable doubts.

It's not surprising that courtrooms must restrain testimony in this way; a courtroom is, after all, a small rigid theatre packed with real enemies, with men and women who might, if given the chance, leapfrog professional intermediaries to sink their claws into the eyes of their antagonists. Passionate testimony is chilled not only by attorneys' objections, but also by the way the attorney's direct examination interrupts the witness's narrative. Trials do not mean to reconstruct or resurrect whole stories or whole people. For this reason, witnessing a trial involving wrongful death is said to be torture for individuals who knew and loved the dead and who, in court, listen to testimony that dissects the victims one more time and then neglects to stitch the pieces back together again.

And what's left after the courts have properly formatted personal testimony? Piles of isolated things: gas cans, bicycle handles, dog hairs in Petri dishes. Disconnected objects clutter the prosecutor's table just as insignificant details clutter testimony. Criminal trials focus on trash, stuff collected, then presented in a way that equalizes the status of a D battery and forty burned human fingers in tubes. The jury must pick through this bereft collection at the end of a trial and discard whatever it finds useless. Our trials, though conducted on a kind of stage dignified by as much regal paraphernalia as a democratic country can tolerate, are inevitably trashy.

And frequently boring. In fact, an actual criminal trial may be intentionally undramatic. Unimportant details smother important ones, so that trials, though rigidly structured, grow shapeless in the center. Bill Sullivan, Shirley Kinge's defense attorney, asked interminable questions about dog feces discovered on the second floor of the crime scene: Did the police test the sample? Did they have proof it came from a dog? "What's he trying to prove, you guys?" a female journalist asked a cop in the hallway. "One of you pulled down your pants and took a shit at the scene?" (Days earlier, Sullivan posed this question: "Is it generally true that when the sun rises the day gets brighter?" "Yes," replied the witness, a Cornell meteorologist.)

A critic may suspect that such things happen because an unspoken goal of any criminal trial is to make the vengeful, intestinal passions stirred up by a particular crime *forgettable*, rather than memorable. If a Shakespearean tragedy, acted on stage, reaches for catharsis and for a kind of resurrection, a tragedy examined in court reaches in the other direction: towards burial, towards landfill. Few legal theorists dwell on a courtroom's inclination towards the city dump; men and women fascinated by our Anglo-American legal system are much more likely to emphasize ways in which the law preserves events by keeping strict records and by placing even mundane disputes into an historical context.

But the fact is, professionals who do trial work daily call trials perfectly forgettable. They know where most of this collected stuff finally winds up. Jerry Spence, attorney for the likes of Imelda Marcos, has cheerfully described his own professional "bathtub memory"—trial's over, pull the plug. He claims that he usually fails to recognize former clients when he meets them on the street after the verdict.

Down the drain go gas cans, VISA gold cards, wigs, photographs of long brown hairs caught in ligatures made with the adolescent girl's own nylons, Vaseline jars, names, dates, autopsy reports.

Judge William Barrett, who presided over Shirley Kinge's trial, quoted Jerry Spence's "bathtub memory" comment with sympathy. What sane professional would choose to keep his memory stocked with the sort of private trash that gets investigated following an act of violence? According to the "inventory upon return of search warrant," New York State police investigators secured from 520B Etna Road, Michael Kinge's apartment, the following articles:

1 Panasonic television

1 JVC VCR

1 box of pornographic material

1 police scanner (Bearcat)

1 pocket phaser (eye irritant)

1 grey Colibri cigarette lighter

1 brown notebook containing list of police radio frequencies

1 black bag containing burglar tools

1 bandolier containing 20-gauge shotgun shells

9 knives

2 diamond sharpening rods

1 pair binoculars

1 black leather holster

1 two-point spike

3 pocket-size batons

1 camouflage blowgun

2 .22 caliber sawed-off barrels

2 black rubber pistol grips

1 Mizzel flash suppressor

2 packs Benson & Hedges

1 paperback book, *The Executioner*

1 credit card case containing miscellaneous credit cards (Michael/Anthony Turner)

7 boxes .11 caliber ammunition

1 black bag containing seven .22 caliber magazines with ammunition, and burglar tools

1 red carrying case

1 Charter Arms .22 caliber rifle sawed-off with pistol grip and equipped with a silencer, fully loaded

1 Ithaca .22 caliber rifle fully loaded

1 New Haven 20-gauge sawed-off pump shotgun with pistol grip, fully loaded

Unspecified hairs and fibers on clothes

1 knit cap

15 throwing stars

1 blue duffel bag containing leather holster and ninja costume

■ ■ ■

It is impossible to reconstruct exactly what happened early in the night, December 22, 1989. The witnesses to those events are dead. A swarm of horrors was let loose in the grey house and that swarm consumed an entire family—parents Anthony and Dolores (Tony and Dodie), their adolescent daughter, Shelby, and their eleven-year-old son, Marc—but people driving by on Ellis Hollow Road didn't notice. Shelby Harris was tied to her bedroom chair with ligatures made from nylon hose, then raped and sodomized; her attacker used her green prom dress in some way (according to the medical examiner's testimony, it was fastened to her wrists), but the court let that detail fade. The parents and son were bound and shot in the boy's bedroom. The invasion, the outdoor silence and the fact that the night contained the execution of children in the presence of their parents all make the story an indelible nightmare. The additional fact that the killer of the white family was a black man, and that, therefore, this true event perfectly recreates old *racist* nightmares, white ladies' cautionary tales about "nigger" rape and vengeance, makes it worse—a tortured dream with a false floor in it.

The Harrises' new country house, regularly described as their "dream house" by journalists, anchors the nightmare. A spacious saltbox, it was constructed on a rural lot broad enough to accommodate a skating pond (Marc played ice hockey), a gift and antique shop called The Grey Goose, and a decorative old sleigh full of empty wrapped Christmas gifts. The house was elaborately wired to protect the family's property and their safety, but no one activated the alarms. Neighbors never heard a thing, no alert sounded until the morning of December 23, when the house itself finally trumpeted its warning for fire.

According to Dominic Bordonaro, who sold the complex $1,500 security alarm system to the Harrises and eventually testified at the trial, the system at 1886 Ellis Hollow Road included buttons for alerting police and for calling fire fighters and medical assistance. There was a literal "panic button." There were magnetic contacts on the doors and infrared motion detectors in the basement and living room. But, Bordonaro testified, "As long as the control is in a disarmed mode, it will not work." On December 22, it appears that the alarm system was operable, but no one pushed the actual panic button.

This security system had keypads located at various places throughout the house. Tompkins County Court Exhibit 531A, a close-up photo, showed the keypad in the master bedroom, where Shelby Harris's body was found. In the close-up photograph, there is a Cornell cap and a toy chalet that appears to be a music box. All objects are heavily coated with brown soot except the keypad, which shines oddly bright white.

The Harrises' security system activated for the first time in response to fire at about 6:40 in the morning of December 23. Dennis Regan, the neighbor to the west, heard it then. He left his bedroom and went to his own front door, opened it. The morning was frigidly cold. The sound came through the air from the grey frame house. He called the state police and told them his neighbors' address—"1874 Ellis Hollow Road"—as near as he could figure it.

New York State Trooper John Beno was the first officer to pull up into the Harrises' wide, white front yard. He had been forced to hang behind a snow plow for a while on his drive down Ellis Hollow Road. He had the slightly incorrect address—1874 Ellis Hollow Road—written on a scrap of paper in his car. Square-faced, moustached, with a piping voice, Trooper Beno appears on a television screen to have a bright pink complexion, but in person he solidifies. His hair is the color of pewter, as is his uniform. He has broad shoulders. John Beno got out of his car that morning in the sharp cold. It was dark, but the sun would be coming up soon and he could see well enough. He had no idea who lived in this house. He had done this kind of thing before. There were tire tracks leading from the garage of the residence, across the lawn, through the snow; in photographs later, these paired tracks would turn peachy and the snow lavender-blue. The trooper himself was now making footprints in the snow.

Trooper Beno walked into the tall peaked garage through its left stall door, which was wide open. Only one car was parked inside, a black Chrysler New Yorker with a small air compressor, cord wrapped around it, set strangely on the hood. Beno started making some noise: "I was identifying myself. I was yelling to see if anybody was in there, to try and get a response." No response. By this time the house alarm had gone silent.

He entered the house through the Harrises' back door and smelled smoke. He passed through a mud room first and went by a half bath. The lower floor of the Harris house was designed to wrap around a massive central fireplace that had openings into three rooms: the high-ceilinged family room, the formal living room and the kitchen. Going around the house counter-clockwise from the rear door, a lone visitor would step first into the windowed family room, which ran along the back of the house and had stairs leading up to the second floor balcony; three bedrooms were located on the second floor. In December, Christmas greenery wove through the square bannister posts. The Christmas tree stood against the back windows.

Circling still counter-clockwise, a visitor would pass the door to the study, cross the formal living room where the couch was fronted by a chest topped with trumpet-shaped candle holders, pass the entranceway and the front door, and enter the long, spacious kitchen. Only at this point would he step off deep, wall-to-wall tan carpet.

Smoke and darkness filled the house. Upstairs, along the balcony, the air rolled with smoke. Trooper Beno hadn't smelled it outside, or if he had, he never mentioned it in court. The new house was well-sealed and had a triple chimney. Outdoors, any scent of smoke would be pale, unremarkable. Indoors, however, the scent was criminal, sweetened as it was by fumes from some combustible fuel. John Beno walked quickly around the house. He noticed a yellow plastic gasoline nozzle lying in the family room and a red plastic gasoline nozzle lying on the carpet in the front living room, not far from a red and yellow metal gasoline can with the word "GASOLINE" printed diagonally up its face. He didn't touch these things, according to his testimony. In the kitchen, Beno saw the phone cord had been cut.

Court Exhibit 515 (close-up photograph) pictures a spiraling white phone cord against teal blue wallpaper. Small flowers in rows decorate the wallpaper. The cord is severed. The Harris kitchen is a firm, cheerful blue, highlighted with red, a color scheme that extends into the family room. Exhibit 514 (photograph) is back a step and shows the entire white kitchen phone with its cut cord. Beside the phone a wooden tulip, a wooden watermelon and a wooden potato rest on a narrow shelf. The coffee machine is next to the phone, with Santa Claus mugs near that. In the center of the kitchen is a cooktop island (Exhibit 513A). A collection of mugs on a narrow shelf lines the kitchen's outer wall, up near the ceiling trim. Four chairs have been pushed in around the kitchen table. The Harrises had no formal dining room. According to friends, their house was always open to visitors.

John Beno was already walking among clues, thousands of fragments that had so recently been part of a coordinated family household. Christmas ornaments, ashtrays, baseball cards, mugs, telephone cords, red and yellow plastic gas can spouts had *all* been severed from their context that morning; in photographs, they look orphaned, magnified. Dodie Harris sold pretty things in her front yard shop, The Grey Goose. But all the chosen things in her house were instantly changed by tragedy, as if the magnetism that had held scented candles close to mugs was now reversed, so that near objects repelled one another. Constructed just four years earlier, her home was going to be analyzed, taken apart, deconstructed by the police who were beginning to arrive, police who would value the objects in her house not as touchstones signifying "Here is Home," but as surfaces on which to find fingerprints.

Beno recognized some of the clues already. He had noticed the air compressor. He had noticed the tire tracks and the open garage door. He had noted the gas spouts and the gasoline can. He had not yet noticed the dim dust circle in the garage that silhouetted (according to the prosecution) the outline of a missing gas can, or the bright cigarette butt on the kitchen floor, a cigarette butt that would later be placed alone in a Petri dish and photographed. In just a few hours, many things would already be *secured*, but they weren't secure yet. For now Trooper Beno was walking around strange rooms in the dark, knowing that some cop or some fireman must eventually ascend to the second floor.

The smoke in the house was powerfully invasive. John Beno opened two windows near the kitchen telephone to ventilate the place. Eight months later he would be asked by the defense attorney whether these two windows were "lift-up" or "crank," but in December, the trooper just wanted air. No one inside the house had called to him yet. When dogs barked, the sound came from a distance, from outside.

Now Trooper Beno returned outside, bent into his own familiar car (scent of decent gasoline, scent of coffee) and radioed the Varna barracks for assistance.

On television, eight months later, Bill Sullivan (defense attorney) would be shown handing Trooper John Beno (witness for the state) a paper bag and asking him to open it. Over the air, the paper bag would crinkle loudly. Beno would lift the air compressor out of its plain wrapping as if it were a gift. From another paper bag would come a telephone receiver. Lots of paper bags would collect on the prosecutor's desk, finally suggesting a lawyers' picnic. Bill Sullivan would call the court's attention to every staple hole in every bag to suggest that the police had tampered with the evidence. Whenever Mr. Sullivan spoke, the court's stenographer (slender, professionally reticent, a gentle woman and an old friend of Dodie Harris) recorded and secured his words without changing her expression.

Courthouses are erected as buffers against civil frights. Professionals, jurors and visitors to a courthouse generally do not feel afraid. In fact, watching a trial can be restful, pleasant. Arranged in our accustomed places when the bailiff calls "All rise," we feel secure because courtroom ritual relies on separation, limitation and a wide variety of proper silences which promise to keep chaos at bay. A courtroom is crammed full of invisible walls. Legal professionals understand *limits* very well, not only established limits to their authority, but also professional limits to their responsibilities and their imaginations.

Shirley Kinge, capped by a wig, shielded by large glasses, spent hours mechanically taking notes on a pad during her trial; seeing her, one academic spectator muttered, "Bartleby." Weeks later, a photographer walked up during a break and poised her light meter in the empty spot that Shirley Kinge's head usually occupied. Ironically, a framed print of that empty space would have provided as much information as a snapshot of the defendant's face, because it would have illustrated an elusive fact about the law: the law does not attempt to penetrate mysteries so much as to enclose them, to wall them in with the magic masonry of prisons, the borders of photographs, the boundaries of ritual.

Our legal system does not reach for comprehension so much as for categorization and decision. There is a satisfying, masculine neatness in its design, but the essential elements of a violent crime fit no given structure. To know Anthony, Dolores, Marc and Shelby, Michael and Shirley in even a small way, one's imagination must admit rumor, guesswork, ambiguities, maybe belief in ghosts or at least the human spirit, certainly belief in mortality. No one will be safe forever. But these legally "irrelevant" bits of understanding are not welcomed in court.

Even minor participants notice the static, "walled-in" quality of a courtroom drama. One witness, a neighbor of the Harris family, described his minutes in court this way: "I walked in there, it was like walking on the set of a long-running play. Everybody else there seemed to be so comfortable with where they were, and they were like set-pieces—you walked in, and there's the jury, the judge, the bailiff, the court reporter and camera crews and all, in exactly the same spots they always were when you saw them on television and they hardly ever moved at all. And Shirley Kinge was that stoic fixture over in the corner. Sort of a vacuum that your eyes couldn't . . . your eyes wandered over to see her. That was it. And then it was less than five minutes for my testimony and I was there and gone. And everything else seemed frozen. I was inserted in that." He added a minute later, "It reminded me a bit of my marriage ceremony."

The judge in court knows his place. He understands that tomorrow he will not be required to trade places with the defendant and sit in that warmed-over chair, nor will the fourth juror be asked to jump the gate and sit as a witness. The courtroom as a theatre assures us that Justice will not turn her head suddenly, unexpectedly, and cry, "YOU there, with the pink necklace and the notepad. YOU are guilty!"

But this strict civil theatre deludes its audience when members of that audience, the "unaccused," trust its implicit promise to shield them, wall them off, from guilt and danger. Terror, a fluid beast, can knock anywhere at any time. Both Shirley Kinge and Dolores Harris heard the knock on the door.

■ ■ ■

After radioing for help, Trooper John Beno, alone in the Harris house, tried three times to get into the rooms on the second floor, but the smoke was so thick up there he couldn't see or breathe. "There was a door in front of me that was closed. . . . I turned on the light switch and the light blew out." He had no flashlight. He did find his way into one room, but discovered nothing there. By the time he came down the stairs the third time, three other troopers were pulling up outside. The doors slammed. Trooper Michael Simmons (rounded jaw, dark hair, moustache) had come with a colleague who was just getting off the night shift. Trooper William Standinger (bullish face, massive moustache) had driven up alone. The sun was beginning to rise. These policemen made more footprints in the snow, snow so cold it squeaked like leather.

Somebody went back out and got a flashlight from the car. With the light, John Beno managed to make his way through the smoke into the second floor bedroom—the master bedroom—located above the kitchen.

The body of a naked girl was in the room, stretched out face down on the carpet with her legs tipped up against the dresser. Near her lay evidence of a spent explosion: ripped, ransacked Christmas presents. The victim's body was "dark, charred, split. You could see the flesh inside of the legs," Beno remembered. "It appeared lifeless and I just went downstairs."

Exhibits 527 and 527A, both photographs, show the master bedroom. The two small legs are not obvious until a person knows to look for them. The exposed springs of the burnt mattress are much more obvious.

John Beno came down the stairs for air and told the others. This time William Standinger took the flashlight and climbed up into the part of the house that was swimming in smoke. He too was stung and choked by the smoke and forced back downstairs repeatedly so that his stories of climbing *up* into the second floor of the Harris house resemble stories of a swimmer treading water in a murky lake and diving *down* again and again, trying to feel his way, to touch wreckage or the blind lake floor itself.

Standinger did make his way into the master bedroom and discovered the dead family dog. Asked by the district attorney if he remembered seeing a "green party-type dress" near Shelby Harris's body, Standinger said, "I don't recall it specifically." On his third trip up, he walked down the hallway and made it into a room with posters on the wall. His fourth trip up, he checked the bathroom area near the room with the posters. His next trip up, he turned right and found a third door, a third bedroom. He had a dishtowel over his mouth and flashlight in his hand. He opened the door of the room quickly, and felt heat. There was "a glow" towards the center of the room, but no live flames. In the dark, he said, "There's a fire in here." Trooper Simmons, who was behind, ordered, "Close the door." Standinger said in court, "I could see the glow and the smoke and that was the only thing I could see in that room." He shut the door without discovering the three hooded bodies kneeling in the fire.

Rolls of yellow police tape were brought indoors. Fire trucks from Varna and Dryden pulled up, and the flat hose was unrolled and dragged through the house and up the stairs. The firemen, equipped like divers with air packs, trooped in heavily. Already state police had sealed off the family room and living room, where the gas cans and spouts had been found, and Trooper Standinger had brought his 35 mm camera upstairs and snapped a few pictures because he was worried that incoming firefighters would disturb the evidence. The firemen came in tidily two by two, at least according to the testimony of prosecution witnesses, so that we imagine these pairs of equipped men as both dainty and forceful. One volunteer did secretary's duty, keeping a list of the men who took the hose upstairs; this list would be provided to the lawyers, who would come marching into the picture soon.

The first volunteers opened the door where they had been told the fire was, saw a glow, shut the door and called for water. When they opened the door the second time, the fire grew and raced across the ceiling. Smoke was thick from their knees up. Darren Miller's air pack ran out, so he and his partner descended the stairs. Ron Flynn and his partner took over with the hose. On his hands and knees, Flynn crawled into the room where the fire had been largely doused but was still pouring out black smoke—"I proceeded into the room and bumped into an object."

In this way he discovered that he was crawling in a twilight space that contained at least two corpses. The victims' heads, fallen forward, were at eye level, if he stayed on his hands and knees. He would have gone farther, but then he heard a "muffled flutter," the signal that his air pack was running low.

The bodies of Anthony and Dolores Harris knelt one behind the other, with the husband slumped forward over his wife. The victims were tied to the bedstead with wire from metal hangers, and their heads were covered with pillow cases. The body of Marc, legs folded under, elbows tied behind, knelt alone with head tipped backwards near a wall in the room. It would someday be described as "the smaller male body." This had been his room; it contained two twin beds. Ron Flynn came down the stairs, removed his air pack and told the gathering men that there were more bodies upstairs.

Trooper William Standinger went up the stairs again, diving upwards. He noticed the old paper wasp's nest on one of the twin beds near the bodies of Anthony and Dolores Harris; in the murk, "I thought it was an animal's head." He distinguished between the husband's and wife's corpses by noting the width of their wedding rings.

By the time Standinger took his sixth trip upstairs, Dr. Maines, the coroner, had entered the house and been directed to the second floor. The smoke was beginning to clear. Standinger testified,

"Dr. Maines inspected the leg area of the female body in the first bedroom. He prodded it with his fingers." Investigator Porter, a senior officer, arrived while the coroner was upstairs. He ascended and informed Bill Standinger, who by now must have been both sweating and freezing, that his presence wasn't required any longer.

It was cold inside and outside the house; an icicle hung from the kitchen faucet and a portion of the side yard was covered with a great fan of ice since firefighters upstairs had blasted water through the window to create a vacuum and help clear the smoke. Standinger left the house and drove over to the police command post that had been set up temporarily, suddenly, in an old white frame church past a **Y** in Ellis Hollow Road.

By the time Investigator David Harding arrived, the carpets upstairs were frozen with water from the fire hoses. The four bodies would not be removed from the house until the end of the day. Outdoors, the large front yard was ringed with yellow police tape. The snow was marred by ice, tire tracks and countless footprints. Neighbors drove by. Some stopped and asked questions.

Major Robert Farrand of Troop C, New York State Police, was Captain Farrand on December 23, 1989. He got to the Harris house in the evening: "I was at the house that night; they discovered the bodies that morning. To make a long story short, I was away. It was Christmas weekend, as you know; I was at my girlfriend's. By the time I got involved and got all the way up to Ithaca, it was late afternoon. I got there about 2:00 or 3:00 and went over to the house maybe 4:30. Of course, at that time of year, it's dark. The bodies had not been removed yet, although they were getting ready to remove them, and just the tree—here's this Christmas tree—Christmas tree, ornaments, lights, Christmas presents lying there, soot-covered for the most part. And I remember, I think this impression will be fixed in my mind forever. Shelby, the girl, her room, her bedroom—there was this Christmas present there to her boyfriend and it was all wrapped in red paper and she, like—I think it was silver glitter, or whatever—had his name spelled out.

And I remember the night they were killed, Shelby's mother, Dodie, was going to take Shelby to her boyfriend's house to exchange gifts, right? And of course they didn't come. And her boyfriend kept calling the house and of course it kept ringing; there was no answer. And you know, I kept thinking, here's this poor kid that. . . . He can't understand. His girlfriend's going to come over to see him, they're going to exchange Christmas presents, and they don't come. He's calling the house, there's no answer, and he's thinking, 'Gee, what happened, what's going on?' And she's never going to come."

■ ■ ■

In county court months later, the testimony of New York State Troopers Beno, Simmons and Standinger lasted four days. They told the court what they recalled about the morning of December 23, when they entered the smoking, decorated house.

Attorney Bill Sullivan gave Beno a hard time. On August 5, the third day of the Kinge trial, the defense attorney called for the entire case against Shirley Kinge to be dismissed because Trooper Beno admitted to having discarded the scrap of paper that said "1874 Ellis Hollow Road," the incorrect address phoned into the state police barracks by the Harrises' neighbor. Faced with this sort of courtroom logic, logic that would attempt to overturn a trial by using an inaccurate, irrelevant scribble as its lever, the police witnesses adapted. They presented their stories in emotionless fragments, retooled to fit the courtroom's legal machinery. Trooper Standinger had faced defense attorney Bill Sullivan before, and responded to his interminable queries with "I don't recall," "I don't recall," again and again and again as he was questioned about his memories of December 23. His responses were anti-dramatic, professional and boring. At one point during his testimony, Goldie the bailiff was falling asleep, one alternate juror was falling asleep, one guard was falling asleep and a reporter in the front pew was falling asleep.

On another day, I was sitting in the county clerk's office with a fellow writer. We had photographs in our laps and steno pads open. I picked up Exhibit 536, a photo. There was a distinct red plastic gas can in the corner of the picture near the white doorway. A white telephone clearly lay on the carpet inside the doorway. It took a while, though, before one more object emerged: deep among the shadows between the lines of the doorframe, that cloudy shape was actually a head encased in bloody fabric. I looked down at my notes. This was the woman's head.

I took notes: "536, 537. Charred posters on the wall. Wicker chest. Second body (male) a black sunlit mass. 534. Dead dog, sun-lit eye. Flat on its side, feet look like frayed rope. 538. Ceiling blackened. Body so charred it looks tarry. One arm seems dissolved into bedframe."

A juror from the Kinge trial would explain, "I guess I was im-pressed that the presentation of the information was done pretty professionally. I didn't feel that the prosecutor tried to present the information in such a way that your emotions overwhelmed you, and that certainly could have been done with a crime this horrible. And yet I didn't feel overwhelmed in that regard at all. Most of the information was pretty dry and clinical in the way it was presented."

Judging by this account, courtroom ritual and discourse had succeeded in making horror stretch itself out dry and flat so that it could be mapped. This doesn't mean, however, that legal profes-sionals, jurors and spectators maintain full immunity to horror, to passionate impulses, pity and rage. We can expect that they—we—do not, and that jurors imagine terrors even though witnesses on the stand are forbidden to speak words like "terror," "soul" or "grief."

On the basis of two fingerprints, Shirley Kinge was convicted of burglary in the first degree and arson in the third degree. She could not be convicted specifically of burning the bodies of an entire family, including two children. The photographs of the crime scene, however, give the strong impression that the Harrises' bod-ies were insulted and even awfully pained by gasoline fire. This is not true; the victims were dead before the fire started. But we can wonder about the power of the photographs and how those pictures, which appear to show a lost husband and wife kneeling close to one another for comfort, influenced the verdict.

■ ■ ■

Because the suspects used the Harris VISA cards to go shopping on December 23, investigators were able to take descriptions offered by sales personnel at the Camillus and Fingerlakes malls and publish composite drawings of the suspects' faces in most midstate newspapers by early January. The composites showed a black man and a black woman. The woman had a thin jaw and was wearing a knit hat; the man looked hairy, especially around his lips.

(According to the plump, young white clerk who sold Michael Kinge the Colibri cigarette lighter at Things Remembered on December 23, the customer was a black male who looked "discombobulated—he was messy, his hair was messy." The clerk testified in court that when he bent to get the lighter, he smelled gasoline on the man's pants. The clerk also tried to say he thought it odd *this* guy had a gold VISA card, but defense objected.)

Telephone tips began to come in, and officers at the Varna barracks were assigned to screen the calls, some of which came from citizens who believed they had psychic powers. On January 5, *The Ithaca Journal* reported that the state police denied Shelby Harris had been raped. In this case, police spokesmen lied to journalists. On January 10, *The Ithaca Journal* reported that there had been thefts of checks at Cornell on December 23 and investigators were going to track the thief. This report was true. Investigators Donald and Douglas Vredenburgh were dispatched to follow that lead, and soon found themselves tracking a black man, a forger, named Charlie Hanes.

"Charlie Hanes, that cost us two weeks; my brother and I worked there up in Syracuse two weeks," Don Vredenburgh said. "We found him in a pile of clothes, second story. A pile of dirty laundry on a Sunday afternoon." But Charlie Hanes was soon eliminated as a suspect: "He would no more shoot anybody than the man in the moon."

The state police began to focus seriously on Shirley and Michael Kinge after receiving a number of tips from people who called upon seeing the composites, and after an officer dropped by to check on the Etna Road duplex. The officer, who said he was doing a "neighborhood survey," was rebuffed by a black man who came to the door holding a baby, and also by a black woman who responded from the second floor window of the adjacent apartment.

All this accumulated—cops working liaison, cops questioning forgers in Syracuse (how do you find forgers? "Just pick a guy on the street and talk to him, he's probably a forger," said Don Vredenburgh), cops taking phone calls, checking out leads and alibis. The most detailed work went on inside the large Harris house, where Investigator David Harding directed the forensics investigation in early January. But probably the *oddest* work took place in the Peregrine House bed and breakfast in Collegetown, where Mrs. Kinge had worked as a part-time employee for about two years.

Late in January, Investigator Harding, disguised as a slightly injured grants administrator (a particularly apt college town disguise) checked into the Peregrine House to meet Mrs. Kinge, photograph her, obtain a handwriting sample and get her fingerprints. This all had to be done without alerting her suspicions. The undercover job was a partial success in that Shirley Kinge, tricked by the investigator with his bandaged right hand, signed envelopes addressed to *Harris*burg, Pennsylvania and met with him next day for a chat at Friendly's; she was photographed entering the restaurant.

David Harding would testify that he was unable to obtain fingerprints from Mrs. Kinge, however, because she had very dry hands which left no marks on the objects she touched in the restaurant (a drinking glass, a photo overlay) or on the objects police collected from the Peregrine House. But according to Harding, this failure to capture the suspect's prints in the ice cream shop turned out to be unimportant since Kinge did divulge an important piece of information during their hour's meeting; asked about previous employment, she told Harding that she had worked years earlier at a federal job in New York City. Her fingerprints were on record. Those prints would convict her.

They would convict her even though, examined from one perspective, they had no substance: only photographic *prints* of the defendant's prints were available for the jury to examine. Shirley Kinge's "real" fingerprints had been lifted from the rectangular gasoline can by David Harding early during the forensics investigation, police witnesses explained. This—"lifting" prints—is common procedure. Unfortunately, Investigator Harding did not photograph the telltale gas can at the time, and later Harding, according to his own testimony, wiped the can clean so that its resemblance to a matching can in the victims' house would be clear to the jury. (This was important because if the telltale gas can had *not* belonged to the Harrises, then Shirley Kinge might have touched it prior to the night of December 22.) The immaculate gas can offered as evidence along with the detached, magnified reproduction of two fingerprints caused some trouble. Jurors were not able to determine exactly where the fingerprints had been located on the big tin can originally; police testimony shimmied on that point. At last, however, the jury decided to have faith in the prints of the fingerprints.

One juror, a Cornell professor, described the situation: "This is probably one of the most sobering things I learned in the process of the trial, that at some level you have to trust the police agencies. We got the can and we brought it in and also another can. And there was one place on one of the cans where you could see where the lift had been. Not *the* can—that one had been rubbed down—but I'm speaking about the other one, which hadn't been rubbed down after it was dusted. The point is, once you lift the print, there is nothing left but a square, blank area the size of the lift."

The prosecution of Shirley Kinge stood tiptoe on a "square blank area."

■ ■ ■

The state police were able to practice for their raid on the Kinge house in a duplex identical to the one where the Kinges lived. This was a great advantage; in more common narcotics raids, officers are likely to go stumbling from room to room, kicking doors, calling out. When February 7 dawned, there were a dozen—two teams of six—experienced state police investigators ready. Other officers had already fetched Joanna White, Michael Kinge's companion and the mother of his son, from her night shift job at the nursing home and questioned her about the likely situation of the baby in the duplex.

Donald Vredenburgh and his brother led the two assault teams into the two halves of the Etna Road duplex. The team that entered 520B Etna Road, Michael Kinge's apartment, was led by Douglas Vredenburgh. Two officers used a pry bar to open the screen door and then smashed open the interior door with a battering ram, a metal rod approximately five feet in length, with four handles, flat on one end, weighing about sixty pounds. It took one blow.

Douglas Vredenburgh ran to the foot of the stairs. Up two steps, to the landing, turn right. In the bedroom on the second floor he saw the black male sitting on the bed, his right shoulder pointed to the door, his feet on the floor. There was a scanner there in the room, but the police had been careful to avoid radio transmissions. Kinge was waiting, poised on the bed. Douglas Vredenburgh testified, "His head was facing partially in my direction, so I could see part of his eye."

The black man on the bed held a shotgun (pistol grip, pump action) with the stock end near his stomach, barrel pointed under and towards his own face. Douglas Vredenburgh ran to the end of the bed and planted his elbows on the mattress. He held his gun in both hands, pointed at the suspect. His friends behind him also had their weapons pointed. The suspect stood rapidly and turned. His shotgun fired, according to the police.

Vredenburgh's third shot caught Michael Kinge in the left side of his face. Kinge fell backwards to the floor after the third shot. Others shot. Somebody also killed the Doberman in 520B.

Next door, Donald Vredenburgh didn't hear gunfire: "When you're pumped up, you know what you have to do. In fact, here's how concentrated we all were on what we were doing. We never heard the shots next door and they shot fourteen times or something, and I never heard a shot and we were right from here, from me to you, just one wall away."

Donald Vredenburgh had broken down the interior door of 520A with his shoulder. One blow. His team didn't need a battering ram. He ran up the apartment steps with two backers. A Doberman scurried in front of him and dodged into the back bedroom (this dog, Shirley Kinge's, reportedly disliked men; it was saved and eventually adopted). Don Vredenburgh ran into the back bedroom. He pointed his gun at Shirley Kinge who was in bed, awakening. She screamed, "Don't kill my grandbaby! Don't kill my grandbaby!" Then he was pointing his gun at the Doberman. Then back at the woman. He realized after a moment that the woman didn't have a gun.

Shirley Kinge was "small," said Vredenburgh. "She was startled. She was shocked. She never did say ten words all day and I was with her from seven o'clock in the morning until five o'clock . . . except for the interview. But she never spoke. She was just quiet. It was almost like she couldn't, couldn't . . . like she was . . . I don't know. When she first sat up, she looked like a frail person, but again, she didn't immediately comply with my orders to get her hands out where I could see what was going on. She covered herself up, but that's probably natural. At that point I knew I wasn't going to have any trouble with her. . . .

"She was startled but, you know, my own opinion is that she had to know some day we'd be coming."

Shirley Kinge was ordered to get dressed and to put her dog in the bathtub. Don Vredenburgh does not recall ever hearing the baby cry. At one point, Shirley Kinge reached for a pair of new Reeboks, and the police told her no—put on some other shoes.

High above the conclusive raid, the trooper who'd been first to arrive at the Harris house on December 23 rode in a helicopter reserved to transport injured officers swiftly to a hospital. What did John Beno see as he looked down? Small men in vests. Dots of orange. Twelve cops disappearing into two doors. Cars pulling up. The roof.

Tip the helicopter and within minutes Trooper Beno could have flown over scattered houses and yards not so far away. He might have passed above the roof of the Harrises' abandoned house. If he hovered in place for weeks, keeping watch over *that* square, blank area, he would eventually see another band of men armed with wrecking tools disappear inside. The last invasion of the Harris house was accomplished by friends and a relative of the victims, and described by one participant, Tom Schneider:

"What happened is—Kevin White and Mark Walker, Bill Brown, who lives three houses up, really close friends with the family, and Don Lake, Dodie's brother—when the police had given the house back to Don, what we had done on a Saturday morning, we had gone in and torn all the sheetrock out of the bedroom, Dodie and Tony's bedroom, that Shelby was killed in, and Marc's bedroom, where Tony and Marc and Dodie were killed. We tore out all the sheetrock that had all this blackened stuff, and also tore the subfloor out—there was a lot of blood. That was astounding. We tore the death out. It worked. Then we hung out and ate and had doughnuts and coffee and sandwiches, and stayed in the room, and Don Lake was there, talking to everyone. . . . We used crowbars. Sledgehammers didn't work, so, you know what Miracle Bars are? They're little teeny crowbars like this, and one end is turned up; it's a teeny, small black crow bar. Then we just pried the sheetrock off and just dropped it out. And that was really nice because all the sheetrock dust—we're all white and grey and black and loaded with it, and the nice thing also was, after having that finished, it was this bright, bright snowy day and there were people. People were bringing food. Not that many people were going upstairs. We had a lot of work to do, and we just wanted to get it done, but the more we worked there, the more we weren't in such a rush."

Here at last is a vigil for the dead. A courthouse is too small for a true vigil, which necessarily floods higher than any invisible wall, as it reaches not for a solution, not even for comprehension, but for placement, a thoughtful spirit's *placement* in a trackless space. A vigil requires attention, and one's stubborn, quiet refusal to be lulled to sleep by practical men. Walt Whitman described a vigil for a dead Civil War soldier:

> "Vigil for comrade swiftly slain, vigil I never forget,
>   how as day brighten'd,
> I rose from the chill ground and folded my soldier
>   well in his blanket,
> And buried him where he fell."

Rising, folding, the speaker attends to his dead friend. This action is irrelevant to the outcome of the war.

We build our private homes and public courthouses to keep off the rain. We build our houses also because we know and we resist our knowledge that each evening, a particular day's architecture becomes dust.

2 deduct

WARREN ANTHONY HARRIS, described by one of his friends as "sort of corn-fed, milk-fed, just a real nice guy," earned his living as a high-grade salesman. Nobody called him Warren. He was *Tony*. He'd been Deanco's sales rep for New York State (Deanco designs and manufactures electrical components, especially cables and electrical harnesses, for cars, planes and computers), and when the company asked him to move south to Raleigh, North Carolina, and then Marietta, Georgia, he agreed, and things worked out.

His wife Dolores liked Georgia. She seemed Southern in many ways—hospitable, a touch girlish, happy with nicknames, pleased by homesteads. What's more, the Atlanta doctors earned her trust. Dolores had been in and out of the hospital; she went through a double mastectomy and treatment for uterine cancer. Friendships helped her recover. So did mild combat; she played tennis steadily in Georgia. Nobody called her Dolores. She was *Dodie*, the name she'd settled on after outgrowing her childhood tag (Dodo) and one adolescent experiment (Kelly). Tony and Dodie's children were young in Atlanta. They knew something about their mother's medical situation. Father, mother, daughter, son learned to maneuver around it and nearly climbed past it.

Georgia was home for years. But when it came time to return north to Ithaca, where Deanco had its central office, the family readily pulled up stakes. Most of their relatives, including Tony's mother, Mary, and Dodie's father, Don Lake, lived within easy driving distance of Ithaca, so this transfer would bring the kids near their grandparents; it would probably be the family's last move. With Shelby entering high school and the parents heading into their late thirties, they were ready to settle. Dodie's father, a Syracuse contractor, had offered to build the family a house to spec if they could find a piece of land that pleased them. Dodie would design the house herself. She had studied "house planning" in college, and though she did not earn a full degree in architectural design, she could handle and draw plans; a few friends considered her plans more workable than stacks of proposals they'd received from licensed architects. She understood site elevations, dimensions, light, answering parallel lines.

The lot they chose in Ellis Hollow lay between blue hills, on a band of field land that had not been cultivated for years. Soon after they bought the property, Dodie planted a wooden sign, a grey goose with the name "HARRIS" painted under it, out front by the road. Eager to join the neighborhood, she erected the goose as her calling card.

The valley of Ellis Hollow radiates east from the vast Cornell University grounds. On that side of Cornell, the animal science, agricultural engineering and veterinary medicine facilities are clustered near the experimental orchards, between two strong creeks, Fall and Cascadilla, that eventually cut deep gorges across campus. For years, the Hollow had accommodated professors who chose to live out in the rural hills, but not too far out and not too rural.

Property values were rising there in the mid-Eighties. The old Ellis Hollow community center now had tennis courts and a good swimming pool. Volvos and Saabs skimmed under the trees. Long-time residents who flipped barbecued chicken at the annual Ellis Hollow Fair were likely to hear chatter about law, computer link-ups and Vienna econometrics symposiums drifting through the tent with the smoke.

At the same time, the community was mixed. The belt of rural upstate poverty that surrounded Ithaca cut through the Hollow, so that a high number of poor white kids attended Caroline Elementary School, where Marc would go. Buffalo Road, just south of Ellis Hollow Road, was so pocketed with rusty mobile homes and hardscrabble shelters that a local anthropologist had driven up and down it for years, collecting interviews she used to write a book about the social disintegration and destitution that blighted central New York after its many small farming communities died.

Some hills around Ithaca turned fashionable. Some did not. Tony and Dodie understood the trends, and knew which old country highway promised to lead homeowners towards an immaculate, new, scenic neighborhood. Ellis Highlands, a hidden garden of $200,000 and $300,000 houses constructed on a subdivision lane that wound through shadowy trees, was just a stone's throw from their new lot. Tony and Dodie liked neat country, not rusty, jerryrigged, pig-stinking country. They were friendly and warm. They were also sensible. When a sub-standard modular house got nailed up suddenly across the road, Tony contributed funds to help sue the contractor.

Dodie planned her own new house to stand out in the sun. Tall, coordinated, disciplined as a Maine landmark, commanding as a Southern home, it would be set at an angle in a wide clearing open to the road. Everybody watched as it was being built. A few, like the Browns, wandered over to say hello and met Don Lake, Dodie's father, who climbed all over the construction site whenever he had a chance. Pitched steeply, the roof timbers for the main house and the garage mimicked the near hills. At last the roof settled on the house, the tarps and tools departed. The family's furniture was hauled out from their Lansing West apartment and moved into this home, which smelled like cut wood and fresh carpet backing. Leaves blew across the unfinished yard, but Dodie had sheets on the beds and snacks in the refrigerator by November 1986, in time for Christmas.

Once moved in, the Harrises joined in. They were participators, volunteers, community organizers, ambitious and generous, visible but not showy. Both Dodie and Tony took turns driving the full-sized van full of children. As they did, from November 1986 into 1989, their children grew taller, sportier, and the closets of the new house filled with equipment: rigid hockey skates with skate guards, hockey sticks, big protective pads and mouth guards, skis, bright ski jackets, tennis rackets, mitts, bats, pucks, balls, various gloves, short golf clubs, small black cleated soccer shoes. Caroline Brown, the neighbor whose kitchen window faced Dodie's across a wide field, remembered when Dodie bought new skis: "She just said, well, she wasn't the best of skiers, but she was going to be out there and be with her kids."

Dodie attended all Shelby's Ithaca High School varsity tennis matches and regularly volunteered food and encouragement, earning the team's "Happy Award." She also helped out at Marc's school: she was an active member of the Caroline Elementary School PTA, secretary of the PTA Council for two years and rep for the Pep Focus Team, also hospitality chair, homeroom parent and classroom volunteer. One acquaintance called her "restless."

Tony had the front yard pond dug so Marc could practice hockey. He was the sort of husband who honestly did not seem to mind going on errands, carrying equipment bags for the hockey coach at six o'clock in the morning on a Sunday, helping out with Kiwanis baseball or soccer, climbing into the van to fetch or deliver packages at his wife's request. A friend remembered him running out of the front yard gift shop "waving his arms frantically" one evening just to say good-bye, although it was bitterly cold, ten degrees below zero. He supported his wife in her efforts to start up a business at home, and helped when Dodie's father built The Grey Goose shop to resemble a little barn. Unfortunately, the fully stocked, out-of-the-way gift shop was never very profitable. But it was not without purpose; Tony understood that his wife's long-distance shopping jaunts and sociable hours behind the cash register functioned as exercises to keep the fear down. She had swallowed bleak diagnoses for years; whirling activities counteracted a different, frightful vertigo.

The whole family helped out in the shop, which was outfitted with a pot-bellied stove, table, chairs and checkerboard. On sale in The Grey Goose were big bonnets with ribbons, candles, carved wooden ducks, decorated mailboxes, antique chairs and other pieces of furniture on consignment, quilts and framed pictures of old-fashioned little girls. Dodie kept the basement of The Grey Goose stocked year-round with Christmas items.

But even Christmas didn't guarantee high profits. Caroline Brown had heard that Dodie was only going to try and keep "the Goose" afloat for another year, maybe a year and a half, before the family gave up on it. State police going through the receipts found that in the last week before Christmas, 1989, the shop took in only $100 dollars net. This amount—sufficient for a few bags of groceries—would pain a burglar.

Dodie Harris had brown hair, fairly straight, that covered a small café au lait birthmark on her forehead and came down just about to her shoulders. In the family photograph the newspapers reproduced, she sits in front of the fireplace holding a stuffed goose and wearing a print dress with a bib and belt. Tony stands behind her. His moustache is small, his hair receding, his smile modest, compressed. To Dodie's left is Marc wearing a rumpled Izod shirt, clean but not tucked in. His hair, parted down the middle, looks golden at the top. To Dodie's left is Shelby with hands clasped just under her slouchy belt and a thin bracelet on one wrist. Marc stands slightly off-balance. Shelby, the adolescent, has her head tilted, asking the camera to be generous. The mother's face is central and sturdy even in the grey picture. Her eyes, rather small, look at ease. She most closely resembles her son, Marc. Her right hand is so nicely arranged for the photograph it appears gloved.

There were other pictures. Caroline Brown remembered, "She had pictures in her house, you know, and there'd be ones where she had wigs on because she'd lost all her hair from chemotherapy and she proudly displayed them; it was fine with her." While she lived in Ithaca, Dodie's cancer was in remission, but her experiences with the disease had been prolonged and harsh. "When she'd get over one, she sort of had another episode. It was separate incidences," Caroline Brown said. "I think that's why she felt that the time with her kids was so precious, because she always said she didn't know how much time she might have."

At one time, before two new houses were constructed on Ellis Hollow Road, Caroline had been Dodie's nearest neighbor on the west side. They walked together for exercise—Dodie couldn't play as much tennis as she liked because of her tendonitis—and even tried the big hill for a while, though usually they chose to wander through Ellis Highlands, checking out the new construction and landscaping. When they spoke on the phone they joked, "Can you see this?", each woman gesturing from her own kitchen window though her view was obscured by intervening trees.

Caroline hadn't joined the bridge group, but she did often meet up with the Harrises at the Community Center swimming pool. She says Shelby was a bit of a scamp at the pool — "borderline obnoxious" with her crew of girlfriends, giddy, goofy, but "she never crossed the line into obnoxious. Close sometimes, maybe." On the tennis court, Shelby's long, permy hair was pulled back, some of it ponytailed, some of it loose, and it flew around her face like a mane. She was tall and looked older than her actual age. Teetering between childhood and adulthood, she made a very good babysitter, ready to sit down on the floor with her charges and try out varieties of toys. Neighbors remembered the big birthday party her parents staged for her in the front yard. Advertised with a wooden Happy Birthday sign "big as a billboard," the party came complete with a lawn tent and a truck serving flavored ices. The green prom dress Shelby had bought before Christmas was her first strapless dress; she and her mother had gone out together and had a great time shopping for it. Dodie "had a rein" on Shelby. Earlier, when Shelby had dated a high school senior, the family repeatedly invited him out on their boat to get to know him and "try to feel more comfortable with him," but the mother felt relieved when he drove off to college.

Marc, four years younger than his sister, was a sports-minded kid, successful and well-liked. He handled classroom assignments with more ease than Shelby did. Some private, quiet element defined him; his Squirt House League hockey coach could remember no other boy on the team who always asked to skate defense rather than offense. Tony accepted the lead in responsibility for Marc. Dodie kept her eye on her daughter.

The family stayed in gear. Mother, father, daughter, son repeatedly set out from home and returned. They enjoyed food, shared food. According to friends who contributed entries to a memorial journal, Dodie organized cookie exchanges and prepared hot cider for customers, thanked coaches with gifts of homemade fudge. Tony grilled hot dogs and corn for friends. He lost 53 pounds at Weight Watchers, where he arrived on time to every meeting.

Sports and church: Tony and Marc arrived punctually for early Sunday practice at the ice rink, then headed straight to Immaculate Conception church afterwards. Neighbors: Dodie invited a passing neighbor's big dog, Rastus, into the house despite the wood floors, and she offered one acquaintance free pick of the butterflies—"small skippers and blues, big monarchs and swallowtails"—in her yard. She delivered books, food baskets and blueprints to neighbors. There were parties: pancake breakfasts, sports banquets, newcomers' welcomes, apple festivals. Drives: to Atlanta to buy things for the shop; to Syracuse to find gifts for friends' children. Tony especially liked driving with troops of kids to the hobby shop to buy rockets, then returning home to shoot those rockets, one by one, into the sky.

And holidays to mark the seasons. Dodie welcomed holidays. Each season proved that the large gears above and underneath her house were still turning. She loved Christmas mugs. She filled up the chicken feeder outside her shop with cornstalks and pumpkins on Halloween. Tony helped. He towed kids behind a tractor every Halloween down into the space near the hedgerow, where he had set up a crew of autumnal white-cloth ghosts.

Jurors would look over the owner's manual for Tony Harris's Kubota tractor, as well as the manuals for his Honda lawn mower and Stihl chain saw when it came time to examine three gasoline cans retrieved from 1886 Ellis Hollow Road after the holocaust. Duct tape that Tony had applied to the gasoline cans one unremarkable day would be exposed to microscopic analysis, and that analysis would catch Shirley Kinge by the fingertips. A juror recalled, "The cans looked alike, the duct tape matched, the fiber count in the duct tape matched, the kind of adhesive in the duct tape, the fact there was writing on it, the fact that there were three cans in the Harris home, the fact that there were only three appliances on the Harris property that used fuel, that they used different types of fuel and the residues in those three cans were those same three precise things. We saw the owner's manuals for all those various pieces of equipment to verify what kind of fuel they used. The circumstantial evidence was overwhelming."

The circumstantial evidence *was* overwhelming. Collected and organized by the prosecutor, it was sufficient to convict Kinge. Fibers and residues recovered from the garage made fine evidence for a courtroom, where microscopic details are always welcome. It is unsettling, however, to move from this close, legalistic examination of scraps to a fuller vision of the animated family that once occupied the house. If clinical evidence obscures or replaces them, our chance to understand this tragedy will be lost.

■ ■ ■

Caroline Brown attended the neighborhood cookie exchange at Dodie's house on Monday of the last week. Women circled the big kitchen selecting Christmas cookies. Dodie was relaxed. She loved her house, but she was not a fanatical housekeeper. When Caroline came near the stove, she thought, "Come on, Dodie, get your stove clean." There were some cobwebs up in the rafters and the smoke alarm on the ceiling kept beeping. Dodie said it didn't need a battery; it probably just needed to have the dust wiped off the contacts.

In short, normally, Dodie's house would have been covered with fingerprints on the stove, on furniture, on tables, Caroline said. If it was strangely immaculate underneath layers of soot as state police investigators claimed, then the thieves must have spent hours wiping it down.

Just before the Browns left for California in the middle of that week, Bill took their fish tank over to the Harrises, who had agreed to keep the fish through the holidays. Marc would shovel their driveway as usual if it snowed. With preparations complete, the Browns caught their plane before the weekend.

Saturday morning, December 23, the alarm at 1886 Ellis Hollow Road went off. A neighbor who lives one field east of the Harris house said, "I always remember twenty of seven, because that's when we heard that piercing sound that turned out to be their alarm. And what happened was, we heard this—it was so cold, it was just freezing—and we heard the alarm, even in our bedroom. And you," she turned to her husband, "went downstairs to see what it was."

Her husband descended and listened, then told his wife he was going outside to check on the weird noise. But she said, "Oh, don't; come on, it's freezing cold, just go back to sleep."

Neighbors living directly on the other side of the Harris property went through essentially the same motions. Dennis Regan, a
professor in psychology at Cornell, owns the brand-new, cedar-
shingled Victorian erected in the field that lies between the Harris
house and Caroline Brown's kitchen window. In court, Professor
Regan explained that he and his wife had taken their daughter
out to celebrate her graduation from high school the evening of
December 22. That night was very cold. They noticed nothing unusual when they came home. Then, the next morning, at 6:45,
Professor Regan heard a loud noise. He looked around his own
house, then opened his front door to the cold and realized the
high sound was reverberating from his neighbor's home. He
phoned the Harrises and got no answer, then called the state police, called the Harrises again, called the police again. Within
twelve minutes, the alarm stopped. Looking out, Professor Regan
saw one of the Harrises' garage doors was open. Urged by his wife,
he returned to bed.

At 7:50 he heard voices and saw activity. He got up, dressed and
went outdoors, walked through the snow. In front of the Harrises'
house, a policeman said to him, "Get back, something very bad
has happened in here. We'll come down and talk to you shortly."

The Harrises' neighbor on the east walked from the opposite
direction later that morning. He encountered an ambulance driver
who said he didn't know why he was hanging around: "If I'm still
here, obviously I'm not needed."

In this story, help comes too late: the ambulance driver turns off
the ignition and waits outdoors near his vehicle by the road. Occa-
sional cars pass quickly on the two-lane Ellis Hollow Road. One of
Dodie's friends made a pass that morning and kept going, figuring
there must have been a chimney fire at 1886. All these facts are
part of a true story. Oddly, though, the story doesn't sound true
because it's so exaggerated, as if it had been written by a didactic
ninth-grader. The killer enjoys too many hours undisturbed in
that house where visitors were frequent, and the $1,500 security

alarm system waits for just a touch, one number struck out of sequence. Too many neighbors sleep peacefully through the night. A single alarm goes off too late, just at dawn. Both next-door neighbors sit up; their wives, in unison, tell them to lie back down. It's almost Christmas. Dead, the wife who feared an untimely death kneels in front of her husband. It's bitterly cold. The murderer is black, hooded. His middle name is Anthony and he calls himself Tony, just like the man he torments and kills.

This story is hackneyed, racially charged and, judging from the evidence, true. It slipped out of the closet and got straight into people's dreams, threatening Ithaca householders with both invasion and speechless guilt. More than a year after the murders, some people are still having dreams.

Tom Schneider lives in Ellis Hollow and is one of the group of close neighbors who feel most affected by the crime. A psychiatric counselor, he has met both adults and children who suffered from nightmares after the tragedy. He tells the story of a Cornell professor who lived across the road from the Harrises, who began dreaming repeatedly that, on the afternoon of the murders, he drove past the family's house and thought of stopping in. Schneider also counseled a young woman, a high school student, who felt that she had a chance to save Shelby, but missed it. This young woman "had done a number of things with Shelby, and that Friday afternoon Shelby was supposed to sleep over at this woman's house. And that afternoon, while they're still at their lockers, Shelby says, 'Oh, I can't do it,' and she says, 'Oh, come on, come on, Shelby, please do it,' and Shelby said, 'You're going to have to convince me more than this.' The young woman said, 'Okay, so if you've got to go home, you've got to go home'. . . . She feels she killed her." This young patient has recurring dreams, Schneider said. "It's a night terror, it's worse than a nightmare. This is what she's dreaming when she's asleep, and she's deathly afraid to go to sleep."

Tom Schneider himself dreams: "That I'd be sleeping and I would hear this sound in the living room and I would go out and see these people, sometimes it was one, sometimes it was two.

Sometimes it was more. We have a ranch house and they were walking down the hall to do harm. And there was this whole thing—what would I do? It's pretty standard."

Since the Harris murders, his wife has learned to shoot a twelve-gauge shotgun. It stays loaded in the bedroom closet.

Why a shotgun?

"Because with a little gun you miss."

Tom Schneider and his wife are parents to a young daughter, not yet old enough for kindergarten, whose photographs adorn his office. "Although it sounds strange, the nature of what this showed me is, if someone comes to my house to do harm, I'm going to kill them. I'm not going to ask questions. And with the nature of the loads I have in the gun, all my wife has to do is point it in the general direction."

He knows of many other Ellis Hollow residents who reacted in the same way: "I saw a range of women, for example, whose husbands were professors, women with small kids, and they weighed like ninety pounds, went to Charlie Muzzy [owner of a local gun shop] and bought a .357 Magnum. You ever hold a .357 Magnum? Weighs about eight pounds." The bullet from a .357 goes a mile and a quarter at a lethal velocity. These women bought guns that added approximately ten percent to their weight. They all imagined the same story: he will come to my door next time and I will kill him.

▪ ▪ ▪

An Ellis Hollow neighbor phoned California to tell Caroline and Bill Brown the news. Even at that distance, Caroline felt the murderer close. She and her husband didn't tell their sons; it was Christmas and their oldest boy was just eight years old at the time. When an ice machine rattled in the California kitchen one night when they were alone, Caroline and her husband both sprang away: "We literally came out of our skins. . . . It strips you. It takes you down to nothing."

It was awful returning home. The first night back in Ellis Hollow,

Caroline slept upstairs with her two sons while Bill slept downstairs alongside a small collection of kitchen knives and baseball bats. The boys didn't know about that either. The family's fish tank, which had been sent over to the Harrises for the vacation, may or may not have been recovered, clean or blackened, full or empty. Caroline didn't say.

She doesn't like seeing the Harrises' big grey house anymore, doesn't like the temporary towel stuck over the bathroom window by the pre-school teacher who leases the house. It's worse in winter, when the leaves come down and she can see the building from her kitchen window: "You don't want it to be, but it's like a monument. It's like a monument because it's unkept. . . . It reminds me of a huge headstone."

She had visited the house when it was burned and charred. How did it look? "Burned and charred." Caroline Brown is direct. She has a rounded, decent face, reddish hair that could go where it pleases but remains basically tame, brown eyes and freckles. She wears jeans and a pink T-shirt. When a heavy summer storm comes up and dims the living room, she doesn't notice for a time and neglects to turn on any lights. It's noon, but she speaks in twilight.

She and Bill had gotten to know Don Lake, Dodie's father, as a friend, before the tragedy. While Don was struggling to clean out and repaint the house after his daughter was murdered in it, he used to come over to Caroline's kitchen for lunch: "He built the house, and so he was the one who was going to put it back together." But he couldn't keep going at this dreadful job for a whole day. He rested during lunch, and told Caroline his story: when he was a boy, he had seen his own father place a note on the mantle one day. A few hours later his mother took down the note and read it; it said good-bye. It was good-bye. Don's father never came back. Don's mother developed arthritis that crippled her to the point where she had to put Don up for adoption. He went "from foster home to foster home." One foster father was good to him.

Eventually Don married, but his own wife had difficulties with her health; a bad heart kept her in bed. This meant Dodie, his oldest daughter, took on the mothering. Graduate of foster homes, Don developed a profitable company constructing homes. One of the best he made was for Dodie.

Caroline had met Dodie's father recently by the grey house. Sometimes Don looked like he was doing fine. Other days he looked tired, pale, sick.

■ ■ ■

Trials and detective stories attract an audience because they offer to reveal what really goes on in the dark, to expose the active traffic patterns of shadowed communities—the scum boys' world, the detective's world, secret domestic feuds, human viscera. It's a con. Trials and detective stories, while promising to lead us down into darkness, actually distract and thereby shield us from the blackest underworld: the death of someone we love, especially the death of a child we love. The thousands of dead fictional females whose bodies get rolled over like crankshafts to start up mystery novels remain strangers to the reader; they are mourned by minor characters but not by the investigator himself. The detective looks down and sees a handbag marked by salt water, a leg muscled in a way that signifies "health club member." The investigator does *not* look down and see the face of his own daughter with her eyes permanently glassed.

Dr. Humphrey Germaniuk, the medical examiner for Onondaga County, New York, testified in the trial of Shirley Kinge. Jurors remembered the doctor for his exaggerated, mechanical manner on the stand, the way he would twist his body to face them and then stare just above their heads. It was Dr. Germaniuk who compared the flesh of the Harrises' burned corpses to "overdone chicken or steak." His line of work puts him in touch with large and small corpses; in his profession, dead people necessarily become commonplace. How does such a man testify? On the stand, the doctor adopts a chilly expert's voice. Off the stand, not surprisingly, he talks like a gumshoe.

The Harris autopsies generated more than a thousand photographs, the Michael Kinge autopsy about eight hundred; we can guess the photographic slides are on file in metal drawers similar to the ones Onondaga County uses to store its preserved tissue samples (tiny magenta slices cut from the organs of former county residents). The autopsy photographs of both the victims and the perpetrator in this case would picture an ugly range of injuries to the skin. Some policemen who witnessed the carnage at the Harris house found it necessary to seek counseling. At one point during the trial, Shirley Kinge's defense attorney asked that photographs of dead Michael Kinge be shown to the jury; the district attorney objected that photographs of a "bloody corpse" had no relevance to questions at hand. The objection was sustained.

Dr. Germaniuk knows what it's like to cut through human skin and to look down on men, women and children whose figurative protective "skins" (automobiles, antibiotic shields, bedrooms) have been fatally disrupted or invaded. He knows what happens to a human body when it is suffocated, stabbed, crushed, shot, poisoned, smoked, massively infected, thrown by a tiny clot, drowned, drugged, left outdoors in February and so on. He was not very happy to be questioned about these topics outside the courtroom, though; he preferred conversations restricted by legal boundaries. So the doctor had slides, a projector, a white board, markers and a silver telescoping baton all ready for our interview, which he meant to conduct as a lecture.

The first thing Dr. Germaniuk did on the white board was to set up opposing lists showing how the education and experience required of a coroner was laughably inferior to the ten years of postgraduate medical training required of a medical examiner in New York State. A coroner merely has to be eighteen years old and win the local election. No medical background or training is required. A typical coroner "might be a tow truck operator along a busy stretch of highway where they are lucky enough to have all the fatalities," said the doctor, who then distributed his first hand-out, the reproduction of a newspaper article describing how a *coroner* had identified a skinned rabbit as a dead baby.

Dr. Germaniuk's voice was distinctive. It lilted and swung, as if he were lecturing hundreds, yet it was dry. He had adopted a tough gumshoe's voice in order to get through the hour, and he liked it. He liked the Raymond Chandler ring of it. Oddly, there were times when his detective's ironies intertwined with passages of Victorian cliché: "Forensic pathology is beautiful. We run a clinic for the dead, and as much love, care, attention and affection is given to our patients as any other patients. Just because a person *dies* does not mean that they're no longer a person. If you forget it's a human body, you ought to do something else—flip burgers or something. The human body is really a temple. It housed hopes, dreams, aspirations; it was loved, it loved, so you really can't separate that. . . .

"The things we can be certain of are that we are mortal and we are finite and that's what makes life worth living. Whether you're struck down by cancer or an assassin's bullet," he said.

His philosophical declarations relied on made-for-TV illustrations: "Advantages to this line of work? Okay. We have our roots in Biblical times. You can take a look at, early on, when Cain socked it to Abel, God did not have to say, 'Cain, where is thy brother?' God would have just asked for the autopsy reports, cranial cerebral trauma. Manner of death—homicide. Number two, we are still some of the few, rare physicians who make house calls, okay? Number three, we don't keep appointment books. Right now, there could be a 747 from New York airport on its way to Chicago that is going to blow two engines, bellyflop, that's got a terrorist bomb on board, that for whatever reason may come plummeting out of the sky, and today, which is generally an administrative day, may all of a sudden turn into . . . Okay, suit up."

Dr. Germaniuk was massively defensive, jolly and rigid, not

only because he intended to withhold information about the specific autopsies in question (as the victims' near relatives expected he would), but even more because he had learned over the years that most outsiders considered his profession ghoulish or at least unfriendly, less humane than the work of a traditional physician whose patients hear, see, feel and talk back. The medical examiner insisted repeatedly that his work as a physician who examined the dead was equivalent to the work of doctors who examine the living.

This was his lecture's theme. He argued that his patients did speak to him with their bodies, that his work comforted family members and helped cure larger social diseases like domestic violence, drunken driving ("How about accidents? The family of four that's tootling home from Grandma's house and gets hit by a drunken driver?"). He argued that the medicine he practiced was preventative by referring to deterrence ("If, as a result of my findings and the cooperation of law enforcement agencies, an individual may be brought into custody as a suspect, the next person may think of that") and to faulty car seats ("Remember back in the Fifties, the classic car seat? And all of a sudden, you get enough smashed-up kids, you take a look at car seats today").

Squeak, squeak went the marker on the white board. Would it be possible to see the autopsy room? In response to that question, the doctor tucked his fingers deep into the pockets of his red sweater vest and tipped his head: "Naw, I don't know what's going on back there. And again, every time a patient—a lot of people think once you're dead, it's over—but every time a physician sees a patient, we enter into a physician/patient contract, one of the boundaries of which is confidentiality. Right now there may be an examination going on back there; well, hell, I wouldn't want someone in the room while I'm being examined. To do an autopsy, all you need is a steel table and that's about it. Scalpel and a pair of scissors."

As it happened, an icy jail guard had responded in a similar manner a few days earlier when asked if he would lead visitors back into the real belly of the Tompkins County Public Safety Building (the jail) to see the dorms (glass-walled barracks used to house a number of male inmates) and cell blocks; the guard replied no, he couldn't allow the inmates' privacy to be jeopardized. It seems unlikely that these two men—the medical examiner, the jail guard—were shielding the privacy of the corpses or prisoners so much as they were shielding themselves. Both these men work in rooms where other people are awfully exposed. They may dread the ultimate payback, the *reversal* that would lock the guard inside the glassed dorm with the exposed communal toilet or lay the doctor out nude on the steel table.

Some do dread payback. Others dream of it. Our dreams of reversals are born of psychological need. We hope that justice will be done someday, that the rotten city judge will find his crimes exposed and his body pushed towards the maw of a legal machine he formerly controlled. Our hopes are answered by fantasies; thousands of detective novels conclude with hypocrites overthrown, police captains jailed. The heroes they had attempted to throw behind bars offer them farewell cigarettes through those same bars. Even our religions promise upsets—"But many that are first shall be last; and the last first."

But for citizens who have no faith that the county judge will someday stand before the Omniscient Judge, no faith that a perfect day of reckoning will truly unbake history's cake, exposing secret villains or, more important, showing a particular lost child home to the woman who has been checking school buses, standing for years in the middle of the two-lane road where her son was last seen—for the realistic, the faithless, murder stories are terrible. Terrible. They finish people. They defy deductive solution.

■ ■ ■

"We received a call we got a dead baby, upstate." The slide carousel had been plugged in, the beam of light activated along with the familiar windy hum of the projector's fan. Dr. Germaniuk had his baton on the screen. There was a child's face, rounded; the boy could not have been more than one year old. His face did not look sleepy, though the eyes were shut. Some dry blood showed under one nostril.

"On the back of the kid's scalp is this curious little triangular-pattern lesion. That was the only sign of external trauma." Click.

Was that the skull? It was. The skin had been sliced and peeled down like halves of a rubber swim cap on two sides of the child's skull. "There's his ears right there." The skull, oddly clean, not bloody, was round as an eggshell but gave the impression of being tough, damp. The ears looked like bits of rolled dough and they hung much too low now, near the neck. This child had been propped up on some kind of seat to prepare his head for the camera. He had chubby shoulders and his hands were not visible.

Click. "Again, if you go beneath the skull, this is the back of his brain and, lo and behold, that's the only injury he's got which is responsible for his demise. Well," Dr. Germaniuk's voice lilted, "what's the cause of death? Cranial trauma. What's the manner of death? Suicide is out. But we still could have either accident or homicide." Homicide if the mother intended to run into the tree, killing both herself and her child. The child's brain viewed through the window cut in the skull was bright red, not grey. The kid remained anonymous in order to protect his privacy.

There were also photographs of the dead mother, who had been killed in this automobile accident along with her infant son. Her breasts hung sideways. She had great lumps of wadding stuffed in her cut abdomen. We looked down her body from above her head. "I didn't do the autopsy on her because she was an out-of-county case, already signed, sealed and delivered," said the doctor.

The medical examiner had worked exactly like a detective. He had checked the road and the tree where the woman crashed. He had photographed the brake and gas pedals of her car as well as the undersides of the woman's shoes, which somebody had removed from her feet: "When you get on the inside of the car, one of the things that becomes important is shoes. If, all of a sudden, I'm committing suicide and I'm stepping on the gas pedal and I come to a complete impact, you'll get a complete imprint of the *gas* pedal on the bottom of the shoe, or the *brake* pedal if they're trying to stop."

And at last he checked the infant seat. He had discovered that the peculiar lesion in the kid's skull reproduced the shape of a small, branched crack in the turquoise car seat. "Can Dad sue the car seat company?" asked Germaniuk. "He's just lost his family. He's just lost his first-born son. I mean, there's someone who is mourning and grieving. Can he get financial compensation?"

No. According to the fireman who extracted the dead kid from the automobile, the car seat had not been properly installed. So that's settled. "But it doesn't explain why Mommy crashed into a tree," said the doctor. Eventually Germaniuk solved that mystery too. Three things must have happened. Mommy turned toward her son, who may have been fussing. Her car floated contrary to a slight deviation in the road. She accelerated accidentally. Crash.

"The two most important tools in forensic pathology are not the scalpel and the microscope. The two most important tools are the camera and the telephone," he said.

Would it be possible to see the equipment Dr. Germaniuk usually took to the scene of an accident or crime? Out came a camera box, containing a Minolta grip, Vivitar flash. In the box he kept a Dictaphone to take notes, a narrow Mini-Mag flashlight and a Swiss Army knife to cut ligatures, cut off jewelry, get through clothing. A ruler to measure fractures and the height of bruises. Film, rubber bands. A silver probe, which was nothing more than a smooth little baton, "to explore a wound." (When the doctor said that, an image surfaced: one stainless probe touching the rim of a surprisingly gentle, juicy bullet hole.)

And a compass to see which way the body is pointing. A human body does not dissolve into wet sugars or sparks of light at the instant of death. It stays. It is convincing, made of familiar components, workaday legs, bellies, cold precise ears. It declares: "This is *it*."

The effort to move closer, to know *it* better, paralyzes the investigator, who might as well pull up a chair, sit for a couple of minutes and attempt to locate his or her own brain. A brain, the center of consciousness, is not physically conscious of itself; it doesn't feel gravity or even its own shape and cupped place. A brain is less aware than the gut, which knots, or the heart, which quickens, or muscles, which feel gravity. The human brain is an empty space draped in a moving load of sensations and voices. Like death, one's own brain is obvious, familiar, commonplace and unreachable.

"Every case is so different, every case is so unique," the doctor said, but he could not say which, if any, had been most memorable. "Basically all of the cases, I guess, I don't know."

The autopsy report found that the Harris family died of gunshots to the head. Each of the children was shot three times, the adults two times. It did not appear that the parents and Marc had struggled at all after they were tied to the bedsteads. Pieces of broken glass littered the father's back. Shelby Harris, whose nude body was found alone in the master bedroom, had been raped and sodomized; the autopsy reported no traces of semen, however. (Police examined the master bedroom using a special black light that would "make semen give off a purplish glow," according to *The Ithaca Journal*. They found nothing.) When Dr. Germaniuk entered the master bedroom of the Harris house, he pulled a sock and another cloth gag out of the younger female victim's mouth. He attempted to remove the green prom dress that had been placed over her body and had apparently been tied to her wrist at one point. It was Dr. Germaniuk's job to amputate the Harrises' fingers and send them in tubes to the state police investigator, Robert Lishansky, who would try to get prints from them by using clay, ink, Q-tips and rubber gloves. Many of the fingers were too badly burned to read. (This part of the forensics investigation led to early rumors that the victims' fingers had been cut off by their attacker. On December 30, 1989, *The New York Times* reported that "Ellis Hollow residents and local reporters have heard persistent rumors—which the police will neither confirm nor deny—that fingers were cut off some of the victims and that one of the women may have been sexually assaulted." Before many weeks had passed, one of these details would be confirmed, the other transformed.)

■ ■ ■

Barbara White organized the memorial book about the Harris family. She did not choose to sit for a long interview, saying, "What I need to do now is be positive." She did speak briefly over the phone.

Her son Daniel still has nightmares. When he wrote his piece for the collection his mother was editing, he finished with: "Do you ever wonder why such bad things happen to such good people? So do I. There are some things that we just don't understand. But they're even closer now and that's all that counts. Well that's life." Barbara White did not include her son's final line, "Well that's life." It was the only passage she cut from all the submissions. It was unbearable to her.

She works as a nurse and knows something about the gut. The loss of her friends, Dodie and Tony and their children, hurt like an actual knife wound, not like a figurative one: "I was talking to a surgeon up at the hospital and I was telling him, 'A person who has surgery couldn't hurt as much as I do. It's a physical pain.'"

It stayed. "'Yes,' you think, 'my God, I went five minutes without thinking about it. I went ten minutes without thinking about it.' . . . The first time you giggle again or you laugh again, you think, 'What am I doing?'"

She had crazy thoughts. Not only did she imagine bringing her friends back to life. She also thought about how good it would be to rejoin them, talk to them all again, by crossing the boundary line in the other direction: stepping forward herself into that sky or pit where they lived now—"You don't feel like being alive. . . .

"Your kids make you survive."

■ ■ ■

Tom Schneider worked with kids. Specifically, he counseled teachers and children at DeWitt Middle School who had known Marc. One class decided to keep Marc's empty desk in the center of the room, one decided to put it in the front of the room, one decided to keep it in the back of the room. Schneider also took a bunch of kids on a tour of the Harris house after it had been repaired. A few went up and sat in the bedrooms.

Tom Schneider's daughter attends the Montessori pre-school that's located in the Harris house now. She plays and naps close to a secret place, a tiny buried cache in Marc's old bedroom that her father saw when he was part of the crew that accompanied Don Lake, Jr., Dodie's brother, when it was time to rip out the bloody floors and walls in the bedrooms where the murders occurred.

Marc was "quiet-natured, nice, quiet voice. Very polite. Sensitive," Caroline Brown said. "The way he asked questions and the way he treated Dodie, the way he treated his father, you could tell. I'd see Marc and Tony walking their dog together at six o'clock in the morning, and that's really nice. Just the two of them talking, walking." The father and son had an extensive baseball card collection. Marc's favorite player was Carl Yastrzemski. When Yastrzemski was inducted into the Hall of Fame, the whole family went to Cooperstown. Dodie and Shelby headed straight for the antique shops; Marc and Tony, triumphant, walked to the Hall of Fame.

The worst fire damage was in Marc's bedroom. Tom Schneider worked in that room with a lever and accidentally found Marc's private cache: "After we tore the sheetrock out of his room, there were these rafters exposed in his bedroom, these underneath floor joists, and Marc had these baseball cards lined up underneath the sub-flooring, and he also had these little people, weren't G.I. Joe, not army people, but people people, like a three-year-old would play with. Little plastic people on little bases, they were also lined up. It was a set-up. My five-year-old daughter makes set-ups, and when I think about Marc, that's what comes into my head. . . . The baseball cards were lined up, not stacked. Maybe he was doing his trades or something, or he was having a baseball draft. . . .

"So we left it. We put a piece of sub-flooring over it."

Since uncovering those poised baseball cards and tiny arranged figures, which touched him because they were so gently sweet, Tom Schneider has learned something about hatred.

"If there would be an execution of Michael Kinge, could I pull the switch? Without blinking an eye." He imagines it sometimes. "Oh, I had all kinds of fantasies. A lot of therapists were talking about that; all kinds of weird fantasies. I imagined I'd be working after hours, that I would get an AIDS-infected needle, that I would give him a razor. You know, I think the same stuff that anybody would imagine."

Tom, whose own brother was found dead, inexplicably, in a beached boat, and whose parents both died within a single year of cancer, will never give anybody a razor; these are just dreams, stories he told himself. Tom loves his young daughter and when he imagines her hurt, a buffaloed rage makes his blood speed. Fantasy is one way he prepares himself against shadows that might be waiting in his future, and in hers.

A lot of scary stories promise to inoculate us against *real* horrors. They tickle or sting. The cold shivers they induce feel therapeutic.

But other stories, the worst stories, make every hour of safe passage, every plain, happy hour, feel like a dream. We try to dream harder, to *dream it all*, so that the diabolic shadows will be hobbled by our foresight, robbed of their power to catch us off guard and thereby restrained from entering our bedrooms and the bedrooms of our children.

This exercise doesn't work very well, but neither do locks and guns. The real gun that Tom Schneider keeps in his bedroom is actually half dream. He asks it to come with him when he falls asleep. Solid objects grow ghostly. The reverse theorem works too. Good dreams, bad dreams, horror stories, salvation stories—all come true some place on the solid face of the world.

trailing Shirley

IN OTHER WORDS, just because someone lies about something doesn't mean it isn't true.
　　　　　　　　　—*The New York Times Book Review*, July 14, 1991

■ ■ ■

For generations, exposure has been a key civil punishment; adulteresses bow their heads to the razor, rowdies slump in the stocks. Every trial exposes the defendant *and* the victims in a manner that makes exposure appear perfectly well-mannered, civilized. But it is actually a cruel business. Faced with the civil exposure of the defendant, a stripping-down which essentially constitutes that citizen's first punishment, spectators in a courtroom remain at ease because they have been assured that, here, it is not rude to stare. Here, it is proper.

And yet the exercise of staring at a defendant can be unexpectedly frustrating, perpetually baffling, because any thoughtful spectator realizes early that the skull of the accused person is not going to spring open and display its ticking secrets and memories. In fact, defendants maintain privacy to a startling degree in court. This is most obviously true of individuals who, like Shirley Kinge, do not choose to testify on their own behalf. An actual jury trial almost never acts as a stage for confessions, or any other sudden, electric acts of conscience or revelation. TV courtroom mini-dramas are electric; real trials are not.

Shirley and Michael Kinge once owned themselves, kept to themselves; captured, Michael died and his mother remained to stand trial, to be analyzed, exposed, photographed. It is here that an interesting story begins, because Shirley Kinge resisted exposure. During her own trial, she did not choose to give herself up; she held her face still as iron or sleep.

Shirley Kinge became a local public figure the day of her arrest, when the videocam taped her stumbling out of the duplex in old belly-slung jeans, her grey hair matted under a wedged wool hat shaped like a golfer's cap, hands cuffed behind her waist by the police. Months later in the courtroom, she would look different. Coiffed (bewigged) and slender, outfitted in low heels and dress suits, she maintained a strict poise that slowed down her movements, as if the element she lived in now were sharp. Sometimes her eyes would close. When Investigator Doug Vredenburgh described the last twelve-gauge shotgun blast that caught her son in the face, her eyes closed. But her chin stayed up. Tight muscles bound her jaw to her skull, and her lips were pursed, soundless, conclusive. Coming out of court, Shirley held her hands together at the waist. It was difficult to notice that she wore a broad leather restraining belt under her jackets and that her wrists were locked to it whenever the court broke for lunch.

This transformation, from sloppy prisoner to crisp defendant, was not Shirley Kinge's only metamorphosis. Even the most polite defendant appears shifty in a courtroom because opposing lawyers busily dress her up, costuming her alternately as good girl, bad girl. The defendant who contests the charges leveled against her wears different masks at various times in court. Which mask dominates is determined not so much by the actions of the accused as by the projections of the audience and skills of the opposing lawyers. A woman's upright face may appear frank and clear one moment, stubborn and deceptive the next, though her eyes and mouth do not move.

Ironically, Shirley Kinge's impassive face in the courtroom took on a dizzying variety of masks. Was Shirley a bereaved black mother punished as substitute for her son, the murderer? If so, then this was both a witch trial and a Bad Mother trial. Or was she a hardened moll, "the brains" of a little family of thieves? One juror called her a "blank slate," one witness called her a "vacuum."

One man from Syracuse, watching her image on television, fell in love with her and began visiting regularly at the jail. Laymon Herring described his first impression of Shirley Kinge in custody between the guards this way: "I saw her on TV . . . and I noticed how her hair was blowing . . . and that's when I got the feeling, you know, like the Righteous Brothers' song, that loving feeling." They got engaged in January, 1991, just before she was sentenced.

Defense described Shirley Kinge in one way, the prosecutor in another. There are many stories about her, and plenty of people who, not knowing her, feel convinced they understand her. At times the stories combine to produce a tense, breathing composite of a woman. At other times they seem to offer the investigator nothing more than a long strand of paper dolls with faces drawn in crayon: mother doll, black woman doll, housekeeper doll (include the little vacuum cleaner), loner doll, victim, villain, thief, dupe, witch, bitch, cold-blooded arsonist doll, prisoner doll.

The same Tom Schneider who counseled adults and schoolchildren in the wake of the Harris murders, volunteers after hours in the hospital emergency room and county jail. As it happened, he was on duty to interview Shirley Kinge at the close of February 7, her first day as a captured public figure, in order to determine whether she would be at risk for suicide in jail.

She had been arrested early that morning when state police raided her apartment. According to Schneider, she told him that when the police guns exploded in Michael's side of the duplex, "that house shook." Shirley was arrested and videotaped immediately after the house shook, then transported in a police car to the police barracks in Cortland, New York, where she was interrogated, informed that her son was dead, interrogated some more, then driven to Syracuse and placed in a line-up alongside five other black women who were all approximately four inches taller and twenty years younger than she. (The defense would make much of this discrepancy.) Shirley was then returned to Ithaca so police could take fingerprints, photographs and handwriting samples, driven to Dryden for the arraignment, and finally returned to Ithaca, to jail, where Schneider met and spoke with her for two hours in the holding cell: a glass-walled unit containing one cot and an exposed white toilet.

She was distraught. She had her arraignment papers, which showed that she was being charged with four counts of second-degree murder (the charge was later reduced). "She was shaking, she was crying, she was nervous," Schneider said. "She was rocking back and forth, she was smoking endlessly, she was alternating between states of total dissociation and total immersion. She was in numerous places at once. It was constantly repetitive, what she said." Shirley went in circles "as if to find her core. But there wasn't any. She was scattered, as if she were hemorrhaging. . . . She wouldn't have been able to lie to me because she was too scared."

And? "She said there was someone else involved. Actually, she said words to the effect of, 'The two people who know are dead and no one will ever know.' . . . She told me that she had nothing to do with the house, she was not near the driveway, she was not in the van; she owned up her guilt relative to the credit cards and the spending spree. . . . But, I mean, it's not my position; I don't know if she was there or not." (Shirley Kinge's courtroom defense made no mention of a secret male accomplice who helped Michael Kinge in his assault on the Harris family.)

Tom Schneider's statements indicate that he judged Shirley Kinge to be a distressed, vulnerable truth-teller the night of her arrest when she told him that she had never set foot in the Harris house, never splashed gasoline through the Harris house. Pressed on the question (does he conclude Shirley Kinge was wrongly convicted of arson and armed burglary?), Schneider, a personal friend of the victims, twists loose and broadens the equation. "I'm being pulled towards confusion, genuine confusion," he says. "The bad guys took a hit, but the good guys really took a hit. The Harrises died, they just died. They were rubbed out. . . . What changed? Shirley gets this, Joanna gets that, my friends are dead and what the fuck do I do with that?"

■ ■ ■

Policemen sitting relaxed for interviews call her "Shirley." Policemen sitting in the witness chair refer to her as "Mrs. Kinge."

Senior Investigator H. Karl Chandler and Investigator George Clum testified in the Kinge pretrial hearings and again in the actual trial. They were the two officers who "interviewed" Mrs. Kinge in the Cortland state police barracks immediately after her arrest.

According to their testimony, it was about 9:50 in the morning, February 7, when they announced to the suspect that her son had died in the raid. In response, the mother sat down on the floor. "She gasped and said, 'God' or 'Oh God.' Then she was sobbing very heavily. She got off the chair, sat on the floor next to the wall. She was on the floor about five minutes sobbing," Clum testified. He continued, "She asked for a cigarette and I gave it to her. Her hands were shaking so she couldn't light it, so I lit it for her. . . . She kept asking us, 'Is he really dead, is he really dead?'"

Officer Charlene Hippenstiel testified that she heard Mrs. Kinge cry out through the shut door of the interview room: "It was loud. It was part scream, part wail maybe." A few minutes later, the two investigators who had been in the room with Mrs. Kinge called for Officer Hippenstiel's assistance. She brought Mrs. Kinge tissues and water in her distress—"I helped her with the water. She was spilling it. So I helped her carry the water to her lips and she drank the water. . . . I picked her up and placed her in the chair."

Within about fifteen minutes, Mrs. Kinge was up, off the floor, and the "interview" had begun again. Police testified that Mrs. Kinge began to talk more freely once she learned her son was dead, and that she told them "her son had threatened to kill her if she talked about the crime. He was better off dead. He had been a beautiful child, but at the age of 15 had turned into a monster." Everybody smoked in the small interview room, though the door was closed. Chandler had Camel Lites, Clum had Marlboros, Shirley had Benson and Hedges Lights. By about 11:00 a.m., according to George Clum, "I was out of cigarettes and Chandler was out."

Somebody was sent out of the barracks into the daylight to get more cigarettes and some food. By this time, Senior Investigator Chandler was taking down Mrs. Kinge's statement. Now and then, Officer Hippenstiel would accompany Mrs. Kinge to the bathroom, where "I got her a drink of water. She would wash her mouth, wash her face." Preparation of Mrs. Kinge's statement was completed at 1:55 p.m., but before she could sign it, she had to read it, and she had no glasses. Someone was sent back to the duplex to get her reading glasses; policemen were able to enter that house when they pleased now. At about this time, Chandler started to turn up the heat. He told Shirley that he knew she had been in the Harris house. He mentioned the gas can and fingerprints; she responded that she had borrowed a rectangular gas can recently from a neighbor on Etna Road.

The reading glasses arrived, but now the suspect, distressed by Investigator Chandler, refused to sign the long document of recorded questions and answers that the investigators had typed up. The unsigned statement was presented as evidence at the trial. No surprise confession was hidden here; the defense attorney's version of events echoed the statement. This—an unsigned statement recorded by a police interrogator—was the nearest the audience would come to hearing Shirley Kinge describe her own (alleged) memories of December 22 and December 23, when she saw Michael for the first time after the murders and drove with him up to the shopping malls.

According to the unsigned statement as it was reprinted in *The Ithaca Journal*, Shirley Kinge told police that she never entered the Harris house, and that the first time she saw Michael after Friday night was late afternoon Saturday, December 23: "He came to my side of the house, he came into the house, I had dozed off and I had heard the noise of the door and that's what woke me up. I got up and went into the bathroom, I was brushing my teeth, he knocked on the bathroom door and asked me what I was going to do later. I told him that I had not planned to do anything, that I planned to be home. He asked me to drive him to Auburn, NY. I told him that I didn't really want to. He said that it was Christmas, so I told him to wait until I showered and got dressed. He told me that he would buy the gas."

According to the unsigned statement, Michael and Shirley Kinge went up to Auburn. "When we got to the Auburn Mall, he told me to come on in and I said that I didn't like shopping in malls because they are noisy and crowded and I just don't like malls. I don't like to shop. He told me it was cold out and to come because it was warm and that we could meet back at the same entrance we would be going in.

"I went in and we agreed to meet at the entrance. I walked around and looked in some stores. I ran into Michael again and he said, 'Why don't you go and buy yourself something.' I told him that I didn't have any money. He reached into his pocket and he came out with this envelope and took a card out of the envelope and gave the card to me. He told me to use the card, saying that it was blank. He said that all I had to do was sign it and that I could use it. I asked him where he got it from and he said that he got it from a guy down by the Commons [Ithaca's downtown pedestrian mall]. He gave me the telephone number and address for me to use for identification." The name on the card was *Dolores E. Harris*.

In the malls, according to court testimony, Shirley Kinge purchased a pair of diamond stud earrings for pierced ears, Reebok sneakers and two sweaters, one purple, one black and white, which she gave to her mother (the police claim she also purchased Sizzlers underwear). After leaving the mall, "We went home, I rode in the back seat, I fell asleep and when I woke up, we were home. I went into my house and Michael went into his. When I came in, I fed the dog and took him out. When I came back in, my mother told me about some people out in Dryden that had been killed. I asked her what their names were and she told me 'Harris' and that's when I made the connection."

Later in the document, "The next day I questioned Michael about the murders. The first thing I said to him was, knowing that he did it, why did he get me involved, why didn't he tell me and let me make the decision about using the cards. We had a big argument about this. My thing with him was that he should have told me. He said that he knew that I would react the same way as I was at that time.

"Q. How were you reacting?

"A. I was outraged.

"Q. Go on.

"A. I asked him how he got onto these people, why he did it, he never answered me. I asked him then and several times after that why he did it and why he would get me involved. He never gave me an answer. He said to me that I didn't know those people, why did I care. That about sums it up. I asked him if he had planned it or why there or why it wasn't John Doe or Mary Doe and he never answered. He just looked at me."

Later, "Numerous times over a period of time, he has voiced the fact that if the police ever came to arrest him, he would kill himself rather than go back to jail."

And, "Deep down, I don't think he would have harmed me. But he had said that if any of us went to the police, that we could just forget it. I interpreted that to mean that if anyone told, he would harm me or some member of the family. I told him that if he felt that way, why don't just come over here and blow me away while I'm sleeping."

In the pretrial hearings, Officer Hippenstiel testified that she heard Mrs. Kinge say to Senior Investigator Chandler in the smoky interview room, "You're lying, he's not dead, he's not dead. You're lying to me." Senior Investigator Chandler replied, "Shirley, we would not lie to you about something like that. He is dead." In that room, he was calling her Shirley.

■ ■ ■

Policemen and policewomen are our most practiced trial witnesses. Central New York's Troop C state police officers are skilled in court, prepared even to face the lawyer who defended Shirley Kinge: Bill (Sully) Sullivan. A local official who had encountered Bill Sullivan many times told me that the best way to prepare for Sully was to "drive for miles with your face stuck out the window and the air coming at you, coming at you."

Troop C officers understand how to format their testimony in court; this skill is a vital part of their job as law enforcement agents. Seated in the witness stand, a trooper's chief goal is to avoid contradicting detailed statements he (the great majority of officers who testified in the Kinge trial were white males; no officers testifying were black) has made earlier, in signed reports or before the grand jury, and also to avoid contradicting statements his colleagues have made. Hesitation (thoughtfulness) in a police witness is suspect. Cops speak as if the witness chair were refrigerated.

Of course, we expect professional detachment, self-control, from professionals who must deal steadily with violence or horror. Physicians practice it, as do judges and cops. But what distinguishes a police officer's attitude from a judge's is the fact that an officer's detachment usually camouflages visceral responses and memories. The law enforcement universe features villains ("scum boys," "scum bags," "scum buckets") a trooper has literally touched and been touched by. His memories have grist, and so do the memories of his teammates, other law enforcement officers. A police officer works as a team player more than an attorney or judge will. The New York state police investigators I interviewed knew very well which team they were on. They simply *were not the bad guys*, despite accusations made by the defense attorney, whose exaggerated portrait of police folly and dishonesty would make any cop feel wronged—and righteous.

The restraints on a police officer testifying in court are nearly visible. Practiced police witnesses don't let themselves get riled, even though the white-collar attorneys, who probably haven't been on the receiving end of a good, hard shove in years and who are privileged to deal with suspects only after those suspects have been captured and placed under guard, try to make them look like bullies, fools and liars. Police witnesses guard against the defense attorney's attack by erecting hard walls of unemotional responses. What these walls hide—allegiance, anger, conviction—is not hard to guess.

Listening to policemen speak first on the witness stand and then later, in interviews, one begins to notice something about our entire Anglo-American court system. Our courts, which aim to conduct objective trials by using controlled antagonism, finally serve up a very peculiar concoction—impersonal discourse accompanied by melodrama. Spectators in court consume big helpings of this stuff, this cardboard cake with hot fudge icing, from witnesses and, ultimately, from attorneys on both sides.

Antagonistic portraits of Shirley Kinge as Villain and as Victim created two caricatures during her trial. Police investigators and troopers generally pictured the defendant in the same way the prosecutor did. Though the district attorney, George Dentes, presented his case in a subdued, formal, even whispery voice, his Shirley Kinge emerged costumed as the Deadeye Cleaning Lady. Capable of ironing doilies with one hand and splattering gasoline with the other, this villainous Shirley presided over a dirty nest where her boy, cuddling his semi-automatic, hid behind her feathers.

To counteract this portrait, the defense presented Shirley as Dependable Grandma, a woman who would never have relegated child care to her own mother and left their apartment in the dead of night, even if her grown son pulled up at the door and confessed to a quadruple homicide. As portrayed by her own lawyer, Shirley Kinge became a dazed, maternal black woman endlessly victimized, duped and tormented by males, men like her son and the deceptive law enforcement officials who kept offering her Benson and Hedges cigarettes during the interrogation to prey on her addiction to nicotine.

■ ■ ■

One police officer who played a key role in the Kinge investigation was Investigator David Harding. Investigator Harding happened to discover the only survivor of the holocaust: the Harrises' pet cat, Shadow, crawled out from under a charred bed when Harding was in the room, looking over the bleak crime scene. "It had plastic or something melted on its face and it had difficulty breathing," he said. Harding supervised the gargantuan forensics investigation of the Harris house. The card showing reproductions of fingerprints lifted from the gas can in the Harrises' front room, the fingerprints which were responsible for convicting Shirley Kinge of major felonies, is signed with his name.

Following up the forensics investigation, it was also Harding who took up the unusual undercover pose as "David Savage," a grants administrator and Peregrine House guest. He met Shirley Kinge, photographed her, noted her cigarette habits and, pleading injury to his splinted right hand, took a sample of her handwriting on envelopes. During their meeting at Friendly's the next day, they talked about how she might apply for a grant to help fund a sort of hospice or retreat for "underprivileged people" (Harding's words) on a tract of land she owned up near Watertown, New York.

He also learned enough to track down her previous employment record, including a stint at the U.S. Treasury Department. He obtained copies of her fingerprints from Treasury sources on February 3 and, on that day, according to his testimony, an expert matched them up with prints found on the gas can recovered from the Harris living room.

During a personal interview, Harding's version of events was both cool—frequently he pleaded loss of memory as if he were still in the witness chair—and melodramatic in its final portrait of Shirley Kinge, whom he considered to be the willing, practiced partner of her son Michael. Viewed from Investigator Harding's perspective, Shirley was the "brains" of the outfit, a woman decisive, responsible, criminal—not a victim of anybody or anything, not a character who deserved pity. She was purely villain.

The lobby of the State Police Command Post at Sidney, New York, where the interview with Harding took place, is homey and panelled in a way that recalls an Adirondack lodge. In it, brochures listing the salaries for New York State police officers ($24,308 to start at the Academy, $41,724 after five years) are available from a painted shelf, and there's a display case full of nice old county fair trophies (Troop C started out as a mounted troop nicknamed "The Grey Riders") near a plaque showing that no officer from Troop C has died in the line of duty since the early Seventies.

Investigator Harding appeared in the lobby fifteen minutes after I arrived. He has a pale cowboy's face, a lean American face. His forehead goes deep where his hair parts, but still he looks young. His voice, hurt by a pneumonia that had caught up with him in December, soon after the conclusion of Kinge's trial, sounded damaged. The interview was conducted in a large back room near a water cooler.

Since Harding mentioned at one point that he was a writer too ("mostly short stories, teleplays"), and that he'd been thinking about doing his own book on the Harris investigation ("I think it's a hell of a case"), provided he could get permission from the State

Ethics Commission, it was to be expected that many details he considered interesting would be kept secret. At the same time, his general descriptions of the archaeological tracking work he and his teammates completed in the Harris house began to make sense; the work began to take shape as he talked.

According to his own description, Harding's days inside the house had been spent in meticulous searches for fragile bits of evidence which might or might not exist and which, if they did exist, could be located just about anywhere in a large space. It involved little soft-bristled brushes used over wide areas in an attempt to uncover, to make clear, the decipherable marks of past events, past life. "It would take three people all day to dust this room," Harding said, gesturing around the conference room. "You're using a half-inch brush on an eight-foot wall."

Police searched for evidence in the Harris house for approximately two weeks. According to Major Farrand, that was the longest piece of forensics work he knew of in twenty-nine years with the force; the house was "huge" and, at the same time, oddly clean of household fingerprints, according to the state police. Walls, doors, tennis trophies, banisters, doorknobs, window shades were dusted with black fingerprint dust, but little showed up. Fingerprint dust is blue-black; in the Harris house, it was frequently applied on top of black soot (". . . the ash and soot generally is fine enough that it's compatible with the dust," Harding said). Whole doors and walls were illuminated by lasers. Many objects were put into little, jerryrigged plastic tents and exposed to SuperGlue fumes to help fix any fingerprints so that they wouldn't be destroyed when the police tried to take the lifts. Absorbent surfaces were tested with chemical reactors, all of which respond to traces of salts and amino acids; in this way, investigators can identify fingerprints traced delicately in criminal sweat rather than in criminal oils. Hundreds of things in the house wound up bagged and transported to the state police lab (according to defense lawyer Bill Sullivan, this "lab" is about the size of a closet and does not contain much equipment beyond a microscope and a few shelves of chemicals).

But Harding (like a medical examiner before him and a judge before that) said no particulars stuck out in his memory: "When you initially process the scene, you're looking for everything and anything. Trace evidence, like hairs and fibers, footprints, loose buttons torn off in a struggle, pieces of earrings—you don't know. That's why, quite often, I'll be in on my hands and knees crawling around the place and somebody'll say, 'What're you looking for?' I don't know. 'Cause you don't." Harding had crawled through the Harrises' charred house on his knees. Some days he wore special glasses in the dark to protect his eyes from laser light while he and his partners examined blackened, glowing doors. Other times he must have cursed trying to pick leaky SuperGlue tubes off his fingers. He was careful testing Christmas wrapping paper from the ransacked gifts in the house. As he explained, much of it isn't really paper, it's plastic-based stuff that, tested with the wrong chemicals, will dissolve on contact.

Despite these efforts, *no* prints or traces of Michael Kinge, the established murderer, were found in the house or in the getaway van besides scattered cigarette butts, which yielded no fingerprints. Harding agreed with the prosecutor's theory that the Kinges had done a cleaning job at the scene of the crime. Wasn't it difficult to credit this tale of lunatic black housekeepers who whipped out their dust rags and wiped down the kitchen one last time before attempting to burn the Big House to the ground? The investigator responded by saying that prints are fragile and easy to ruin: "Again, we're talking about atomized quantities of salt or acid. It takes nothing to wipe them away. You've got your prints on that table and just go like that—", he said, wiping near the tape recorder with his coat sleeve. "They're obliterated to the point where there's nothing for you to work with."

What was it like then, generally, to hunt down these fragile traces in order to work backwards to a monstrously violent event?

"I never thought of it like that," he said.

■ ■ ■

David Harding firmly believed that Shirley Kinge never suspected he might be an undercover cop those two days when he
posed as David Savage, grants expert, at the Peregrine House and
then at Friendly's restaurant: "She had no idea. I know she didn't.
Anything she would say contrary to that just isn't true. A person as
articulate, well-versed and intelligent as Mrs. Kinge would never
entertain me, go on with the things that she provided us, if she'd
had any idea. . . . Don't think for a second that if she thought I was
a cop, she was going to sit down and tell me about weapons."

Harding was referring to an incident that happened in
Friendly's. According to his own testimony, they had been talking
about her history and facts she should include on the grant
application when he asked her whether she'd ever been convicted of a crime. Leaning forward and taking his hand, she said,
"Do you mean did I ever kill anybody?" Following his bemused
response to that, she reportedly added, "Well, if somebody put a
.357 Magnum in my face, I might make you eat it, but I would
try to get away."

Investigator Harding interpreted this statement as proof that
Mrs. Kinge did not suspect his true identity: "That sounds like a
pretty shocking statement and it was in a way. But, again, we deal
with guns and violence and death all the time, so it's not something that's going to shock me, set me back dreadfully. I was a little
shocked by some of those statements, just because I'd never had a
lady tell me these kinds of things before." Others might interpret
Shirley Kinge's words differently, as part of a half-conscious, edgy
game of hide and seek this woman was playing with this friendly
man. We imagine her as a tough, lost woman who sensed the
hunters were drawing very near, a woman who found herself,
one day, chatting with her polite enemy in an ice cream shoppe.
Such a woman invites both dread and sympathy. She was certainly
living in a nightmare.

Harding was interested in the topic, in Shirley, and felt that he understood her after crawling on his knees and peering through special glasses in search of her fingerprints, then examining objects this woman had touched: following her tracks for so long. "I have a feeling for [the Kinges], just from having worked so closely with them for such a long time," he said. Asked about the weird trail the Kinges would have needed to follow if they acted according to the theories of the police, a trail alternately invisible (so few traces found at the Harris house that the police theorized mother and son, practiced janitors, got down to clean the place) and blazing (finished scrubbing down and igniting the Harris house, mother and son take the victims' credit cards and shop for Christmas gifts), Harding spoke about criminals, what he knew of criminals.

The way he figured it, Michael Kinge never got rid of the murder weapon because "that was a real piece of handiwork. He was very proud of that, especially after he used it to kill those people. Most people kill somebody, one of the first things they do is get rid of that weapon, but this was something pretty special to him, to use again."

To use again?

"I don't have any doubts. They would have."

They? Did Harding see them as a pair?

"I don't have any doubts. Somebody has to be the brains. She's very intelligent."

But the Kinges gained almost nothing from the burglary and murders. Was it intelligent to go parading through the malls with the VISA cards?

"I think, again, they thought they'd taken the evidence out of the house, cleaned it up, burned it t. the ground. You know, they're off shopping, they don't know if that place is smoking in the basement or if the fire went out. . . . That's why they didn't keep the cards. That shows some degree of intelligence there. You know, these are VISA gold cards, thousands of dollars credit ratings; they could have run those for a long time. . . . But here, again, you're not dealing with somebody who thinks like you and I. These are killers. They're not sane, rational people anyway. They view everything from a little different perspective."

Investigator David Harding thought of Shirley Kinge as both contradictory and monolithic. When she needed to be the brains of the outfit, she became the brains. When she needed to be irrational, she became irrational. According to this police theory, criminals are impossible to understand but easy to explain: they're criminal because they choose to be. Having chosen, they are responsible for their own actions and thus deserve punishment.

This legal portrait of the woman Shirley Kinge does not allow her to be helpless in the presence of her son, even though this son happened to be a grown man whose bedroom arsenal included little, sharpened homemade tubes—aluminum stickers—designed to protrude from a clenched fist to make deep puncture wounds.

A more complex portrait would allow for this woman's fears. It might show her, for instance, walking the center aisle of a mall at Christmas, decisive and helpless with a stolen gold VISA card in her hand. To picture Shirley Kinge in this way involves an act of interpretation which legal discourse cannot handle well. Our antagonistic courts, and probably our law enforcement officers as well, are poorly equipped for expeditions into ambiguity, but it is here that characters, not caricatures, reside, their eyes obscured by shadow. The defendant's tracks are everywhere in this fertile territory.

According to her own statement, Shirley Kinge knew by the evening of December 23 that her son had murdered the Harrises. Even so, on Christmas she gave her mother the sweaters purchased with Dolores Harris's stolen VISA card.[1] The gesture is chilling. Five

---

1. Sallie Reese, Shirley Kinge's mother, testified under oath that she had received a particular sweater from Shirley as a Christmas present; the prosecuting attorney identified the sweaters recovered from 520A as the sweaters purchased by the suspect from a Sixteen Plus store with the stolen VISA card. However, since Shirley Kinge's first trial has been discredited, thanks to David Harding's dishonesty, legally this testimony now exists in limbo.

weeks later, in a small interrogation room, when police announced to her that Michael was dead, killed in that morning's
raid, Shirley Kinge sat down flat on the floor and wailed. That gesture is pitiable.

■ ■ ■

Nancy Falconer owns the Peregrine House bed and breakfast
where David Harding played out his undercover scheme. The inn
faces uphill on a slope so pronounced that the sidewalk crosses at a
level with its second-story windows. Nancy Falconer's private residence faces a different slope in town and backs over one of Ithaca's
small cliffs, on the creek gorge that cuts behind Woolworth's. She
lives here with her granddaughter, a blonde child of misty pretti-
ness. Their back yard is a narrow, crumbling shale platform. There
are plenty of such houses in Ithaca, houses whose basements expose themselves where the hill drops down, houses propped on
stilts over deep drops, houses constructed near angular cliff walls
that beckon footloose phantom children.

Falconer is a handsome white woman who wears loose, brightly
colored clothing and keeps her nautical grey hair cropped short.
Our interview was conducted in her front room which, furnished
in antiques set off by tinted, muted photographs of her children,
was as pretty as the inside of an Easter egg. During the interview,
Mrs. Falconer chewed nicotine gum; she and Shirley had smoked
the same brand of cigarettes, Benson and Hedges Lights, but now
she was trying to quit.

Nancy Falconer had lived through a hard year in 1990. One of
her adult daughters had suffered a breakdown just before the year
began. This meant January of 1990, the month following the Harris murders, was shadowed not only by the results of a family crisis
which required Mrs. Falconer to take over the care of her granddaughter, but also by the police undercover investigation of
Shirley Kinge, an investigation focused on the Peregrine House,
where Mrs. Kinge was employed for $6.50 an hour to help iron

doilies, pillowcases and cloth napkins (not sheets), take reservations, serve food, cook food, vacuum and clean.

Falconer had cooperated with the police in January, thinking that the evidence they collected would help clear Shirley, a woman whom she considered meticulously neat, a hard worker, intelligent, sometimes moody. "Shirley would come down from a hot day of cleaning and look like she'd stepped out of a band box," said Falconer. "She said she didn't feel it, but her shirt would still be crisp and there was nothing out of place." David Harding had testified that Shirley Kinge dropped ashes on the floor as she stood at the ironing board in the Peregrine House, but Nancy Falconer did not believe it; she thought he was making up stories: "I never saw . . . I've seen her put the ashes in her hand." Half-heartedly, she wondered if the investigator might have gotten her mixed up with Shirley; she described herself as a "wrinkly, messy person" who had smoked continuously during her own nervous interviews with the police.

When police talked with Nancy Falconer, it became obvious they assumed *every* action of Shirley Kinge's over the course of two years in the company of her employer must have been essentially deceptive. Shirley, the criminal, could not be sincere. When Mrs. Falconer told police that Shirley had often criticized Michael ("She never praised him. . . . She couldn't stand macho men and she commented on that in Michael over and over"), police concluded the sly mother/moll was just trying to distance herself, to camouflage her working partnership with her son. Discovering that the two women smoked the same brand of cigarettes, the police "made remarks to me during the interview about, 'Oh, that was so she could get away with using your cigarettes.' Not true. For two years she was scrupulous." Mrs. Falconer concluded, "She didn't tell me things and act this way for two years to set me up for this event." And "I've had some psychopaths work for me up there, I really have, and they act very differently from what I ever saw in Shirley."

Her own experiences as an admittedly dazed go-between during
the investigation ("I somehow was able to remove myself enough
from it so that I didn't think it was really real") left her with some
odd, strong stories. She remembers which mundane objects David
Harding took out of the Peregrine House to be dusted for fingerprints and how those things were returned to her: "David was very
pleasant, very soft-spoken, very nice. . . . He took a lot of things.
He took the can of spray starch. He took a mayonnaise jar. He took
a glass; I think a mug. There were at least six things. . . . And when
it all came back to me, it was in a big old paper bag and it all had
the black stuff all over it still, I thought it was really . . ."

Here, as she spoke, her eyes widened. ". . . the police came to
return this stuff when Shirley was upstairs cleaning, a week later. I
said, 'You iddddiots!'" Falconer's voice stretched and got hoarse.
"Now that really scared me, because I thought how stupid they
were and how they could have, if they really thought what it
might have led to . . . I suppose some piece of it broke through and
I just said, 'My God.' I yanked them in the door."

Standing up from the couch, she gripped the collars of two
imaginary, bumbling cops. "They come to the front door, they
ring the doorbell, I just have left the upstairs; for all I know,
Shirley's at the top of the stairs. As it happened, she was just
around the corner upstairs. They come to the front door and they
say, 'State police. We got 'cher stuff here, we're returning.' I took
them by the arm, I said, 'She's upstairs.' They said, '*What?* We're
just bringin' your stuff back that we took.' I pulled them in. I said,"
her voice hissed vigorously, "'*Get in there!*' I took them into the
kitchen and now I'm really going—" She makes a guttural, nervous
sound. "Terrified. I said, 'You idiots, she is upstairs cleaning.' They
said—they were just like Keystone Cops—they look at each other,
they said, 'What? She's here?' I said, 'Yes, you idiots.' They said,
'We gotta get outta here!' It was just like a movie. They took all the
stuff and they dumped it out in the sink, it was covered with the
black stuff. . . .

"I should have kept it all. It never occurred to me that they were going to say they didn't get any fingerprints off of it. . . . Some of those things, without question, were slightly greasy. You don't wash and clean a mayonnaise jar."

Fingerprints. Mayonnaise jars. Only one paper bag full of displaced objects was collected from the Peregrine House, while pounds of such things had been removed from the Harris house. Nancy Falconer put out her arms and received the dirty objects back from the police.

State police had testified that Shirley Kinge left no useful prints for them on the water glasses and the photo overlays she handled at Friendly's, and that she left no prints on the objects collected from the Peregrine House, because she had very dry hands; she lacked "the natural oils" in her skin. They said that only when they secured her federal employment records were they finally able to match her prints to the prints on the gas can, prior to their assault on the duplex.

Mrs. Falconer responded, "I find it difficult to believe the only place she ever left a print was on the gas can. And with all this other stuff . . . I'm not sure your hands are that dry if you've been ironing and then you handle a spray starch can."

The prosecution brought into court reproductions of slightly smeared fingerprints and their own assertions about where those prints were found: on the gas can in the Harris house. Only reproductions of these prints were available since the fingerprints themselves had been "lifted." What's more, the gasoline can had been wiped off by David Harding, so it was no longer even possible to tell where the "lift" mark had been.

Nancy Falconer was uncomfortable with the whole thing. She did not want to accuse David Harding of concocting the vital fingerprint evidence. (After all, if he had been foxy enough to change a label, for example, so that fingerprints actually lifted from a spray starch can suddenly became prints lifted from a gas can, wouldn't he also be foxy enough to avoid this gas can muddle altogether and declare that these fingerprints had been lifted from a bannister, a wall, some convincing immovable object?) At the same time, she could not believe the prosecutor's theories about Shirley Kinge, this reportedly intelligent woman who tried to clean a bloody house before setting it on fire and, luckily for her adversaries, neglected to wear gloves in the process. David Harding had emphasized that fingerprints were terribly fragile. Nancy Falconer agreed with him there. The prosecution's weighty case, viewed from her perspective, balanced on almost nothing.

Shirley Kinge told Nancy Falconer the following stories about herself. She said that both her parents were college-educated and that she went to college for a short time. That she lived in different people's houses a lot when she was growing up in the South. That she had once lived on Central Park West, and that she'd had savings of about $30,000 which she invested and lost in a land deal down in South Carolina. She had lived in Florida a while. She didn't like macho men. She loved her grandson, Ronan, and regularly took care of him when Joanna, his mother, left for work at night. Tony (Michael) didn't want to be bothered much with the baby.

Nancy and Shirley talked. They shared Benson and Hedges Lights. They ribbed one another pointedly to help deflate the mistress/maid tension; when it was time to make waffles for the guests, Shirley gleefully offered to go "beat the whites."

No other local people besides Sallie Reese (Shirley's mother) and Joanna White (Michael's girlfriend) who knew the accused woman personally have come forward in her defense. In fact, Shirley does not seem to have been part of a community much larger than her family circle. The police find this easy to explain.

Nancy Falconer chooses to distance Shirley Kinge from her murderous son. When asked what she thought of the fact that Mrs. Kinge must have been aware of Michael Kinge's extensive arsenal since, after all, she lived in the duplex next to him, Mrs. Falconer replied, "I don't know that she would have. I don't think she was over there much. . . . Now that may seem unbelievable and maybe she did and I don't know it, but I think it's quite possible she didn't know he had all that stuff."

This theory—that Innocent Shirley never guessed her son had a cache of weapons in his half of the duplex—is finally not credible. Joanna White's testimony showed she was aware Michael regularly traveled out in the night as a burglar. Shirley knew of her son's prison record and colluded in his use of an alias. Michael shot off the guns for his friends. We can expect that his mother knew his bedroom contained weapons and that the downstairs workshop contained tools to make more.

David Harding thinks of Shirley Kinge as plainly criminal. Nancy Falconer, though uncertain in many ways, thinks of her as essentially innocent. Our courts are equipped to handle difficulties that arise because witnesses have chosen sides in this way; it deals efficiently with "interested" testimony, testimony influenced by allegiances. Our system of trial by jury accommodates for the physical fact that when a light is cast down one wall of a chasm, the other wall recedes and grows more deeply dark. This system knowingly deals in caricatures, it manipulates villain/victim caricatures and thus proves itself to be very, very smart—but not wise.

■ ■ ■

ON JUNE 27, 1992, *The Ithaca Journal* published a story announcing that state police investigator David Harding had confessed to tampering with evidence and testifying falsely in a 1988 case against a man accused of robbery and assault. According to the article, Harding admitted that he had lied in Tompkins County court years earlier when he testified as a prosecution witness against Mark A. Prentice, a suspect accused of striking an 81-year-old man with a metal pipe and then robbing him. In that trial, Harding had sworn that the damning fingerprint in evidence was discovered on a sink in the victim's house. In fact, authorities now allege the print was lifted from a beer bottle found discarded outside the defendant's house.

The *Journal* did not explain what prompted Harding's admission, though it did report that Harding allegedly confessed while being interviewed for a job with the CIA. This interview had taken place nearly a year earlier, in the summer of 1991; Investigator Harding had been put on "disability leave" soon after, and the state police then began their own slow investigation. Reporters who gathered in the courthouse to watch Harding be indicted on Friday afternoon, July 17, 1992, said that they had not been able to get the CIA representative to confirm that David Harding had flunked a lie detector exam during his job interview, only that lie detector tests were generally administered to men and women who applied to join the organization. "The player got played," one reporter quipped. "Yeah," his colleague came back, "and state prison is one place that guy doesn't want to be. He's too pretty."

David Harding was indicted in Tompkins County court on four counts of first-degree perjury, six counts of tampering with evidence and one count of making "an apparently sworn false statement." His lawyer, Earl Butler, entered a plea of "Not guilty" and met with reporters briefly out behind the courthouse to complain that the state police were using his client as a "lightning rod" to attract and deflect criticism of the organization. According to a *Journal* article (July 16, 1992), State Police Chief Inspector Francis A. DeFrancesco had stated at a news conference that "this charge against Harding was the only case of this nature he was aware of in the history of the state police." DeFrancesco called Harding "an aberration." In response, Earl Butler called DeFrancesco's news conference "premature."

Now David Harding has pleaded guilty to four counts of perjury. He has confessed that the fingerprint evidence used to convict Shirley Kinge was faked. He is going to jail.

This chapter was not designed to stretch into 1992. It had a beginning and an end, an introduction and a conclusion, shaped in 1991. At that time, David Harding was generally accepted as a truth-teller. Now his voice has changed, though not extravagantly. The man was always guarded, always masked. A becoming front-page photograph in the *Journal* (July 16, 1992) shows him walking tall alongside a much littler policeman. In wire-rimmed glasses and a sharp blue suit, with hair brushed, face lightly serious, hands clasped, Harding exactly resembles a young lawyer. The bracelets locked to his wrists look like dark shirt cuffs. Harding likes to smile. He refuses to stop smiling. He doesn't like to sit alone with his back to the audience. During the indictment hearing, when his lawyer was called back for a conference with the judge, Harding got up, pushed through the gate that divides participants from spectators, and settled in a courtroom pew to chat with a grinning circle of reporters. He told them he was doing fine. He told them he'd had a bit part in the baseball movie, *A League of Their Own*.

A few minutes later, Harding returned to the front of the room and stood next to his attorney, facing the bench. Judge Betty Friedlander read out the litany of his rights, including his right to remain silent. A small clutch of photographers with tripods, light meters and big hooded videocams stood in their designated corner: front right, same place they had stood for the Kinge trial. Payback, reversals, exposure. We dreamed them; they arrive.

District Attorney George Dentes appeared uncertain during the Friday indictment hearing of his old ally. Dentes moved without his usual briskness; he looked like a man surviving a dinner party where the new husband of his former wife was seated just across the table. The district attorney had been passionately involved in the complex Kinge trial and now that passion was spent and ruined—it was embarrassing to recall. I remembered that George Dentes had said in an interview concerning a different piece of litigation, "This one's not like a Shirley Kinge case, where you're thinking, 'What is this person [Shirley Kinge] all about, and there's something strange here, and she was really involved in something wicked;' that was the impression I had there. . . ." Wicked. Who was wicked now? What did "wicked" mean now?

It's only fair that this section of the narrative, which criticizes the rigid structure of a criminal trial, must itself be stretched and cracked now to fit startling, banal, weirdly predictable new evidence. But it can't stretch all the way to the end of these new stories.

invisible man

SHIRLEY KINGE had no criminal record at the time of her arrest. Her son, Michael Anthony King/Michael A. Kinge/Anthony Turner, did. According to court documents, in early January 1973, Michael Kinge committed burglary in the third degree in New York County and pleaded guilty. He was seventeen years old. In early January 1975, he was convicted of forcible theft with a deadly weapon and criminal possession of a silencer in New York City. Probation, five years. In late November of that same year, 1975, when he was still nineteen, he committed robbery in the first degree in New York County, pleaded guilty and was sentenced to three years maximum. March 1976, burglary third, dismissed. Addresses are listed for him on West 94th Street and West 85th, Manhattan, usually in the narrow blocks between Broadway and Amsterdam, from 1975 to 1977. That slice of neighborhood was not fashionable at the time.

From the Upper West Side of Manhattan he moved to a lone,

dilapidated farm house buried in trees on Sill Road, an unpaved dusty lane that runs for a short distance along the Lansing town line, about twenty-five miles north of Ithaca. There, in December 1977, according to the sworn statement of Steven May, an acquaintance, "Tony and I committed two burglaries. The first burglary we did was on Sill Road one house down from Tony's. We walked to the house and I don't remember if we had to break in or if the house was unlocked. This house was actually a trailer with an addition built on. We went through the Christmas presents looking for valuables and we searched the whole place. I stole a bull whip and a bottle of phenobarbital and I don't know if Tony took anything. . . . I think it was right after the first burglary we drove to a house on Tupper Road in East Genoa in Tony's car. It was about three o'clock in the morning. We parked Tony's car on the road down from the house and walked to the house. When we got to the house we went to the back door and pried the door open with what I think was a long screwdriver and went inside. Tony told me to go upstairs and search and he stayed downstairs and searched. I stole an old leather pouch from upstairs. While I was upstairs I searched very carefully and did not ransack. I went downstairs and discovered that Tony had ransacked the downstairs, throwing everything all over the place. Tony found a safe that was open and took a bunch of antique coins, and in with the coins was some old costume jewelry; we also took a cheap stereo."

Early February 1978, Michael (Tony) Kinge (Turner) was arrested for grand larceny, Locke, New York, no disposition reported. Locke lies adjacent to the town of Lansing, again not too far north of Ithaca. According to the record, Kinge was sent to prison one year later in February 1979 for the robbery he had committed in 1975 and released a year after that. Following his release, he came back home to Sill Road, where he met up with Steven May again; May had just been dishonorably discharged from the army after going AWOL and was living with his father on a nearby country road.

Kinge was living with his mother. In the late Seventies, through the year her son was in prison, Shirley Kinge worked as bookkeeper and babysitter for Douglas Sutton, a developer who managed his successful business from a two-room office in the basement of his Ellis Hollow home, and who, five years later, sold Anthony and Dolores Harris their lot on Ellis Hollow Road.

Steven May had a couple of guns, a Beretta he'd purchased while stationed in North Carolina, and a .22 caliber revolver. "Both of the guns had a blue finish," he told the police. He hid the guns in the woodpile in his father's barn, and couldn't resist showing them to Tony. "Tony asked me if he could borrow the Beretta and I told him the gun did not have a magazine and he gave me forty dollars to get one; I never got the magazine and he never asked for the money back." Later, May couldn't find the Beretta in the woodpile. The revolver was gone too. "My sister Charlotte knew where the guns were. Charlotte in the past had had sexual relations with Tony and it's possible that she could have told Tony where the guns were."

In late September 1982, Michael Kinge was arrested in New York City for possession of a loaded firearm—New York County, return on warrant. Douglas Sutton remembered that Shirley Kinge left his employ in 1982. She told him she had to go down to the Carolinas to help out with family (at the time of her arrest in 1990, Shirley Kinge had a South Carolina driver's license). Steven May's statement: "Sometime around 1982 or 1983, Tony left, he and his mother moved, I don't know where."

Shirley Kinge was back in central New York by 1983; she worked briefly for Douglas Sutton and then did not return to that job. Late November 1985, Michael Kinge was back in Lansing too, arrested this time for petit larceny. Charge dismissed. Judging from testimony at the trial, Kinge had a girlfriend by this time: Joanna White, a local woman with family in the area.

Most of Kinge's burglaries took place in the winter months, in the dark months near Christmas. Kinge dodged from the city to the country, back to the city, back to the country, in New York

State. His record shows a four-year break in arrests *after* the last petit larceny charge, which was dismissed, and *before* the quadruple homicide and armed burglary of December 1989. According to Joanna White, Kinge regularly "worked" as a burglar. It appears that he escaped detection for four years. Steven May's statement: "Tony's attitude is bad, he fancies himself as a professional criminal, he doesn't like cops, people with money, does not like authority. Tony is always saying that anybody ever gives him a problem he'll just bust a cap in their ass . . . I am personally scared of him."

The outstanding New York City warrant for Michael Kinge's arrest on the firearms charge was dismissed in January 1990 at the Tompkins County district attorney's request, so that it wouldn't botch up legal aspects of the planned arrest and interrogation. There was no interrogation. As *The Ithaca Journal* reported, "Michael Kinge, 33, of 520B Etna Road, and the Doberman Pinscher died in a shootout with a state police assault team the morning of Feb. 7."

Police said they were prepared to face violence in 520B because Joanna White had informed them Kinge was armed and did not want to go back to prison, ever. An internal police department investigation and grand jury hearings determined police had acted properly when they shot and killed Kinge in his room because the suspect had risen halfway from his bed, swung his gun towards Investigator Douglas Vredenburgh, and discharged the gun once before the police fired, according to police witnesses.

The search of Kinge's apartment turned up the VCR and TV set that had been purchased with Tony Harris's VISA card (the serial numbers matched) and also the shortened .22 caliber Charter Arms semi-automatic rifle with silencer. Steven May had told police about this gun and said that once Michael shot it outside for him; with the silencer it didn't make much more noise than a pellet gun. May's statement: "Tony explained to me how he modified the gun. He said that he cut the barrel off and he cut it too short and it wasn't long enough to create gas-back pressure to operate the bolt, so he purchased another barrel. This time he cut the barrel again to make it shorter and drilled holes in the end of the barrel and somehow affixed a sleeve over the holes and filled the space between the barrel and the sleeve with Chore Boy and this was his silencer. The grip was like a pistol and the grip had Pachmayer grips. The gun also had a scope on it. The gun is all black. The gun had a black metal clip that was about five or six inches long."

Ballistics tests established that this gun had killed the Harrises. *The Ithaca Journal* explained that an expert "fired several shells into a tank of water because liquid would do minimal damage to the bullets, thereby making them easier to compare to those that were extracted from the Harrises' heads."

Investigators Robert Lishansky and David Harding went into Michael and Shirley Kinge's apartments. During the trial, Lishansky would describe the weapons workshop in 520B, with its homemade sticker knives, boxes of ammunition strewn over the floor, drill press, belt sander, loose gun manuals (*Improvised Weapons of the American Underground*) and magazines about guns. Harding remembered the Etna Road duplex vaguely. It hadn't impressed him: "It's the kind of place, not very well kept up. I've been in a thousand just like that. Half the homicides we have, most of the drug cases, are related in some way to a place exactly like that. Just being unkept, not *clean*."

During his relatively quiet four years from 1985 to 1989, Michael Kinge lived most of the time with Joanna White. She gave birth to Ronan, Kinge's son, in that period (a neighbor said she remembered Michael wanted the baby and Joanna didn't; Nancy Falconer had the impression that Joanna wanted the baby and Michael didn't). Joanna also purchased the .22 caliber Charter Arms rifle for Michael during those years. Joanna White's statement to police shows that she understood Kinge burglarized houses while they lived together. Apparently he didn't get caught. In their pick-up truck, Joanna drove Michael out near the Harris home on December 22, 1989, and dropped him off with his stolen mountain bike. She saw him pedal down the road. When he told her later that he had "burned" some people, she thought that meant he'd robbed them.

Joanna is thin as a stick and pretty, with long blondish hair and high cheek bones, a small mouth, long eyes. Newspaper photographs made her look cocky; she holds her head up, poised on a long neck. In person, in the courtroom, that impression alters. Her chin is up because it's been ratcheted up; it will topple the minute some guy kicks her in the belly, as expected.

Joanna can sit up straight, but she has the sallow American look of a failed country singer who survives on Diet Pepsi. Five months after the capture of Shirley Kinge and the killing of Michael Kinge, she was charged with fourteen counts of criminal facilitation and hindering prosecution. It appears that the district attorney couldn't quite decide what he wanted to do with Joanna, this shy, tense, bold young white woman, mother of a little boy, companion, arms procurer and chauffeur for a man shown to be so awfully violent that it became difficult to imagine any woman looking him in the eye or touching his hand without being hurt. Bill Sullivan, Shirley Kinge's defense attorney, claimed that criminal charges were filed against Joanna in order to prevent her from testifying that Michael informed her he had started the gasoline fire in the Harris house all by himself without any help from Shirley. (Brought up on formal charges, Joanna would not risk incriminating herself by taking the stand to defend her lover's mother.) At the pretrial hearings, the district attorney did say this much was true: he might not have decided to charge Joanna White with crimes if she had been more cooperative, but in July she insisted on having her attorney present during a polygraph test the police wanted to set up, and that did it. Joanna wanted to play legal games? All right.

During the hearings, Joanna White faced the same prosecutor who had succeeded in convicting Shirley Kinge and the same reputedly gentle judge who had sentenced Shirley Kinge to the maximum—fifteen to thirty years in state prison. It was clear Joanna's attorney, Jim Kerrigan, didn't want his client's trial to repeat Shirley Kinge's. Thus, Joanna testified in her own defense; she spoke up in court, whereas Shirley had maintained a granite silence. Joanna testified, for instance, that at about 5:00 a.m. on February 7, just a few hours before the big raid, two state police officers came to Ithacare, the nursing home where she worked, and pulled her out of work, even though her absence might have endangered some of the home's patients. Then they took her to their barracks and began an interrogation that lasted for approximately twelve hours. (When investigators picked up Joanna, the armed police assault on the Etna Road duplex was scheduled to begin at sunrise, in less than two hours. Officers Courtwright and Kelly needed to learn from White where Michael, his mother, his grandmother and the baby slept in the duplex, and they needed to relay that information to Don and Doug Vredenburgh immediately; nobody wanted to charge upstairs in 520A or B and accidentally shoot a baby.)

Joanna said that her interrogators screamed at her all day: "The only time they stopped yelling at me was when they told me Michael was dead." She also stated that one policeman threw a chair against a door and another told her she would never see her child again unless she cooperated and avoided calling an attorney. This testimony about rough tantrums and age-old threats had some effect—eventually the prosecutor and defense attorney settled on lesser charges and Joanna White's case did not come to trial—but it was not enough to get the charges dismissed or White's statement to the police disallowed as evidence.

Judge Barrett looked weary as he listened to this new round of attorneys' duets sung over Michael Kinge and his women. The judge would cite legal precedents to determine whether the defendant had been mishandled by police. But he was aware that Joanna White had known for weeks that her companion had killed the Harris family, yet she never reported him to authorities, and that Joanna had repeatedly lied to Lieutenant Kelly and Investigator Courtwright in the Varna "interview" room, despite alleged threats and flying chairs; only after the police announced to her that Michael was dead, shot that morning at sunrise, did she begin to talk about her memories of December 22, the pick-up truck and the bicycle. Facts like these would make it hard for the judge to credit defense complaints that Joanna had been dragged from her duties at the nursing home by callous cops who refused to notify her superiors properly.

The district attorney questioned Joanna on such points during the pretrial hearings. "He threatened my life many times," she said, explaining her willingness to cover for Michael Kinge. "Yet you mourned him?" George Dentes asked. "I lived with him for ten years and he fathered my son," she answered. "There's a lot of water under the bridge in ten years."

Joanna White was finally sentenced to one year in county jail.

Shirley Kinge was sentenced to fifteen to thirty years in state prison. Nancy Falconer visited Shirley in jail after she was sentenced. At one point, Nancy asked her whether she had been able to mourn her dead son, Michael. Shirley Kinge said no. Shirley also mentioned that when her probation officer asked about her son, "I locked, I froze and I could not utter a word." She was afraid her silence had damaged her chances with the probation officer. She was also afraid, according to Falconer, that the locked silence was damaging her.

The post-mortem trial of Michael Kinge was contained within the trial of his mother. The prosecutor had to establish the son's guilt in order to prove that his mother had acted as an accomplice. The same would have been true in White's trial if that case had come to trial. If Joanna White had faced a jury, many witnesses from the Kinge trial would have been recalled and a lot of gruesome testimony repeated; *The Ithaca Journal* would have begun printing bloody reports about the murders again. People who disagreed in their judgments of Joanna's sentence (some found it too light compared with Shirley Kinge's; others found it too harsh because they thought of Joanna as a psychologically battered woman) agreed that the lawyers had acted wisely in bargaining to avoid a second trial of the phantom Michael Kinge. People were tired of picking up a local newspaper soiled with the name "Kinge." It made them sick of the newspaper itself.

▮ ▮ ▮

David Harding remembered that Michael Kinge's apartment was not clean. Donald Vredenburgh remembered that Shirley Kinge's apartment was not tidy: "Her side was cluttered. It was like they were just moving in. You move your boxes in and you stack them here and then you unpack them one at a time; well, she never got around to unpacking half her stuff, was my impression."

Lots of places in a town need to be cleaned at night, and the Kinges knew all about that network of service jobs; they tidied and wiped for pay, not for pleasure. Steven May, Tony's (Michael's) acquaintance and former companion, started up his own cleaning service in the late Eighties. From an office in his slightly tilted home south of Ithaca, he hires part-timers and sends them out on contract jobs. Steven May sent Tony out to sweep up popcorn and soda cups in Hoyt's Cinema at the Pyramid Mall. But finally the results weren't so good, and May fired Tony. Tony came by a few more times, but after a while May sent his wife to the front door and hid in the bedroom whenever his former friend knocked.

Shirley Kinge also cleaned for a living. She worked for two years at the Peregrine House. Sometimes she hired on with her son to clean department stores, dentists' offices. She was good at record keeping and had worked as bookkeeper and sometime babysitter for two different realtors, Audrey Edelman and Douglas Sutton. In one of the queerest moments of the Kinge trial, defense attorney Bill Sullivan asked Sutton, witness for the prosecution, if he remembered going out to the parcel of land that would someday be sold to Anthony Harris and helping Shirley Kinge bury a dog there next to a cat he had already buried. He said no.

Shirley Kinge interviewed well for independent, pick-up jobs, and seemed to prefer these informal, irregular jobs to steadier employment. (Nancy Falconer said Shirley disliked being bossed around, especially by macho men: "You know the old thing about *boss* is a four-letter word.") Scott Hamilton, owner of Ide's Bowling Lanes, remembered, "Shirley came in, interviewed; I never even took an application because she was running a janitorial service. I hired her as a contractor. And then she employed people, as I understood, to work for her, to do the actual job. So for about the first four months, she was actually involved in the cleaning and Michael was with her. I didn't know him as Michael. He was presented to me as Tony Turner. They also had a young girl they called Bonnie. It's the same white girl [Joanna], but her name was Bonnie, they said. . . . Realize, I didn't pay *them*, so I had no reason to know what their names were."

Both Nancy Falconer and Scott Hamilton, owners of properties that need regular cleaning, remembered that they had met and hired Shirley Kinge before encountering Tony Turner. Shirley Kinge did not tell either one of her employers that "Tony" was her son when she recommended him for hire (she informed Falconer that Tony Turner was the adopted son of a relative). Both Falconer and Hamilton were much more impressed by articulate Shirley than by morose Tony.

"An extraordinary woman. I've interviewed, over twenty-two years, a lot of people for the types of jobs we're discussing, cleaning and menial types of labor. She was in a class unto herself. I never interviewed anybody of her eloquence," said Scott Hamilton about Shirley. "Intelligent" . . . "attractive" . . . "appealing" . . . "articulate" were all words Nancy Falconer used to describe her.

But Tony at the bowling alley: "If you'd ask him anything about, 'Well, how you doing, Tony,' it would be very monosyllabic answers—yes, no, huh, grunts."

And at the inn: "It wasn't anything you could put your finger on; he wasn't really impolite, but he didn't work very much. He painted beautifully, but he smoked incessantly. . . . You can't paint while you have one cigarette after another in your mouth, and I know 'cause I've tried to do it and you can't do it. Either the cigarette burns out in the ashtray or, you know, you're always smoking, so I spoke to him about that . . . and he didn't like that too well. . . . There was something about him that didn't seem open, seemed sneaky, seemed not appealing."

Tony only worked a few days for Nancy Falconer, painting walls (when he made a pass at her adult daughter, that cinched his dismissal). He held the janitor's job at Ide's Bowling Lanes much longer: two years. After about six months, Shirley Kinge, the nominal contractor, pulled out of the arrangement at Ide's, explaining that she had to go down South and asking that Tony Turner be paid directly. Her proposal was accepted.

"Again, he was contract service, so I didn't have a social security number or anything; I was paying for a contract job," said Hamilton. Tony and Bonnie continued at the job for about a year and a half, until sometime in 1987.

There's not much business at the lanes in summer—the summer leagues are thin—so this was a part-time job, minimum wage, six or seven days a week in season. People hired to clean the lanes came to work at about four or five o'clock in the early morning and left by nine. There were thirty-six lanes to wipe down, as well as the bar, lockers, game room, bathrooms, alley-side tables, ceiling fans, ashtrays, trophies, plaques, mirrored columns, windows, tops of the soda machines, carpets. Waxing the linoleum behind the approaches was additional. Carpets were extra if they needed hard cleaning. Ide's had tried a full-blown cleaning service for a while, and they did well, but the price for such a job was stiff. Tony came in at half that price and for about eighteen months, at least, he and his girlfriend did a thorough job.

Ann Reilly was the manager at Ide's during those years. She had to give the alley "the white glove test" after Tony and his shadowy girlfriend had finished up. "I never liked asking him to do things over," she said, and yet she had to. "We really had a bugaboo with those fans. When the fans turned on, people complained these little things would float down in their drinks." So Ann would get up on the tables and wipe the blades of the ceiling fans with her fingertips to test them. About twenty ceiling fans circle in Ide's, which is a cavernous place, red and gold and brown, dark in the morning; full of bowlers, smoking cigarettes, Cokes and punctuated noise in the evening.

The lockers were a problem too. Nobody liked getting dust in his face pulling down bowling balls off the lockers.

And there was a lot of trash. Sometimes Tony would drag out the trash, which included soda cans, along the walkway and leave a wet trail. Ann had to talk to him about that. Sometimes he would leave piles of dust between the support poles, or dust on the carpet edge along the moldings. She had to talk to him about that too. Again, this was not a task she enjoyed, so often she would stand at the other end of the dark alleys and yell to him.

"He always had a hat on and he always kept it down. He just sort of peered out from under it," she remembered. "I felt at the time I worked with him that he was a real spooky person."

Ann Reilly barely spoke with the girlfriend, who impressed her as a "little know-nothing, little frightened thing. . . . She was intimidated by him." When Ann came into the lanes at around nine, usually she found the girlfriend working furiously, doing the windows, while Tony was over wiping out ashtrays.

And yet Tony was dependable for a good long while, compared to the single women they'd hired before. In one year, he only missed showing up for work about four times. Scott Hamilton, the owner, considered him a hard worker, at least for the first year. He had suggested at one point that Ide's could give Tony a scholarship if he wanted to go back to school—they gave out scholarships to employees frequently: "His response was, 'Yeah, maybe.' You could not engage him in conversation."

Ann Reilly and Scott Hamilton didn't believe the stories that had come out in the newspapers about Tony stealing from Ide's. They'd both heard that Tony boasted to his friends he had a "good thing" at Ide's because he could bilk the game machines for about $200 a week. But according to Hamilton, "Most or all of our machines are leased to a vendor and they have fairly good controls, so I would tend to believe that if there was any discrepancy of that magnitude on a regular basis, it would come to light."

Hamilton remembered the baseball cap. Tony always wore a baseball cap and a bandanna around his head under the cap, so that nobody ever saw his hair. Women Hamilton knew, including his own wife, found the man threatening "in retrospect." When all the facts were revealed after the raid, "it scared the hell out of my wife," because Tony Turner had come over a few times to clean the Hamiltons' house.

■ ■ ■

Nobody thought of Tony when the composites of the Harris suspects were first printed in the newspapers. First, those composites had such wild kinky hair and nobody at Ide's had ever seen Tony's hair. And also, "he was just an entity." He worked nights with his girlfriend. He answered the boss's questions with monosyllables. "He was a very inward person" hidden under the brim of a baseball cap in a large, littered, empty bowling alley that had to be wiped in a thousand places.

Only after the police had come back to Ide's three or four times asking about black men (they concentrated on Ide's because the getaway van had been discovered in the parking lot) did one of the mechanics mention that there had been a black guy two years earlier who cleaned, "and bang, the light went on." Police asked for Anthony Turner's cancelled paychecks to look at the handwriting.

They interviewed a woman who had worked in the lanes and who knew Tony had a lot of guns. The investigation focused.

After the raid, the shoot-out, the capture of Shirley, even more people with questions arrived at Ide's. Reporters interviewed the employees at University Pizza, the pizza place that has one counter opening into the bowling alley and a little walk-in space (containing the meat locker, three tables, plastic chairs) accessible to the front parking lot. It turned out that Tony had visited the pizza joint regularly after he quit working as a janitor at the lanes. Bill (not his real name), a crewcut blond from University Pizza, remembered him and thus gained brief celebrity.

Bill was shocked to find out about Tony/Michael. He spoke to reporters and, in the process, contradicted the police surveillance report that Michael Kinge had never stepped foot out of his apartment for more than a week before the raid. Bill disagreed; he remembered that Tony came in for his usual slices of cheese pizza a few times after the murders and that the last time he dropped by was in early February, just one or two days before he died.

Tony liked cars and during the time Bill knew him, they usually talked cars. "He noticed the fact that I had three Trans Ams, which he thought that to be rather out of the ordinary. . . . There'd be times I'd have all three of them here—for some reason, who knows, I don't even. But he'd see them and he'd see me at times go out and get in one, and leave and come back and get in another or something, you know? Strings him out." Bill knew Tony was working on his own truck, a flatbed American-made truck missing a conventional bed so that things had to be lashed down in back if they were going to stay put. "It started out as a low-investment vehicle," but Tony was making it into something.

Tony liked his cheese pizza well-done. That took time, so while he waited he'd talk to whomever was working the counter. Pizza and water, he ordered that every time, maybe because he didn't want the sugar in the sodas. When Bill saw him, Tony always wore plain clothing, one-color clothing, usually work clothes stained from working with the truck, boots (big boots), cut-down muscle shirts and a baseball cap without any team logo. Bobby Brown was his favorite musician: "He'd usually come in by himself, he'd get the pizza, go out in his truck and sit there and eat it, listen to his music."

Bill remembered women employees got along fine with Tony, even though the customer did look a bit intimidating, "especially if he didn't have a smile on his face; he just had that really doubted look. I can't classify him as a city person, because I'm not a bigot in that sense, but he just looked like the harsh, strong type." But when Tony spoke up, he seemed gentle. It was always a surprise: "He was just the most, you know, gentle person who enjoyed everything he did in here."

He was muscular, but small, about 5'9", 5'10", maybe 160 pounds. Never mentioned martial arts or guns in University Pizza, just automobiles, music. Never offered to buy one of the Trans Ams, never asked to look under the hood or go for a ride, never invited Bill to his house to look at his truck: "It was always him coming to the pizza place and we'd talk here and that was it, and what he did outside of here, who knows."

Bill thought it was interesting that after the murders, Tony "didn't run, didn't change his lifestyle." But that was about it, really. "Personality traits, boy, that's a tough one. . . .

"I saw him over at the mall once," Bill recalled, "and he had a very serious look on his face, harsh; that's the only time I ever saw anything but a smile on his face. I talked to him for about half a minute because he was going and I was coming."

■ ■ ■

The Ithaca Journal did not report on Michael Kinge's funeral, though it did report that Shirley Kinge was denied permission to attend. Asked if an attorney's gag order or family request had kept journalists away, reporter Russ Maines said, "No, it was just that

everybody forgot about it; so many other things were going on."
Maines covered the Kinge trial. Son of the Tompkins County coroner who touched Shelby Harris on the lower leg and declared her
dead, Russ Maines is a sociable, reasonable young man, a college
graduate but not yet a spouse, not yet a householder. Most of the
reporters assigned to cover the interminable Kinge proceedings
were about his age.

It is difficult to escape the impression that the body of Michael
Kinge was wrapped in old newspapers and burned. Actually, funeral arrangements were made through Herson's, a small Ithaca
establishment housed in a white frame building, fronted by a
porch built of rectangular grey stones. Herson's has a few pale
churchy windows and a large ventilator on the roof.

Russ Maines said that he didn't know where Michael Kinge was
buried. Of course, plenty of reporters attended the memorial and
funeral services for the Harris family and knew where those victims were buried, at St. Mary's outside Syracuse. A Xeroxed photograph of the single large stone that marks the Harris family's grave
accompanied District Attorney George Dentes's recommendation
that Shirley Kinge be given the *maximum* sentence, which the D.A.
figured at more than 60 years. Yes, said Judge Barrett, when asked
about that touch—the Xeroxed image of a gravestone stapled to a
legal request—sometimes George did things like that.

Over the phone, Russ Maines mentioned that apparently nobody showed up for Lee Harvey Oswald's funeral either. A couple
of reporters, not many, arrived at the cemetery and were standing
around. They got roped in as pallbearers; a TV documentary
showed them gripping the handles of the coffin. Their cameras
hung temporarily down their backs.

Over the phone, the secretary of New York State Police Major
Robert Farrand said that the department had no record of where
Michael Kinge was buried. Over the phone, the assistant who had
consulted the owner of Herson's Funeral Home pleaded confidentiality. A testy dispatcher at the local state police barracks said

everybody was too busy with a new homicide to answer any questions about Kinge. Someone from Tompkins County's district attorney's office said they didn't know, and suggested it would be best to phone Bill Sullivan, the defense attorney. His secretary came back on the line after a pause to report that Mr. Sullivan wasn't available at the moment. She took another message.

5 that night

SOME STORIES are no good. Their internal form is narrow as a serpent's, and they hiss false promises. Michael Kinge liked to read male adventure stories and magazines about weapons and men who concoct weapons. Judging by the list of items collected from his apartment, Kinge had read about Mack Bolan, "The Executioner," whose fictional international renegade escapades filled 146 paperbacks at last count, including *War Born, The Killing Urge, Haitian Hit, Kill Trap, Warrior's Revenge, Vendetta in Venice, Backlash* and *Night Kill*. In book #146 from "The Executioner" series, the hero Mack Bolan, in his fight against evil, wields a black, rubber-sheathed grappling hook, a 9 mm Sola submachine gun—"for close quarters work the silenced 9 mm submachine gun was one of the best friends a man could have," a Heckler & Koch G-3 SB/1 Sniper rifle, a Stinger surface-to-air missile launcher, a Heckler & Koch MP-5, a silenced Beretta, black nylon ropes, a stun grenade, a nightscope, an M-16, a suitcase-sized parabolic satellite transceiver, a twelve-gauge Hilton MPRG shotgun using StarFlash Muzzle Blast shells, and an S6 anti-riot respirator—"Now that they had softened up the opposition, they had to wade into the smoky hell they'd created." Bolan's vicious enemies come equipped with a matching, encyclopedic arsenal. It is impossible to count the dead in this novel because many of them fall down in groups.

The story of the Harris murders was largely invented by Michael Kinge. He decided to make it real. That leap, from fantasy into action, is one that authors and movie makers fear to examine, thinking they might be held accountable for the tall tales they deliver to the world, but it happens. Generals planning a war begin by toying with representational maps. Novels and films are sometimes used as maps of real, accessible countries.

Kinge picked the day for his assault, he packed his knapsack and set out down the road. At some point he tasted ash. The story that he had fashioned could warm him for just a short time. It was a hot, cold-blooded thing. I think it turned on him. It got him like a constrictor at last and bound him to the face of the ground he had hoped to escape through violence. Finally paralyzed in central New York, in a duplex with his mother and grandmother, he never did commandeer a boat to Venice or Haiti for his escape. He died in his bedroom.

The story was not fully told at the trial. The fact is, *any* version of this story will be oversimplified and riddled with error. Here is one skeletal narrative gleaned from testimony in the Kinge and White trials and arranged in chronological order:

Michael told Joanna to drive him south of Route 13 that Friday before she had to go to work. She dropped him off on Turkey Hill Road in Ellis Hollow, and he unloaded the bicycle from the back of their blue Ford pick-up, which still didn't have a finished bed— they had to lash things down to keep them from flying away. The bike had straight handlebars and broad wheels for traction. The gun, a Charter Arms .22 rifle with a barrel cut down and fitted with a silencer, he carried in a pack under his hooded winter coat.

When he mounted the bike and started to pedal, it worked, though at times a wheel skidded. Behind him, Joanna pulled away. In a few hours, she'd go to Ithacare, the nursing home where she had a night shift job. He would meet her there in the morning. She hadn't asked him why he planned this burglary during the late afternoon on a Friday three days before Christmas, at a time when he couldn't expect many houses to be empty unless the families had left for vacation.

Pedaling through the snow on a frigid afternoon, he left some wobbly tracks, but nobody would be able to trace those. His face he kept hidden inside the deep hood.

When he got to the house, he simply coasted down the driveway, past a salty brown van, and climbed off the bike. He knocked. The mother came to the front door, probably expecting to answer some question about the shop. The sign on the fence said "CLOSED."

Briefly, Dodie Harris stood with the jacketed man in her front yard. Kevin White, a family friend, drove by and noticed. The bicyclist may have pleaded low air in his tire. Dodie may have told him to come around into the garage, where she could get the air compressor. She knew right where it was.

Marc was home from school; he had already taken the dog out and come back in. Shelby was up in her room. She and her mother were planning to drive out again in a little while to deliver the gift to Jim. It was wrapped, decorated with red paper and silver glitter that said "JIM."

Kinge brought his bicycle around to the garage and then inside. Dodie pulled down an electric air compressor, not just a pump, for his bike. It was cold in this roomy, organized garage, but protected; nobody from the street could see him or the bicycle in there.

At some point he removed his gun from the backpack and got into the house, or he entered the house and then slipped the gun from the pack.

Michael Kinge shepherded the mother and two children upstairs. He probably bound the mother and son near one another and warned them to keep quiet—the father wasn't home yet. He took the girl into her bedroom and fastened her to a desk chair with nylons he got from her drawer.

Tony Harris came home about half an hour later and parked his black Chrysler in the garage. At Deanco they'd had a Christmas party, so he was dressed in a sweater, trousers and deck shoes, winter coat. He entered the back door, put down his briefcase near the kitchen island, hung his jacket on the bannister and put down the new Syracuse basketball he'd received at the party. The house was silent. A man emerged above his head.

Tony never reached for any blunt object or mashed the buttons of one of the security alarm boxes, possibly because the threat to his family was made instantly clear. He climbed the stairs to join his wife and son. On a slip of paper, he wrote down the correct code number for his bank access card and handed it over. He told the man where to find his wallet and the car keys and even a new set of unsigned VISA cards in a pile of mail. But he didn't have much cash—some in his wallet, but less than $100 in the cash box.

Tony, Dodie and Marc followed orders, bending forward as the intruder tied them to the double beds in Marc's room with metal hangers. Pillowcases over their heads blinded them whitely. They could hear Shelby.

Michael Kinge moved Shelby from her bedroom into the master bedroom. He got the jar of Vaseline from the medicine cabinet because it was necessary, and gagged the girl by stuffing her mouth with a rag and a sock. He attached the green prom dress to her limbs, set her in position and raped her.

The family dog was in the house, but never made enough trouble so that it was necessary for the intruder to shoot it. The police found its body later—dead of smoke inhalation.

He shot the girl. He went into the other room and stood above each member of the family and shot the kid in the head three times, the mother and father twice.

■ ■ ■

Imagination suggests much more, for example:

That Michael Kinge wore lightweight latex gloves and a knit cap to insure he would leave no traces in the house. That he controlled the parents by threatening them with the deaths of their children.

That Michael Kinge instructed Tony Harris to go out, get the van and drive it into the garage. Outdoors for a moment in the plain, real air, Tony Harris felt desperate to return inside, back into the nightmare with his family. He thought that the evening would pass and the intruder would disappear. Later, as the horror escalated, Tony still imagined that he would pick up the phone eventually and call for an ambulance. The big ambulance would drive his entire family to Tompkins Community Hospital. Not a far drive—over the tracks, over the flood canal, to the emergency doors, the fresh, real hospital cubicles.

That Dodie's spirit broke into pieces trying to reach her children. She had bolted down her courage to face death, but she had expected it to approach from a different direction. She knew she had *not* earned this night. She understood that they were at the edge.

Marc behaved with a child's iron courage.

I can't see Shelby.

■ ■ ■

Up to this point, Shirley Kinge has not entered the story. It was the jury's job to decide what part she played in the assault and robbery of the Anthony Harris family which occurred December 22–December 23, 1989. No one tried to place the defendant in the house during the hours when the family was tormented and murdered. The prosecutor argued that she came on stage soon after. The jury ultimately accepted his arguments.

By the conclusion of Shirley Kinge's trial, the twelve jurors had come to know one another pretty well. They had started serving time together during the protracted *voir dire*, a selection process that lasted over a week for this particular trial and ran through a pool of approximately six hundred prospective jurors. Of those six hundred, only about half showed up in court and proved to be eligible for duty; of those three hundred, only five or six were black (the population of Tompkins County is three percent African-American). The final dozen people who made the cut included just one black woman, but she was a strong figure, handsome, with her scarves and ominous name (Cassandra), well-known in the community as a deft, responsible organizer. And then there was the young, newly married girl who had been selected by the attorneys in part because she said she never read newspapers; she got pregnant and miscarried during the trial. The professor, chairman of his department, brought his papers to work on during recess. The wife of the baseball scout had only so much patience with long cross-examinations.

Ironically, these dozen people, selected to decide on the guilt of an accused felon, were themselves entrapped, locked down, by the system. They were never allowed to take notes during the trial, though the accumulation of specific details grew mountainous. They were never allowed to ask direct, searching questions of witnesses, though ultimately they would be the people to decide the verdict. They were forbidden to discuss any aspect of the proceedings with one another or with friends or family, so that the one topic that bound them together was itself bound in mystery. And, finally, they were instructed to disregard information about topics ranging from fingerprint analysis to photography to shopping malls if they happened to encounter that information outside the confines of the courtroom.

An American court's efforts to sequester jurors from "outside" information, to limit what data they ultimately carry back with them into the deliberation room, are fascinating (we can imagine that Lewis Carroll's Alice would greet a judge's demand that she "unhear" some bit of improper testimony with polite disdain). Attempts to sterilize deliberations, to place jurors at last in a sort of germ-free laboratory where they examine only those specimens of evidence and law allowed by the court, cannot really work, since trials require shared language and language richly contaminates anything it touches. But jurors do *try* to think cleanly, and this puts a final lock on the jury box; it adds to a general impression that this captive audience of twelve people, required by law to be patient, obedient and silent, properly attentive *and* properly forgetful, now and then grows listless as a bunch of caged animals.

The jury's silence in the Kinge trial faced and met the defendant's.

That silence lasted through part of summer and most of autumn, from July 23 to mid-November. At last, in November, the final witness testified and closing arguments were scheduled. Bill Sullivan's summation extended over six hours and crossed from one day to the next; he did not want to surrender his grip on the podium. George Dentes's address was more concise.

Judge Barrett delivered his instructions to the jury (to convict Shirley Kinge of burglary in the first degree, the jury had to determine that she "knowingly entered unlawfully in a dwelling" and was armed with a deadly weapon or accompanied by someone armed with a deadly weapon. To prove that, they had to establish: (a) that the defendant entered the dwelling; (b) that she unlawfully entered; (c) that she knowingly entered unlawfully; (d) that she intended to commit a crime; (e) that, while in the dwelling, the defendant or her companion was armed with a .22 caliber firearm; and (f) that the firearm was a deadly weapon. Count 2, arson in the third degree, had its own equivalent defining subtext—to be found guilty of arson in the third degree in New York State, a defendant must be proven to have: (a) "spread and ignited one or more flammable or combustible liquid accelerants;" (b) intended to spread and ignite; (c) damaged a structure by spreading and igniting; (d) intended to damage such building when she started such fire—as did counts 3, 4, 5 and 6, hindering prosecution in the first degree; and count 7, hindering prosecution in the second degree; count 8, criminal possession of stolen property in the fourth degree; counts 9, 10, 11 and 12, forgery in the second degree).

Then the twelve stood up. They walked once more into the back room where they had coats, books and one huge scenic jigsaw puzzle provided by the county.

And *now* they could speak. Their job would be finished once they reached a unanimous verdict: a solution to the trial of Shirley Kinge.

The jury deliberated for a day and a half. No one ever told the participants how their predecessors—millions of jurors past—had organized their own private deliberations; this small group had to establish its own working rules quickly. At the close of the first half day's work, the twelve had supper together at the Manos Diner (big potatoes, heavy plates) and slept at the Ramada, chaperoned by one male and one female bailiff, who were there to make sure no splinter groups gathered apart from their fellow jurors to chat about the trial. The following afternoon, when they filed out from the deliberation room, took their proper places one last time in the box and announced their verdict—Kinge guilty on all counts—the press swarmed. Shirley Kinge placed her hands flat on the table near her attorney's computer and held her chin up. Bill Sullivan covered his face with his fists.

A while later, Shirley Kinge descended the front steps of the courthouse under guard. Swimming through cameras and microphones, at last, after months, she too spoke out. Did she have something to say? "Yes, I do have something to say. Yes. It's about truth, justice and the American way." A quote from the *Superman* TV show.

For the next hour, pairs of TV reporters stood about in various parts of the courthouse, replaying and measuring timed segments of video tape, then taping themselves sonorously responding to the segments of tape.

■ ■ ■

In the back room, the jurors in the Kinge case had moved

towards their unanimous guilty verdict by telling stories.

This process has been studied. W. Lance Bennett and Martha Feldman, political scientists, argue in their book, *Reconstructing Reality in the Courtroom*, that juries regularly construct stories to test and organize trial evidence: "The juror or spectator in a trial may be confronted with conflicting testimony, disorienting time lapses, the piecemeal reconstruction of a scene from the perspectives of many witnesses and experts, and a confusing array of subplots. Without the aid of an analytical device such as a story, the disjointed presentations of information in trials would be difficult, if not impossible, to assimilate."

The authors describe other, foreign methods for moving towards a verdict or decision. Bedouin adjudication relies on oaths; a witness steps inside a divided circle, faces south and begins his testimony by declaring, "A false oath is the ruin of the descendants, for he who swears falsely is insatiable in his desire of gain and does not fear the Lord." The oath has significance because liars must fear that they or their descendants will eventually be punished by an immortal, listening Judge. There is also trial by ordeal. Among the Tanala in Madagascar, a suspect was found innocent if he could plunge his hand into boiling water, pick up a submerged stone, plunge his hand then into cold water, put that hand forward to be bandaged and emerge the next day showing no blisters. The handsomest trials on earth, however, seem to have been conducted by the Anang, a Nigerian tribe that required plaintiffs and defendants to battle one another using proverbs. In one case, the argument "A single partridge flying through the bush leaves no path," conquered "If a dog plucks palm fruits from a cluster, he does not fear a porcupine."

In every exotic or familiar form of adjudication, the writers argue, participants ultimately rely on shared, implicit assumptions about human situations: "Formal procedures must present disputed facts in ways that make it possible for members to use implicit judgment practices to judge those facts." In other words, though formal trial rhetoric and ritual appear to supersede common sense in many cases, individuals taking part in any trial expect that the final judgment will be sensible and *fair* in context. The context is each community's understanding of how people operate. Disputants tell their contradictory stories about past events which have stirred up controversy or resulted in a claim involving debt. Someone, be it god, jury, judge or boiling water, attends to those stories. Dismissal, mediation, payment or punishment follows.

In our Anglo-American legal system, the presumption of innocence puts most of the storytelling burden on the prosecutor, who must "build a perfect house" or a perfect fence of argument, so that by the conclusion of the trial, when the judge explains to the jury every point required to establish guilt for each crime, those points will be set and firm. If, for instance, a conviction for assault in the first degree requires not only that the defendant get into a fight, but also that the victim receive serious injuries, and the legal definition of serious injuries requires a trip to the doctor *and* it happens that the victim never consulted a doctor, "that count's gone," one local attorney explained, and the prosecution's whole case is lost.

The prosecutor's accusing story emerges piecemeal in a trial, its narrative hobbled by interruptions, an elite, impenetrable jargon, and the passionless quality that legal professionals adopt to reassure citizens that their courts are more objective than competitive. Bennett and Feldman argue that scholars have responded to the halting, broken quality of courtroom discourse by studying courtroom situations in bits and pieces, and that therefore most researchers fail to notice the most important, broad task jurors work at during a trial and the subsequent deliberations. They try to place the mother in the brown van after midnight driving west on a two-lane road. They try to reconstruct a plausible story by using reason and imagination.

Jury deliberations in the Kinge trial began November 15 with an outpouring of shared anecdotes: Did you notice this? Did you see that one witness do that with the wallet? After some time, however, deliberations focused.

"It was very clear to us that everything hinged on, to one extent or another, two questions," said one juror. "Was that the Harris gas can, and was that her print on it? And it didn't take us long after the storytelling activities to get comfortable in the process to focus in on those two questions."

This juror continued, "Fortunately, fingerprints are a kind of evidence that, once you've been led through it, you actually can interpret yourself, so by actually having the prints in front of us, we went through ridge by ridge, making the comparisons again in the deliberation room, and what we ended up talking about was the fact that there were differences, but that was irrelevant, and that's what you have to come to grips with. . . . Three points of comparison is conclusive and four's overwhelming, but they require twelve as a standard, and they had the twelve and they were all labeled and there was no question whatsoever that those twelve matched up."

Did jurors find it difficult to convict a woman based on technical, circumstantial evidence when they couldn't feelingly explain why she would enter the house?

"Oh, absolutely. . . . Clearly, it's a process that everyone had to go through because it *is* inconceivable. It's not within anyone's experience to even conceive of the possibility of anyone doing this, and yet you're left with the evidence—the can and the fingerprint—and no charitable explanation for how that could conceivably end up in the Harris household. And you know, we spent time concocting scenarios, trying to find a way, an innocent explanation for the prints. . . .

"Believe me, we spent a lot of time on scenarios that had her [Shirley Kinge] downstairs, not knowing that the bodies were upstairs, but even that didn't wash. The cars were there, the gifts were under the tree, dishes were out in the kitchen; there was all kinds of indicia that there were people in this house."

But what if Michael Kinge had returned to the house without his gun? Then one of the counts required for an armed burglary conviction would be struck down.

"Well, first of all, we knew that he was not going to be taken by the police again. And this was a guy that carried a gun that was a complete—I mean, this was a gun capable of the kind of hideous crime it was eventually used to do. He carried that gun to simple robberies. He would go into a house and, to defend himself, instead of having a small handgun, he would have this enormous semi-automatic weapon strapped to his side. If he did that for a robbery, I find it inconceivable he'd go back to the scene of a quadruple homicide unarmed."

Did the jury figure out who drove the van where and when that night?

"The bottom line was, it didn't matter. She could have been airlifted there by helicopter. The fact is, the prints were on the can."

Questioned about whether he trusted the photographic print of a fingerprint allegedly lifted from a gas can that was subsequently wiped down, the juror responded, "That print could have come from a toilet seat, for all you know, so once it's on the lift, you have to believe the chain of evidence and the expert witnesses of the police, because otherwise you could dust a can, put a lift on it and leave a blank spot and say, Hey, right there, there's where it was. So that's a very scary thing, when you realize the awesome power that goes into gathering that evidence."

So, there were gaps in the story.

"There were enormous gaps that there was no physical evidence, no circumstantial evidence, at all for. Things like, did she know the bodies were in the house? Well, we know she was in the living room. We have no physical evidence she was ever upstairs. Well, that's an enormous leap you've got to make, and yet taking everything into account, including the belief that she willingly used the credit cards, it's inconceivable that she could have gone to the house, put herself in that jeopardy. . . . Again, this is a person who's bright enough not to go to a scene that she thinks is a simple robbery and commit arson, which is a more serious crime, in order to cover it up. Again, to protect her child, but nonetheless, knowingly doing it. Once you take that into account, you have to make all these leaps. In virtually every count, there was some kind of assumption."

Including a broad assumption that the entire story could never make perfect sense because Michael Kinge, the author, was a maniac: "It's so foreign to think about someone who, as a hobby, made these knives that can have no other purpose but to stick someone. They were like little pieces of aluminum tube, and there would be a long piece with a double-edged blade at the end. But then it was shaped like a T; the other end of the handle went across the end, so it's not convenient to hold, to do anything with, other than to hold between your fingers and jam it into somebody. And he had, like, lots of these things lying around; he made these things like a hobby. That is a strange hobby. . . ."

It was all crazy?

"Yes, but then the can and the fingerprint bring your feet back to earth. You still have those to explain."

This juror recalled some witnesses in particular: "Who could ever forget Dr. Germaniuk? He's a very likeable guy and obviously, he does his job very well, but the complete ninety-degree turn of the head to face the jury was so unnatural-looking. It's just unnatural to contort your body that far to face the jury."

And "David Harding is obviously very slick as an individual and you can see where that would serve him well as an undercover person. He was probably best at a natural rapport with people. He would throw you a glance or a smile. So, frankly, you're cautious looking at that. You try not to be suckered in by him and look very critically at the evidence. But I found him very credible."

Then it was over: "Once you reach the decision, then you tell the court clerk that you've got the answer, and they bring you out there and, you know? That's it. So there wasn't a lot of time for particular reactions or interactions, and then you go out there and present the thing and then it's, 'Thank you, good-bye.'"

■ ■ ■

Bennett and Feldman write: "We have suggested that an over-riding value expressed in the legal judgment practices in criminal trials is the purchase (through story construction strategies and tactics) of some degree of freedom from the ambiguities and problematic circumstances that characterize most legal conflict situations."

In other words, jurors hope that they will be able to construct a plausible story that will lock up the troubling past event and put questions to rest, nail down haunting ambiguities. The task jurors have been asked to complete is tightly circumscribed by the judge's instructions. Everybody wants this civic job done . . . and gone.

In the Shirley Kinge trial, however, it becomes clear that no neat story ever coalesced in the deliberation room, though the verdict—guilty on all counts—was uncompromising thanks to what one juror called "the domino effect." If the jury accepts the prosecutor's story of a mother driving with her son to a blood-soaked Christmastime house, cleaning it, then drenching that house in fuel and igniting it, smaller questions collapse, blown down by a kind of explosion. And yet the juror himself, a likeable, humorous, acute man, repeats the word "inconceivable" again and again. He inadvertently pictures himself and his fellow jurors planting their feet solidly on a surface that might be a toilet seat. He describes how they had to leap for conclusions, because the narrow bridge of circumstantial evidence available was so alarmingly full of gaps.

One conclusion the jury apparently did reach: that dark night, December 22, 1989, must have been lunatic. Anything was possible.

■ ■ ■

THE INTERVIEWS described above were obviously conducted long before state police investigator David Harding's confession that he had tampered with fingerprint evidence as he helped prepare the case against Shirley Kinge, and

then committed perjury when he testified as a prosecution witness
in her trial. Re-examined in this new light, statements from people
involved in the trial look and sound different. Some lines have
become electrified, others have deflated. The fact that the fingerprint which convicted Shirley Kinge was probably just a bit of
grease lifted off a piece of trash is disheartening, sickening, because
so many discussed the fragility of that print and yet continued to
believe that it had weight, that it could not be moved.

Since we know now that David Harding cooked up the fingerprints that convicted Shirley Kinge of two felonies, it is *difficult*
to remember how convincing David Harding appeared in court,
in context as a policeman among other policemen, and what a
sharply angled leap the twelve jurors would have needed to
make in order to decide that he was lying. Practiced as a courtroom
witness, he managed his performance smoothly. In any case, this
development suggests that repeated experience in a courtroom
teaches witnesses and attorneys more about staging, dodging and
performing than about integrity. They must learn integrity else-
where.

The jury believed information about the fingerprint. They
bought the prosecutor's story and decided Shirley Kinge did appear on the scene, in the house. They concluded that her print on
the gas can proved that point beyond a reasonable doubt. The second half of the scenario the jurors accepted, but never spelled out
in detail, would have to go something like this (again this is a
sketched narrative, similar to what the jurors must have told
themselves when they voted to convict Shirley Kinge; it is not a
story that most people find credible any longer):

Wearing his bloodless latex gloves, Michael Kinge dialed his
mother from a phone in the Harris house. He had a cigarette in his
shut mouth. When she answered, he told her to meet him in the
lot at Ide's, he needed help. He hung up and threw down the cigarette. Then he walked out the dark passage to the quiet garage.
Most of the lights behind him were turned off, except for the ones

that never stopped—security box lights, digital timers. There in the garage waited the family van, practically big as a house itself. He had the keys. But he was beginning to feel cornered. He picked up the air compressor, put it on the hood of the black car to get it out of the way, opened the rear of the van with the keys and shoved his bicycle into the vehicle. Slammed those doors. Then climbed into the driver's seat and turned on the ignition. He pulled out onto the open road, following the headlights of this full-sized van that had belonged to them.

And drove towards Ide's Bowling Lanes, where a few years earlier he'd worked as a janitor. He pulled over briefly at the intersection of Ellis Hollow Road and Quarry Road. There, he swiftly lifted his bike out of the van and hid it in a corner patch of trees and bushes (it was freezing cold, and too far, too dark for a midnight bicycle trek from Ellis Hollow Road north to the duplex on Etna Road). Later Shirley could bring him back here and he could drag out the bike and pedal down to Ithacare, where Joanna had the truck parked. He had to get the bike to Ithacare, where Joanna had the truck, because Shirley's Subaru was too small.

Ide's was a familiar place; he still got his pizza here, the same pizza every time from the same window every time. He parked the van in the bowling alley's side lot, knowing the alley would close soon. He waited.

His mother drove up. He got in with her, leaving the big telltale van parked behind him in the lot. He told her, suddenly, everything.

She didn't trust what he told her about his precautions. She proposed they use the van to go back to the house.

They did.

He steered into the quiet garage again. Got out. Entered the house and led his mother upstairs. She was quiet. She immediately returned downstairs to start to work. Cleaning soaps were available in the obvious cabinets. He didn't have an extra pair of latex gloves for his mother, but she knew enough. The stove top, the kitchen table got wiped. He smoked a lot of cigarettes. He checked everything again, wallets, gifts, and took just what he could use.

At last, he went out to the garage for the gasoline. Shirley had gathered all the cleaning rags in a paper bag and returned the cleaning fluids to the proper closets. She walked with him and put the bag, which smelled like ammonia and hard pine, into the van, leaving no traces behind, then helped him carry the gasoline inside. He doused the upstairs, heavily around the dead bodies, and lit that fire. In the larger bedroom, he pushed the dead girl off the bed and doused the mattress. He lit two more matches. Running fires sprang up.

He went down to where his mother stood—it wasn't light yet—and they each began to splash fuel in the main rooms, the living and family rooms.

The alarm above the balcony above their heads screamed. Shirley yelled. She dropped the gas can in the front room. He grabbed her. He was wearing gloves; she wasn't. He still had the keys, the cards, some bills. They tried not to run. Climbing up into the van was easy. We're going to drop you off near Joanna now, she said.

She dropped him off near where he'd stashed his bicycle. She was going to park the van in the Ide's lot, then walk over to her car with the bag full of cleaning rags and drive away. They parted.

When Joanna emerged from the lower level door at Ithacare, he was sitting in the cab of their truck, waiting, smoking. He had hoisted the bike onto the truck bed and tied it down. The credit cards lay between folds of paper in his coat pocket, next to his cigarettes. He was going to use them to shop. With his mother.

■ ■ ■

Or: Michael Kinge was not the only man in the Harris house. He had a male partner who arrived later, in some way, not by bicycle. This male partner was the one who drove the Harris van to the lot behind Ide's. One story claims that this other man committed suicide in January.

■ ■ ■

Or: Michael was accompanied by his Doberman Pinscher. Early reports from the police indicated that "Doberman Pinscher-like hairs" were found on discarded clothing in the children's upstairs bathroom. But no witnesses had seen a black dog galloping alongside the hooded bicyclist on Ellis Hollow Road. Speculation about the Doberman Pinscher faded.

■ ■ ■

Or: Michael did it all alone. He never fetched his mother. If he managed to intimidate, bind and murder a family of four, why would he need his mother to help clean up? She slept through the night as she said, and didn't speak to him until Saturday, when he insisted she drive with him up to the malls for Christmas shopping.

■ ■ ■

And: The big house was empty of fingerprints because it had been cleaned by Dodie and Shelby after the cookie exchange to help prepare for Christmas. The fingerprints found on the gas can, allegedly prints from Shirley Kinge, were a police scam. It is impossible to credit theories that the mother and son wiped down the house.

■ ■ ■

Or: There were lots of fingerprints in the house. The police lied.

■ ■ ■

And: David Harding found a good fingerprint on the mayonnaise jar taken from the Peregrine House. He used it to advantage.

■ ■ ■

State police investigator David Harding, Michael Kinge's former acquaintance, Steven May, and Shirley Kinge's fiancé, Laymon Herring, all mentioned that they hoped to write books about the case. It was an incredible story.

■ ■ ■

1990. I walked through the metal detector into the jail's visiting room, signed my name, fumbled with my coat and turned around. I had expected to sit and jimmy myself into place before Shirley Kinge emerged from her cell. Instead, she was already standing against the cinderblock wall, looking straight my way. That scared me. I was not prepared. We spoke for a while about the trial. She said it had exhausted her. Our conversation was legally designated a "visit," not an "interview," and so could not be recorded. Shirley Kinge refused to speak with me again after the judge announced her sentence.

■ ■ ■

1992. I watched David Harding exit the courtroom after he had pleaded "Not Guilty" to four counts of first-degree perjury, six counts of tampering with physical evidence and one count of making an apparently sworn false statement. His hair was summer blond, long enough to brush his suit collar. He made a quick escape; the judge, advised by the district attorney, had released this defendant on his own recognizance.

The courtroom air conditioners were going full blast that day, the blinds were drawn against the July sun, and the walls, painted a wintry, salt-watery color, looked dull to me, like the walls of an empty closet. I was not outraged or fascinated or tickled by this new reverse twist in the plot. My chief emotion was dread: I dreaded going backwards to re-open and re-read the story of this case again. I had thought this meditation on the Harris murders and Kinge trial was finished. It is not.

From a distance, all verdicts and conclusions to this story look small as baseball caps nailed to the lip of a volcano.

*Michael Kinge
in 1978*

Shirley Kinge in court

Courtesy The Ithaca Journal

Shelby, Tony, Dodie and Marc Harris

David Harding testifying at the Kinge trial

© *The Ithaca Journal/David Grewe*

Christine Lane in a courtroom re-enactment

Aliza May Bush

The search for Aliza

Debra Dennett leaving the Court House with her brother

Patricia Reynolds Photography

Nathaniel Knappen

■ ■ ■

PART 2 Christine

6

the cold

ALIZA MAY BUSH's headstone is polished black granite. In summer, more than a year after the child's death, it was topped by a large bouquet of lavender and orange silk flowers, and inside the nest of flowers was a stuffed animal—a small duck with an orange beak.

The Lansingville Cemetery (Est. 1855) resembles many other central New York graveyards disconnected from churches and marked by short lengths of black cast iron. Located on a high green ridge, it faces a cornfield that runs downhill to a hedgerow, then dives out of sight into the valley. Sumacs, black walnut and maple trees fence the graveyard on three sides. During June, grass heads stand up, waiting for the mowers pushed by two teenage kids, Lansing students who both say they don't like high school. The mowers make noise, and so does a pack of yowling, caged dogs hidden somewhere behind the trees. But these noises barely disturb the quiet. One rooster crows. The downhill view from the heights is rich, especially in summer, when the far valley shows itself as a quilt of vivid rectangles and the sky turns lake blue.

The view is rich, but many of the residents are poor. Lansingville Road sweeps past mobile homes that have been in place so long they've sprouted boxy additions and trellised porches padded with morning glory vines. A number of the older farmhouses have mobile homes parked in their side lots, and camper trailers lined up beside those. Not many farm families reside in these tall wooden houses anymore; residents are more likely to be truckers, secretaries, maintenance men or salt miners.

Judith VanAllen, a political scientist and college professor turned activist, explained the fate of local citizens whose families had been settled in Tompkins County for a long time: "Most of the county is a declining farming area. Even though the unemployment rate in Tompkins County is lower than in the surrounding counties, many of the jobs available for people who are born and grow up here and aren't themselves born into the middle or upper middle class, people who lack whatever combination of motivations and luck to be upwardly mobile, are dead-end jobs. . . . There's a lot of service work that's not very well-paid, and then professional, managerial jobs that are very well-paid, and not so many people in the middle and not so much of a chance of moving up if you start low."

Chauncey Bush, Aliza's grandfather, lives on Lansingville Road less than a mile from the graveyard. His son, Greg, Aliza's father, set up housekeeping with Christine Lane, Aliza's mother, in a mobile home parked on Chauncey's side lot. The white mobile home with butterscotch trim has not been moved. It appears unoccupied and has both sets of side curtains thrown open; passing motorists can see straight through it to the sky. This is not the unheated house trailer described at Lane's trial by the defense attorney, who wanted the jury to know that, immediately after her baby's birth, Christine shivered through a New York winter with Greg in a mobile home warmed only by a portable space heater. This is the second mobile home Chauncey made available to Greg and Chris.

But then in late 1989, Greg moved out to stay with friends, and in early 1990, Chris moved out and rented her own apartment on Warren Road. The evening of February 1, a Thursday, Chauncey drove over to visit his granddaughter in the apartment. When he arrived, Chris said Aliza had been sick, so she'd put her in bed early. But Aliza, hearing her grandfather, rattled the crib bars. Chauncey made a comment. Christine surrendered and hoisted the child out of her crib. Chauncey read his granddaughter a few books and crawled around the tan carpet with her on his back. Then he said good-bye and left his son's girlfriend to put Aliza to sleep.

Melvin A. (1880–1968) and Jessie H. (1881–1957) Bush are buried side by side in the Lansingville cemetery. Marian Bush (1909–1983) is there, and so are Harold M. and Jennie Bush Whipple (1917–1979). In a letter she wrote to Greg Bush from the Tompkins County jail, Christine Lane asked that Aliza not be buried next to Grandma Jennie Bush, but Aliza is. Christine said that someday she wanted to be buried next to her daughter. That won't happen.

Chris's letter to Greg, a document written so neatly in a round hand that it looks oddly official (as if it were intended to address a wider audience than Greg alone), was made public at her trial by the defense attorney. It reads, in part:

> I want you to know that the pink teddy bear that you bought Aliza when she was born is with her. I had Mom get it and give it to the funeral home. Also, I'm having Mom put in the books you got her for Christmas.
>
> You know, I don't care how you all treat me, but please leave my parents alone. Jim and Cindie are also being bothered along with Kevin. I heard that Kevin had his keys taken out of his truck, isn't that a little childish?! I'm not saying you did it, but I've got a good idea. And if they took them to see if he had a key to the apartment, so you could get in, well he doesn't. The investigators took his key the night I

was arrested. I've also been told that someone was seen messing around my apartment. So, see, I may be in here, but I still hear about what's going on.

Now, I love you and your family. I realize that's hard to believe at this point, but I do. Also, I am not going to sign the release form for the funeral services. I want very much for Aliza to rest in the Lansingville Cemetery, it's her being next to Jenny that I can't agree to. It's nothing against her or your family. But I love Aliza and when I die I feel that she'd want me to be next to her. If she's buried next to your Grandma, I won't have that chance. I'm not trying to start anything, but up until now I've let everybody handle what goes on with Aliza. This is one thing I can't agree to. I never hurt Aliza and why God took her away, I'll never know, but she has always had me there and when I die I want to be along side of her. That's all I want, is to make it so we have that option.

Look, let me know what it is you want out of my things. Either write or come up and see me.

Take care,
Chris

The Lansingville Cemetery is an old rural burial ground. Names carved repeatedly into the stones are Woolley, Holden, Minturn and Inman, Rogers, Kent, Bunk, Brill and Baker, Stout, Strong and Storm. Josiah, Lucretia, Angelina, Philinda and Mary Ann are dead, their life spans measured in Yrs. Mos. Days. Patience and Caroline Fletcher, the two daughters of Abram and Phebe, both died in their teens, in 1851 and 1867. Edward J. Riley Died a Hero at Gettysburg, 1863. Thomas Pearce also died in the Civil War, 1864. Many of the oldest stones are made of slate. Names carved into this substance are easy to read; they resist weathering. Unfortunately, slate headstones split into layers like a pack of cards.

Granite is strongest. Aliza's granite headstone has been polished so that it mirrors the ground. The verse carved into this black mirror rock will keep for a long time:

Where did you come from, baby dear?
"I came from nowhere into here."
Where did you get those eyes of blue?
"I took a piece of heaven when I came through."
Where did you get that golden hair?
"I stole some rays of sunshine from away up there."
Where did you get that roughish [sic] grin?
"Oh God gave me that from away back when."
Did you come down here on the wings of a dove?
"No, I thumbed a ride with Don Cupid on his arrow of love."
How long do you think you will stay?
"I hope to be here for many-a-day."
And whom do you love the best of all?
"That's difficult to answer, cause I love you all."

In this poem, chosen by the Bush family, the child descends to earth without passing through the body of her mother.

■ ■ ■

Christine Lane telephoned the Tompkins County sheriff's office the morning of February 2, a winter Friday, to report that she couldn't find her two-year-old daughter. It was grey and wet outside; the cold rain would turn to blinding snow by noon. The sheriff's department took the young mother's broken message and immediately dispatched cars, one to the scene and one to the workplace of the child's father, Greg Bush, who was automatically a suspect in his daughter's disappearance. Greg Bush worked laying sewer line, moving crushed stone, for Rob Lychalk, owner of a heavy equipment concern. Bush is a stocky young man with broody, hooded eyes, a dark, old-time beard, no moustache. When the deputies found him with the crew and told him the news, "he was totally astounded," said a neighbor. His response impressed the deputies as sincere. Bush got a ride to help with the search. Heat was on in the cars and the windshield wipers set high. Everybody wore boots.

This was the story they had to go on: the mother had taken her daughter, Aliza, and Peewee, their dog, outside briefly that morning because she had to carry some trash to the dumpster. Aliza was dressed in her snow jacket and sweat pants. They made it to the dumpster, but then Christine's stomach rolled—she'd been suffering from the flu all night—and she had to pick up Aliza and rush back to the apartment, to the toilet. She stayed in the bathroom for just a few minutes, two, maybe five. During that time, her toddler must have reached up with her mittens on, opened the apartment door, slipped out, opened the building's outer door and wandered down the driveway. When Christine emerged from the bathroom, she called. She went outside and looked, circled the building and called and called. One mitten lay on the ground. She grabbed it. But for that, the landscape was empty.

When a child is missing, terrain expands. Boundaries and property lines dissolve, so the world looks both watery and sharp-edged. People searching for a lost child see what a nauseating multitude of doors, shadows, stands of water, gaping gutter drains, woodsheds, garages, unfamiliar automobiles, bushes and muddy paths exist in a neighborhood. Thus, the landscape becomes a nightmare until that *awakening* moment when the child is found.

Christine Lane lived with her daughter in an isolated cluster of flat, two-story apartment buildings on a network of dead-end lanes connected to Warren Road, a main county artery. Warren Road cuts through an extensive tract of nondescript land encompassing the Tompkins County Airport and the county jail, the Federal Express office, the Dairy Herd Improvement Association, damp cold fields and hardscrabble woods edged with a nearly impassable black bush called arrowwood, or "buck brush." To the east side of Warren Road, volunteers would find swamps, farmland, cement culverts, ponds, one old barn, a fenced water tower and awful thickets of frozen buck brush. The fenced airport could be reached by a side road. Lane said that she and Aliza often walked over to the water tower and to the airport to see the planes. To the west of Warren Road was an open field, thick woods and some large stands of pine trees; Lane said they also regularly walked up Warren Road, northwest to the Lansing Post Office. These were both long walks, northwest and southeast, and between those approximate vectors lay a huge, dense fan of territory.

Just outside this fan, to the southwest, on the other side of a small road named Hillcrest, there was a field, a ditch leading to a hole in the underbrush, and an old house with a cluster of white-painted whirligigs in the back yard. The snow was falling heavily and the whirligigs spun in the storm. According to one witness, Christine Lane told deputies that she and her daughter almost never walked on Hillcrest and that she'd instructed her daughter never to go that way.

By ten o'clock Friday morning, members of the Lansing volunteer fire department had arrived on the scene to help search for Aliza. Men and women in snow gear scattered around the apartment buildings and fields. They walked with heads down. Linda Turcsik, a tall, outspoken member of the Lansing ambulance crew, recognized Greg Bush, since Greg was a firefighter with Lansing Company 3. (The town of Lansing relies entirely on volunteers to staff its fire trucks and ambulances.) Sheriff's department representatives told searchers that the little girl was dressed in her winter jacket and boots, but probably had one bare hand; her mother had discovered a mitten lying in a driveway puddle.

The search for Aliza Bush had begun. Men checked around the apartment complex first, looking through the hallways, the laundry rooms, the musty, grey meter rooms. Others began walking sections of land outdoors. Groups of men and women lined up five to ten feet apart from one another and swept the nearest fields in a concentrated line. A small band of men approached an old barn with bolt cutters, making way for Gordon Gabaree, a local animal tracker, who then shimmied into the crawl space under the barn floor, through heavy cobwebs and coon and skunk scat. Snowmobiles appeared. A few local women on horseback arrived.

The Lansing rescue truck was on the scene; soon another rescue truck, well-stocked with radio equipment, arrived from the nearby town of Dryden. It didn't take long before an informal headquarters was established a few miles away at Lansing's central fire station, a spacious, spare building with cinderblock walls and a large glassed bay housing yellow-green fire trucks.

Christine Lane joined in the search now and again, sometimes walking alongside Kevin Dexter, the man described as her boyfriend, but she spent most of her hours with sheriff's deputies and family members in her apartment. Chris Lane is a peachy and stolid young woman with shadows like smoke rings around her eyes. Her voice is young and average, smoky and plain. Months later, a few people would say they suspected her story from the beginning. The mitten allegedly retrieved from the puddle wasn't wet as it should have been. The brief amount of time Christine claimed to have spent in the bathroom didn't sound plausible. One witness recalled that Greg Bush "sat outside in the fire truck, wouldn't come in the apartment, wouldn't talk to Chris," because he knew something was wrong. And Chris's own parents, interviewed by the FBI, had little good to say about their daughter. Joe O'Brien, FBI agent, testified at the pretrial hearings that "Mr. Lane didn't believe Christine would cover up for Kevin or Gregory, but she would tend to cover up for her own wrongdoings. . . . Mrs. Lane said that Christine would never admit to having hurt Aliza and would never tell the truth about it. . . . The parents both told me that Christine liked attention and she was getting plenty of attention during this investigation."

But on Friday most people did believe Christine Lane's story. Said one man who had known Chris Lane well and asked to remain anonymous: "She's got that effect on you, man. You sit face to face with her, then tell me you don't believe what she said. Go do it, sit there and talk to her."

Snow had begun falling heavily by noon Friday. It fell in a series of weightless veils; the most distant looked drowsy and massive.

Nobody on the search talked much as they walked the fields through rain and then through damp curtains of snow. "It was real quiet. We were just walking. . . . Most of it was tall weeds," Jeff Walters, fire department chief, recalled, "and then you did get some where it was briar patches, pricker bushes and stuff, but not a lot of that."

It was cold, cold. Walters had a stitched cut in his hand: "I'd just had surgery and it was so cold my stitches were pulling; they were supposed to come out the next day, so I was taking them out up there because they got so dry from the rain and cold that my skin was starting to tear." He clipped his own stitches during a rest break. He remembered the child had one bare hand.

Now and then, a volunteer in the field would straighten up to holler through the snow. Others nearby would "just stop," and a few detach themselves from their places to go see what had been found—a print, a piece of cloth? Some people on the west side of the road thought they saw something, but it turned out to be just a clump of brush. Greg Bush managed to obscure himself in the snow; TV and newspaper cameras never found him. Fire fighters interviewed months later at the station said that firemen got together and shielded Greg, a fellow Lansing volunteer, from reporters. And anyway, "He's quiet, a very quiet guy," said a fireman. "As a member, he's quiet. We've got your typical loudmouths who are, like you say, LOUD, and he's more a quiet type."

Day rolled toward night. Representatives from the Department of Environmental Conservation (DEC) had arrived and were now directing the search. Four snowmobiles buzzed the freezing woods until eight, but after eight the fields were cleared so that DEC officials could set up "bump lines," quadrants of land numbered on big aerial maps and then marked outdoors by foresters carrying flashlights and reels of white string.

Early Saturday morning, in the dark hours after midnight, some little boot prints were discovered in the woods across Warren Road. Already, the shallow prints had partly filled with snow.

When the sun rose, a core group of searchers returned to the spot with a camcorder. On the video tape taken that morning, a hazy, bluish gloved hand, a man's hand, reaches forward and gently shovels the loose snow from the imprint. Then a narrow tape measure appears on screen. It measures the stride, the boot length. When the focus shifts, we see black sticks, dry, snowbound goldenrod stems swinging into view. Background voices sound chipper, as the guys encamped around the aimless little footprints trade information: "Seven inches again" . . . "The heel's this way, the heel's there" . . . "Somebody walked right over these tracks yesterday" . . . "Let's dig this one out here to get an idea. It's not a deer track because it's smooth, you've got the heel" . . . "It's not deer, bear or nothing else. That's a kid's track" . . . "There's ice underneath, which shows she was in here before the snow" . . . "These ain't deer tracks" . . . "At night it was perfect, with the lights, I could see them."

But these prints had not been made by Aliza Bush. The trackers eventually called for the little spare boot that the child's grandparents had a local shoe store put on emergency order the day before. The boot refused to fit. Its tread was wavy and deep. The snow print showed straight lines.

By ten o'clock next morning, Saturday morning, the main rooms of the Lansing fire station looked like "a zoo". . ."a war room." Maps lined the walls. Tables were set up. The night past had been frigid and the little girl was still out there in her small puffy boots, with her one bare hand. But people were telling each other that if she'd crawled among the pines, she could have stayed warm, "because there was a ten-degree difference between the woods and the open fields." The DEC reps reminded everybody about the lady in Watkins Glen, "old lady in her late seventies, early eighties, nightgown, wandered out in the middle of the night, cold. Found her in a swamp two days later. She was still alive."

The massive search increased on Saturday. News reports informed mid-state residents about Aliza Bush. Reporters arrived in their vans; one of those vans slid into a ditch when the driver pulled over frantically to corner the professional tracker, Gordy Gabaree, who had just ducked out of the woods. State police helicopters, landing in the field on the other side of Ridge Road, battered the air. School buses and TomTran buses, engines fuming, shuttled volunteers back and forth from the rescue site to the station headquarters where "tons" of food and coffee were available, donated by women's auxiliaries, by Mr. Donut, pizza joints, the Wegmans, Tops food stores. By midday Saturday, the entire large bay of the fire station was packed with volunteers and the big country parking lot overflowed with cars, many from downstate or even Pennsylvania. Men and women who came unprepared for a two-hour trek in the cold were turned away. Others lined up, many in fire fighters' "bunk gear," and gave the DEC their names, phone numbers and addresses. They were assigned leaders, given instructions: *"Don't go around anything.* You've got to walk through, over or under."

Outdoors, diagonal lines of volunteers paced a slippery landscape that white string on white snow had transformed into a vast, dim checkerboard, a grid erected against the mystery of a child's disappearance. First, the lead man of each crew would step off the bump line. When he had progressed about three steps, the next person would start up, just back and inside the leader's heels. Faced with a barrier, men and women got down on their bellies in the snow and crawled with their elbows "through, over or under."

Linda Turcsik remembered the rabbits: "Every time I'd be crawling on the ground, oh, the rabbits would run in front of me and we had one of the rangers that was funnier than . . . well, just a riot, and you always knew where I was 'cause the rabbits were running and I'd usually scream. . . . One time they had to pull me out because I was stuck. There were some thickets so bad you couldn't get through." The following day, Sunday, Turcsik would break a rib searching for Aliza—"One of the trees snapped back and caught me." The fourth, last day of the search, Monday, February 5, she spent inside temporary headquarters, working the phones.

She spoke to Christine briefly each day—Saturday, Sunday, Monday—to ask how she was doing and whether she needed anything: "She wasn't much of a talker. No emotions. Not much of anything. It was like she was numb."

Another volunteer, Scott Hollister, fire department captain, agreed: "The mother. Mainly she just looked kind of flat."

On Monday, February 5, Christine Lane, Greg Bush and Kevin Dexter were transported to the Onondaga sheriff's department in separate cars for polygraph examinations. After the usual, gentle introduction, Christine was asked by the polygraph operator, private investigator Michael Carberry: "Right now, could you take me to Aliza?" . . . "Did you lie to authorities about Aliza disappearing?" . . . "Did you falsely report that Aliza was missing?" No, no, no, she replied, and passed the test. So did Dexter and Bush.

That same Monday, in the evening, the search for Aliza was called off. Lansing volunteers at the station weren't informed of this decision by the DEC; they heard it on the six o'clock news. Some of them were still cold, with frozen hands, numb feet, chill, sweated pant legs. The reporters on the six o'clock news looked solemn and very clean. That was a bad moment. The group had invested muscle in the four-day search. They had crawled on their hands and knees, eye level with an imaginary, huddled child, through ice and black brush. They had imagined grabbing her arm, rolling her over—her face might be caked with snow, her one poor hand dark—stumbling up and shouting at the top of their lungs for help. Laughter and a cascade of victorious rescue teams! Bring oxygen, blankets, toys. Now they were being told to surrender the girl child they'd carried in their imaginations for four days. This was it. The bustling map room, the "war room," would be dismantled the next day, leaving the station with its old cinderblock walls and nothing much on the horizon.

There was no news on Tuesday. People trusted the sheriff's

department had deputies out and other deputies recording phone leads. Posters picturing Aliza's round face multiplied in bookstore and grocery store windows. A local dairy ordered 70,000 milk cartons with her picture.

Wednesday, February 7, Christine received a child's mitten in a large envelope through the mail. No message or demand accompanied the mitten. Christine and Kevin Dexter were out at the time distributing flyers with Aliza's picture; they were hailed by a deputy at the post office and then accompanied to the Tompkins County Public Safety Building with the suspicious package. At one point during their drive, the deputy's red roof lights began dancing. Dexter pulled over and was told he'd been driving too fast.

Mid-state news teams prepared for a mad evening because on this same day, February 7, state police raided Michael Kinge's apartment, shot Kinge and arrested his mother, Shirley. Local stations shared the video tape. It showed a handcuffed black woman in a hat, gripped by police, stumbling from her apartment. And it showed the covered body of the murderer, her son, lifted through a near door. These clips would be juxtaposed against "Aliza is alive!" stories.

Thursday, February 8, the sheriff's department arranged for Christine Lane to speak on television and address the person who was presumably holding her daughter, the same person who had sent the child's mitten through the mail. It was a delicate situation. Law enforcement officials did not believe that Aliza had been the victim of a planned kidnapping; if the child had been out of her mother's sight for just a few minutes, that didn't leave a sufficient "window of opportunity" for a kidnapping. Therefore, they theorized that a man or woman might have seen the little girl wandering outdoors in the cold, picked her up and then been afraid to return her. How should a mother address this frightened, confused "good Samaritan"? Investigators did not want Christine to frighten or anger the person who had Aliza, so they contacted the FBI's behavioral sciences unit and received a script to help guide this mother as she made her plea.

Lane did very well. She looked over the script, then walked into the room with the cameras, took her seat and, when it was time, improvised a short speech with her head tilted down: "I just want to say to this person who took Aliza that I understand and I forgive that person, but I need to have her home with me . . . I miss her very much and the family and everybody . . . " She caught her breath. "I don't know, if you could just contact me," she had to catch her breath again, "or the police department or the press, or somehow, and maybe drop her off somewhere, but let us know where so we could pick her up. I mean, I want her home before her birthday. The family and all have bought her presents and . . . " Her voice faded. Christine dropped her head and cried into her palm.

Faces of investigators on the tape appear sincere and concerned. Judging from their trial testimony, they *were* sincere and concerned, and busy. Busy checking out reports about a little white girl spotted with a black man in Elmira. Busy checking out Christine Lane herself. Lane was not aware that Tompkins County deputies, assisted by FBI agent Joe O'Brien, had a growing list of her "Inconsistencies" taped on a wall in the station, or that the sheriff's department had received a phone call from a young woman in Lansing who reported that she had seen Christine Lane remove her hands from a mailbox on Tuesday, February 6, the day after the search for Aliza Bush was called off.

Friday, February 9, an investigator drove around Ithaca, pulling in at one stationery store after another. He had been assigned to search for large envelopes matching the one that had contained Aliza's mitten, and to ask salespeople if they recalled Christine Lane, whose face had been broadcast repeatedly and so was familiar to most locals, purchasing such an envelope.

On Saturday, February 10, FBI agent Joe O'Brien, tracker Gordon Gabaree and a sheriff's department investigator all arrived at Chris Lane's apartment with camcorders. They knocked on the door and asked Lane to re-enact, please, the sequence of events that took place early in the morning, February 2. They had their cameras, and they even had a little girl named Rachel who could pretend to be Aliza. Lane got her coat on. Somebody gave her a sack of trash to carry. The dog was a problem. Should they try to involve the dog? The three men decided it would be best to forget the dog.

The tapes filmed that morning show Christine Lane walking through huge doorways, up slanted steps, then outdoors onto the sidewalk. The filming goes better in the light outside. Lane is understandably hesitant. Rachel doesn't know her and so darts from side to side among the parked cars. Near the dumpster stands Rachel's mother, an anonymous figure. After Christine has thrown her bag of trash properly into the dumpster, she must try to lift Rachel in her arms since her statement said that, on February 2, she picked up Aliza and ran with her back to the apartment, to the bathroom, impelled by terrible pains in her stomach. But Rachel refuses to be touched. Her anonymous mother bends forward, coaxing, and it's no use. The scene falters and continues.

After Christine emerged from the bathroom on February 2 and discovered Aliza was missing, she reportedly hurried outside and walked around the building, calling her daughter's name. This sequence, too, is re-enacted. Again, misfit adults appear. One tape clearly pictures Joe O'Brien, a tall man in a long coat, walking a few steps behind Chris and solemnly videotaping her back and hair. He moves without apparent emotion. He would make a very nice figure in a self-aware experimental film if we could imagine that Joe, the actor, appreciated the ironies and farcical aspects of his role as one of three overlapping cameramen following a half-hearted actress. But we can't. This FBI agent is taking a dead serious home movie. The loud wind that blows across the camera's mike sounds hungry.

It must have been shortly after Saturday that Christine wrote Greg Bush's brother, Andy (who had just about finished serving his time in a youth detention center) a letter about her situation. Lane's defense attorney, convinced that the letter would illuminate Christine's love for her daughter, submitted this document as evidence in the trial:

Hey Andy,

Happy Valentine's Day! Hey, Dad says you've got just a few more weeks and you're out. You must be really counting the days down. He said they're leaning on you a little because you're [sic] time is almost up. Well hey, hang in there, I know you can handle it, you're tough. Just keep thinking about getting out and being with everybody. . . . Hey, you could live in mine and Greg's trailer, he lives with Fenner's. I hate to see it just sit there. Well hey, as long as you're happy, that's all that really matters.

Well, I suppose you're wondering about how things are going with Aliza. I'm sorry to say, but not much is happening. At least I know what it feels like to be held in a place that you don't wanna be. The FBI won't let me go out. I have to stay in here all day and listen to the phone. But it's hard because it gives me too much time to think about things. Somedays I'll drive myself wacko because all I think about is what is Aliza thinking, is she being taken care of? It's something I'd never want to experience. I've been doing a good job of keeping my hopes up and not losing it. But I'll be honest and say that I can't go on without her, she's my life. I have such an empty feeling in my heart. I don't think I could go on trying to live with that emptiness.

Greg doesn't talk much. I keep asking Dad about him all the time. I want to call him or go see him but I can't stand to see someone hurting. I know that this was my fault. I blame myself for leaving Greg, if I hadn't this would of never happened. And if I had put the chain on the door, she wouldn't get out. I'm sure a lot of people blame me, now I've got to live with it.

Well hey, you hang in there and you'll be home soon. Hopefully Aliza will be home when you get out. Look, I sent

you a picture of her and if you get a chance and can make a
call, give me a hollar [sic]. Hope to see you soon!
Love,
Chris

Christine Lane broke down February 15—right after Valentine's
Day—during a second lie detector test administered this time by
an FBI agent in a rented room at the Sheraton. (Said Special Agent
Thomas Donlan, "I didn't want the atmosphere of the police
around . . . I wanted a nice, quiet setting.") Lane's father had accompanied her to the Sheraton, but he was kept outside the room.
Agent Donlan had Chris sit on the hotel bed. He furnished the
subject with an "Advice of Rights" form and a "Consent to Take
a Polygraph" form. He explained things. She signed. They began
the pre-test interview. Bands were strapped comfortably around
Lane's chest and fingers. Then came the in-test phase. The little
black arms of the machine jumped nervously as compass points.

The confrontational, post-test interview began at about a quarter to four, after Agent Donlan had examined the test strips and
found indications that the subject was lying. Donlan described his
post-test interview technique during the trial: "They're very emotional, they're very upset. They're on the verge of confessing. You
don't want to antagonize them. You want to coax them, you want
to hold their hand." By the end of this phase, test strips were scattered over the bureau and the suspect was sobbing, shaking, on the
edge of the bed. Donlan was pleased with the charts: "These charts
were not flat. For a polygraph, they were beautiful charts. They
were great reactions." Agent Donlan radioed the sheriff's office
and told them to send Joe O'Brien up to the room because Chris
Lane had flunked her exam this time and was in the process of
changing her story during the post-test interview.

Christine Lane told her new story three times in the motel
room, first to Donlan, then to Donlan and O'Brien, then to
Donlan, O'Brien and sheriff's department Investigator Emery
Guest. At first Special Agent Donlan tried to keep Guest out of the

room because he understood this was a federal case. In fact, the case more properly belonged under the jurisdiction of Investigator Guest. The FBI agents had a right to pursue the investigation only if the crime involved a kidnapping.

Lane confessed that she had hidden Aliza and knew where the child's body could be found, but she *did not* confess to killing Aliza (no evidence offered in court indicated that Donlan tested her on this central question). Her new story went like this: early Friday morning, February 2, she had discovered the child tangled tightly in her blankets. Bending over, she found the baby stiff and cold. She carried Aliza to the big bed and tried to resuscitate her, but failed. She reached for the phone to call the police, dialed a few digits. And hung up. Now deeply in shock, she panicked. She dressed Aliza in her snowsuit, wrapped her in three garbage bags and carried her.

They were suddenly out in the night. Christine hadn't brought a flashlight and she didn't know where she was going—she'd never ventured into the woods across Hillcrest Road before. Her feet crossed asphalt and followed a ditch. Finally she stopped and put the slippery burden on the ground. There were branches nearby. She used them to cover the bag.

A while later, back at the apartment building, she planted one pink mitten outside in the driveway. Then she phoned the sheriff's department. The other pink mitten she mailed to herself Tuesday after learning that the search for her daughter had been called off.

In heavy rain again, through the afternoon's half-dark, Lane led investigators to the place where she had buried Aliza in garbage bags under long-needled pine branches. They hiked alongside a small ditch full of slush and water. To their right stood a Greek Revival farm house with a cluster of silent whirligigs turning in the back yard. The men came to a wall of narrow trees. All but one of them ducked through a hole in the winter forest. The one who couldn't face what lay ahead crouched on the edge of the field.

It wasn't difficult to follow the ditch. They actually had not come very far from the apartment buildings, the epicenter of the search grid; it seemed odd that no volunteers had clumped around back here. Some volunteers claim that searchers did comb this area, but the snow was deep and they weren't looking for a child who had been partially buried. Gabaree, the tracker, says that the DEC grid stopped short of Hillcrest Road because Christine Lane told the rangers that she and her child never walked along that property to the southwest.

One of the deputies in this wet entourage carried the department's camcorder on his shoulder. Another one offered Lane a rain poncho. She draped it around herself and stood while the deputy with the still camera ripped open a box of film, tossed the trash onto the ground and loaded up. The deputy with the camcorder managed to keep the machine on though his hands were growing cold. Slowly, Joe O'Brien, FBI agent, uncovered the black plastic egg and broke it open for the picture-takers.

A series of photographs made public at the trial shows first a close-up of a postage stamp against a weird green background. Next, a manila envelope in a plastic bag; this envelope contained one pink mitten. Next, an aerial photograph of a brown landscape divided into rectangles. A little snow is on the ground. Next, a cut brown field walled in on the far side by bushes. Next, a tangle of narrow brown tree trunks; a few carry looped strands of barbed wire. Next, a heap of pine branches with long, graceful brown needles. The narrowing focus is at once tedious and unbearable, framing a mystery which won't quite fit inside the margins.

The last photographs in this pile show the opening of the black and brown garbage bags. The child's body is dressed in grey sweat pants and puffy winter boots. Finally a man's arm, distinguished by a large wristwatch, droops across the corner of a picture. The job is done. His face remains outside the frame. The bare fingers of the child are visible.

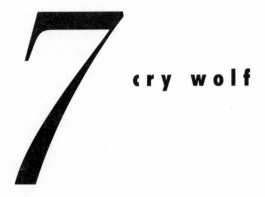

7 cry wolf

... SEEING, as he sat down on the log the crooked print, the warped indentation in the wet ground which while he looked at it continued to fill with water until it was level full and the water began to overflow and the sides of the print began to dissolve away.

— William Faulkner, *The Bear*

■ ■ ■

Gordon Gabaree, owner and primary asset of Nuisance Wildlife Control, Inc., often works in the dark. If he's been called to eliminate a New York State coyote, for instance, he will drive his truck onto a field at night, switch on the tape-recorded coyote call and wait with his shotgun (he can *do* a coyote bark, but the tape recorder gets better results). His partner accompanied him once on a coyote job and found the wolfish shadows plainly terrifying. Gordy isn't afraid of the dark. "Dark, light," he says, it "doesn't matter." But one night he got so far into something that he heard a preternatural voice. He had been warned by his police friends that someday, if he kept getting involved, a case would bite him. It would stay in his memory and infect his dreams. This was the case.

Gordy is a wiry man who answers to the nickname "Bear." In his job as an animal tracker, trapper, sometime exterminator, Gordy kneels to examine paw prints; crouching and straightening, his body inadvertently strikes one mythic pose after another. He can read green grass. He can read an absence of bird song: "If I walk in and your property is completely dead, there's not even a bird singing, the coyote is there and he's there now. It's something about the predator. When the predator walks in, everything quiets down." Gordy has followed the trails of both animal and human predators. He lost one partner that way because the young man's wife didn't want her husband mixed up in law enforcement—too dangerous—and she made him quit.

Gordy has a new partner these days, a level-headed woman, for-merly wife to a Cornell professor, who now accompanies him on assignment in Nuisance Wildlife Control's tan pick-up truck with the raccoon logo on the side doors. They wear thick, khaki work clothes and heavy boots. Gordy carries a holstered gun with bul-lets. A sticker showing that he is licensed to use poisons has been pasted in the truck window.

Nuisance Wildlife has captured pet boa constrictors, extermi-nated flocks of bats, handled skunks and raccoons (mean little bas-tards that boil out of the trap), shot coyotes and herded swarms of bees from residential bathrooms. Gordy tells stories about his en-counters with animals. There was one eight-foot boa constrictor that escaped its cage, leaked through the plumbing of downtown Ithaca and finally emerged to wrap itself around a shower head. The unsuspecting tenant of the apartment, a football player, turned on the shower, got in, hoisted himself to wash under his arm and. . . . When Gordy arrived the path the man had blazed from his shower was easy to track. He had thrown his body against the toilet, against the bathroom wall and against the door frame, leaving big splashes and bits of skin to mark his passage. Gordy caught the big snake. He says he wore it under his coat, around his neck, a few weeks later to a Cornell football game, went down to the benches where this player was sitting and . . . "You know how the head slithers out along your arm. . . ."

County sheriffs' departments contact Gordy not only to trap or shoot "nuisance" animals (he has killed bears and coyotes, and claims there's an Eastern puma living in the woods out by Dryden), but also to help find injured dogs, disoriented men, lost children and criminals. Gordy can follow paw prints; he can also read boot prints in the pine mulch under a smashed window and the direction of a burglar's passage through grass. When a woman was bludgeoned to death in the woods south of Ithaca, it was Gordy who theorized that the attack had been accomplished *not* with two weapons—a hammer and a little axe—but one, a carpenter's tool fitted with a head that has one blade end, one blunt end, used to pry loose shingles. Gordy relies on common sense, experience, instinct and some pieces of machinery for his investigative work: in his truck he keeps a hearing device invented for military use which lets him pick up faint sounds of voices miles away. Sometimes he hears deer poachers chatting over cups of coffee. Once in 1989, in the middle of the night, he walked down a dirt road on Connecticut Hill, pointed his device and heard a lost boy crying deep in the forest:

"I got called from the sheriff's department that this boy had got lost thirteen, fourteen hours, and they asked me to respond. I walked into the area and I asked about the location, and they said, 'He's out there. A lady's with him, their dog got lost . . .' and this and that. So, I went to this one section and just stood there a second. Scott was with me, my partner at that time, and I said to him, 'This ain't right.' He said, 'How do you know it ain't right?' I says, 'This ain't right, they're not here. I'm going to go down and cut back in another road.' So what road I was on, I have no idea.

Connecticut Hill's got all these little dirt roads; it's big. So I pulled in there and it's like I got goose pimples and I said, 'They're here.' Scott says, 'How the hell do you know?' And I said, 'I know they're here. Get the hearing devices.' Got the hearing devices, heard that boy holler, I says, 'I got him.' Scott says, 'I don't pick him up.' And I says, 'I got him.'" Gordy called the sheriff's department, and managed to direct the boy's father and the woman's husband through the extensive maze of dark dirt roads to his truck. Headlights struck a wall of tangled, colorless forest growth where the cars parked. Flashlights were switched on. And then, "We walked right to them." The boy was miles in.

The boy Gordy tracked down on Connecticut Hill was named Ben. Not long after the abortive search for Aliza Bush, Gordy went over to visit Ben, just to talk a while and touch him. Ben still has nightmares about the night woods. Gordy says he has bad dreams too, not about the woods or darkness, but about "the little one"— the buried two-year-old girl he heard and couldn't find.

■ ■ ■

Sometimes Gordy speaks, sometimes his partner does. He's leaning near the ashtray; cigarettes burn constantly when he describes the search for Aliza Bush. His partner—call her Lee—stands a few feet behind him mixing sugar cookie dough in the kitchen of Gordy's mobile home. The house trailer is situated on a big hill above a big field above a grand, big valley in Alpine, New York; he and Lee own about fifty of the surrounding acres. Gordy's home, exceptionally neat and clean inside, has been decorated with drawings of Iroquois braves and, above the teal blue couch, a trapper's basket full of furs—the red and sable fox tails look richest. It's quiet in the house. Neighbors live far away downhill.

The first day of the search for Aliza May Bush was wet and snowy. Most volunteers described it as a tense, *quiet* day. Gordy remembers it as a day marred by din and chaos. He was trying to listen for a small voice, trying to discover small tracks, but always he met with galloping interference. They got the call at noon. "We responded right away and by the time we drove from Tompkins Community Hospital up Route 13 to Warren Road, you could barely make it up the hill and you could hardly see in front of you. The snow was just blinding and very thick," Lee remembers.

"When I got there," says Gordy, "there was no organization. And once I talked to the mother, then I went back to the rescue engine and I asked who's in charge of the search, and I told this man, the chief, 'I want these people *out of here*. We've got people out here walking with their *kids*, for Chrissakes, and we're trying to find this child!'" Gordy's face tightens as he recalls children at the search scene stamping hundreds of misleading little prints in the snow. "We got out into the woods and they had people on horseback, all-terrain vehicles, and I'm screaming. They got about four women out here on horseback, riding through the woods just as fast as the horses could take them through here, hollering, 'ALIZA!' Even if the child had answered, they couldn't hear."

Christine Lane had told the sheriff's department that she and Aliza often walked over by the water tower: "So I went to that area. We had a snow pile there from the previous snows, and the snow drifts were this high where they plowed, so a two-year-old would have to climb up it and slide down the other side." In other words, a booted child would have left a broad track. "So I cut that perimeter quick."

He cut a lot of perimeters quick, following the directions relayed to him from Lane by the sheriff's deputies. He crawled under the old barn, through cobwebs and skunk scat, because "the child's going to want to get underneath something, it's going to want to have that closeness. I was told the child was still in diapers at two; her diapers are going to be soggy. You know how cold it got."

He "wallered" all through the woods across Warren Road, and stayed out in those woods Friday night with the DEC: "I'm out here, freezing my wazoo. I mean, it rained on me then it turned to snow then the temperature dropped right down to nothing, and I'm colder than nobody's business. I haven't eaten. I haven't had a cup of coffee, which burnt me because every time we went back to the rescue truck, all the volunteers stood around in big groups drinking all the coffee and us guys who were doing all the work couldn't get a cup of coffee, so that irritated me on top of everything else. But I had found out something, because of the questions the mother asked me, so I started doing my own investigation."

Something was wrong. Gordy says that he kept trying to tell people that day something was wrong, but nobody heard him over the din.

"Say your child is lost," he says. "And when I come to you and I say to you, 'I'll do my best for you,' and I reach out and I touch you, and if you pull away, I know you got problems, because I've worked with so many people. Regardless of whether their children are lost or their dogs are lost, you almost had to handcuff them to the vehicle because you didn't want them to mess up the scene. But a person who doesn't respond to you emotionally . . . "

He first met Christine Lane out on the sidewalk in front of her apartment: "I hugged her and she was very cold. She pulled away. . . . She had her Levis on, and a grey sweat shirt, make-up on, hair all brushed, clean. Dry-eyed. Very quiet. And I asked her if there was anything of the child's that I could look at. I walked into that house, it was like this house. There was no evidence of a two-year-old in that house, period. No toys, nothing."

Later, Gordy runs the video tape of Christine Lane's apartment. The camera loops and swings, doors careen. The atmosphere is unfocused, foggy, pearly grey. The apartment pictured on-screen contains Christine's weight-lifting equipment, a slumped, brown-checked couch with wooden arms, ceramic horses on a window sill and a wall poster of horses (soon after she left Greg Bush, Christine and her friend Brenda discussed moving south to work at a horse farm in Virginia). In the bedroom are two small teddy bears fastened to the wall somehow; Gordy insists those elevated bears and a little tricycle were the *only* toys in the apartment.

"So anyway, a little later John Huether [one of the sheriff's department deputies first on the scene] went back into the apartment to get something with the child's scent on it, because I asked him, I said, 'We need something for these dogs,'" Gordy says. "Because now we've got the state police dog there and the state police dog is a crackerjack. Jeez, can't think of his name, but the dog knows what he's doing out there." But the dog responded to the end of the driveway and that was it. The trained German shepherd gave up, trotted in circles.

There were other dogs on leash out in the snow, pulling, eager to track. But "the things the mother was willing to give the police department and the search teams that came in with these dogs from all over the country! And I'm thinking, 'What's the matter with these people? They know damn well that scent can't stay on plastic.' See, she had something like four or five plastic blocks and one sneaker that had been washed, and these people are putting the bags up to the dog's nose and I'm thinking, 'My god, what are we all doing?' . . .

"See the thing that happened here was, I know about plastics and knocking the scent down. I also knew she had to know. . . . See, if I want to kneel down here on the ground and I don't want to disturb it for wildlife or a tracking dog, I will put a piece of plastic down and kneel on the plastic, because otherwise my scent will go right into the ground."

As Gordy recalls, Christine Lane walked up to him later on Friday after the frustrated dogs and their owners had scattered, and "she says to me, she says, 'Could the dogs pick her up if she was in plastic?' Asked me that point blank. Well, then I came unglued. Because already now I know that me out here in the snow is wasting my time. . . .

"So, by the time I saw Lee about 3:30 in the afternoon I'm out of my bonkers."

Lee explains that she returned to the scene and met with Gordy that Friday afternoon in the storm. He told her then about the plastic blocks for the tracking dogs, and she asked him, "What about the bedding, couldn't they use the child's bedding?" And he told her, "She washed everything. That morning. Before she even called the police."

He goes on, "Everything was washed, everything was put away; it was erased that the child had ever been there. There was no emotion, the make-up being on her, not a tear shed," Gordy counts off the details that aggravated him. The apartment's doorknob had been difficult to work; he didn't believe the child could have managed it with mittens on. And the mother was so calm: "I came back approximately two o'clock and I wanted to talk to the mother again, because I wanted to know other locations where maybe she'd gone for a walk with this little one. I went to the apartment and she was asleep on the couch. . . .

"They all kept saying, 'Gordy, you're on the wrong track, she's a distraught mother,' and I kept saying, 'Distraught, my ass, this mother knows.'"

He believes he was steered away from the burial site throughout the four-day search by Christine Lane herself: "During that search I got within twenty yards of that burial site I don't know how many times, and she had to be watching like a hawk, because every time I would get there, I'd get a call from the DEC saying, 'Gordy, we need your expertise over here, mother says.' . . . And that's the way I was steered." Gordy stubs out his cigarette. "I was steered in so many ways," he repeats later once, then again.

"I'm still out looking when the main search is over. Oh my god, I'm wet completely from head to toe, cold, I'm shaking and everything else but I'm hanging in there because of the little one. I should have went back in by the little crick, but I'm glad in a way I didn't. But something kept calling me back there. I kept looking for crows, for coyote tracks, 'cause they'll go to carrion. . . . But she carried the baby right up the crick, 'cause when I got there . . . see, that's where I kept going during the search, right up this damn crick. It's only a little stream, about two foot wide. Just a ditch. And I kept going up there, but every time they called me back."

Too much interference, too much *interference*. Gordon Gabaree failed in his attempts to find Aliza because men with radios kept calling him back from the dark round space where his instincts told him he ought to go. The failure galls him. The child haunts him.

At some point early in the search, Gordy started tracking a new quarry: the child's blank mother. He met with better success on that trail. "I started to talk to people and I'm playing the sympathy thing right up to the hilt. And I came out one time point blank, and I says to somebody, 'She was a trapper, wasn't she?'"

Gordy's independent investigations turned up some lurid gossip. One of his informants claimed that Christine Lane was lover to one of Greg Bush's relatives. Another said she had seen Christine Lane partying in a Lansing bar that Friday night, the first night after Aliza's disappearance. "What about trapping," Gordy asked, "did she know about trapping?" Yes, Christine liked hunting and trapping, people said. She went out for quail, squirrel, red fox. She liked the outdoors.

Gordy contacted one young woman, Heidi, who lived in the same building as Lane but was reluctant to speak with police; he found her, thanks to the intercession of a lady who literally had bats in her attic. Heidi said that she'd been outside the apartment building in her car early Friday morning when she saw Christine walk past to discard a paper bag full of trash in the dumpster. Christine was not calling for Aliza and she didn't bother to approach the car to ask if Heidi had spotted the baby. Later, they met in the hall and chatted. These events took place before Christine phoned the sheriff's department. According to Heidi, her neighbor never mentioned a lost child.

By Monday, February 5, the day the freezing search was cancelled, Gordy had his trapper's sack bulging with information on

Chris Lane. At about that time he caught the attention of a man in power. "Joe O'Brien, FBI, called me in. And he says, 'Gordy, tell me the story.' And I told him. And he says, 'Why didn't you tell me yesterday!?' I said, 'I thought you knew.'"

From that point on, Nuisance Wildlife Control worked closely with the FBI. The path they had to follow was a narrow one; if Lane was, in truth, the distraught mother of a missing child, they owed her sympathy and aid, but if she had been spinning lies, they wanted to "break" her and get a confession. A few guys thought it would be nice to get her hypnotized; Lane balked at the idea, then her boyfriend talked her into it, but the proposal was never carried out. Somebody else suggested the police could surprise Lane one morning by arriving at her door and asking her to re-enact the events of that Friday when she had first discovered Aliza missing. This plan was implemented.

It was Gordy who contacted the two little girls who arrived to play Aliza during the re-enactment (Gordy and his estranged wife formerly ran a day care center). They used Rachel first; Rachel's mother stood near the dumpster to talk her daughter forward. On tape, Rachel darts, she balks, she calls for "Bear." She's dressed warmly in a pretty, buttoned coat. Gordy says that the following day he spoke to Rachel and she told him she didn't want to make any more movies.

Probably it was Joe O'Brien who decided they didn't need to unveil the second little girl (law enforcement agents were satisfied with their first take, since Lane's re-enactment deviated in many ways from her statement). This second child, who remained off-stage, " . . . looked almost exactly like Aliza and we had her dressed exactly like Aliza," Gordy said, "which would have made the mother shit in her pants." This nameless girlchild, a stand-in for a stand-in, was costumed to haunt Christine Lane. She proved to be unnecessary.

Three camcorders, run by a sheriff's investigator, a trapper and an FBI agent, dogged Christine Lane that morning as she tried to re-enact a little horror accurately. Gordy frankly admits that he and his companions hoped Lane would break down and confess. She didn't. She attempted to pick up Rachel, but appeared patient when the attempt failed. She walked behind automobiles calling, "Aliza . . . Aliza." She bent over plainly to pick up the mitten officers had dropped on the concrete as a surprise for her. Gordy has copies of all three tapes from February 10. Watching his tape, he explains, "According to her statement, she should be coming around the corner of this house right here and she never comes." The recording showed a white door, a white door, a white door— then black.

Five days later, when Special Agent Thomas Donlan "broke" Lane in the Sheraton motel room, then called Joe O'Brien (who radioed for assistance and a camcorder), before driving with her out to the site where she had buried her daughter, Gordy was invited to come along again. But he didn't make it into the woods that time. Drenched in rain, he literally fell down on his knees at the edge of the field.

The pathologist came over to the Tompkins County Public Safety building after officials recovered the child's body. Gordy was there: "I asked about how was Aliza laying in her grave. And she was laying in the prenatal position, face down. She was in a ball just like this, not on her side. And I says, 'Oh Jesus Christ,' and he says, What's the matter? And I says, 'Holy shit, I'm sorry but I come from the old school. Back in our history, if you was a no-good person and you wanted to be erased, they buried you face down so you could not face your god.' These guys all ask me, 'What significance has that got?' I said, 'She could not look at the child and didn't want the child to look at her when she put her there.'"

A small bag containing Kleenex had been found tucked in with the body. "And they said to me, 'What's the significance of the bag with the tissues?' . . . And I says I thought really what was on the tissue was her tears, and also she tried to clean Aliza up, and I also thought that she had put some kind of a chemical on the tissue to distract any wildlife or any dog being able to dig this child out."

Gordy's own investigations continued; he couldn't give up walking this territory, the scene of a chilly failure for him. He read Christine Lane's new statement about finding her daughter entangled in her blankets. Like the jury that would eventually convict Lane, he didn't believe it. The lady had cried "Wolf!" one time and brought him in at a dead run; he didn't plan to listen to her again. The predator in this neck of the woods, as Gordy saw it, walked upright on two legs, had pretty hair, make-up and laundered her daughter's bedclothes in secret.

So "I walked the route and I'm figuring she claims now it happened at four o'clock in the morning. She carried this child a mile, buried her, walked back and had to hide herself so the traffic couldn't pick her up on Warren Road and Hillcrest, and get back to the house, wash all the clothing, put her make-up on, take a bath, wash her hair, do all this kind of crap. Mathematically, it can't come out."

Unlike the jury, Gordy thinks that the killing of Aliza Bush was premeditated—murder 1—and that Christine had help. He says that investigators discovered the photographs of Aliza which Lane gave to authorities were taken just two days before the child's disappearance, developed immediately and picked up by the defendant on February 1: "The next day she had them ready to hand to the police department." In one of these photos, Aliza wears her snow jacket and sits alone in snow with her legs out straight. In the other, her round face comes in close. She wears a warm, soft cap tied under her chin. (The local dairy that ordered 70,000 milk cartons imprinted with that face had to discard the cartons when Lane was arrested.)

Gordy adds that the white pine branches found covering Aliza had been cut with a saw: "I'm looking over these photographs with another guy, and I hand him back three pictures and said, 'What's wrong with these?' He says, 'Nothing. . . .' I said, 'Look at the branches, they've been cut.' He grabs the pictures, he's looking at 'em. I says, 'I want Joe O'Brien and somebody from the sheriff's department with me when we go back there. I want to go to the grave site this afternoon.' So we made arrangements, we all met there, and this is as true as I'm sitting here and you can ask Joe O'Brien, there's photographs of the whole nine yards. I climbed up that tree carrying branches, putting them back up and holding a piece of paper so you people could see the cut and where she'd broke them the last part of the way, all the way down this tree, to match up and make sure that all these branches that covered Aliza came from this tree."

When police asked owners of the property if they had pruned the tree, they said no. Gordy looked everywhere for the saw; he feels certain Lane used it to cut the branches a few days prior to Aliza's disappearance. He crawled into dumpsters and kicked along the ditch, but it never turned up for him. During Lane's trial, Jim Church, the prosecutor, asked the defendant a few tentative questions about these *cut* branches, but then dropped the topic. He couldn't prove premeditation; to suggest it might ruin his entire case. Could a mother efficiently snap photographs of a child she planned to kill? Could a mother go out with a saw and prepare a bed of pine branches for her daughter's grave? The story, neat *and* bloody, defies belief.

But Gordy Gabaree believes it. He believes Lane got a ride to Hillcrest Road (she herself had no car), then, with her daughter in her arms, waded through the freezing slush in the field ditch, leaving no trail as she headed straight for the pine branches. Her friend waited in the car. In Gordy's judgment, it would have been impossible for Lane to carry Aliza from the apartment, in the dark—she would need to dodge through heavy brush to keep out of sight of the traffic on Warren Road—and make her way by happenstance to the pine tree. The garbage bags showed very few rips. The old white pine isn't obvious from the street.

"You hear her laughing?" Gordy asks as we watch the February 10 re-enactment tape. On screen, Christine Lane wanders near her apartment building, obediently calling out, "Aliza? Aliza?" for the cameras. She walks behind a few cars; in one of the cars is a woman, a female FBI agent pretending to be Heidi. A few seconds after she picks up the mitten from the ground, Lane's face does appear to be poised near a laugh. Did she almost laugh? We were curious, so we replayed her. What we saw might have been a hyena's grin. Or it might have been the hysterical murmur of a woman who knows she's being hunted by these men armed with camcorders, these men with their shoulders half-draped in sheep's clothing.

■ ■ ■

A few weeks after our first interview, Gordon Gabaree and Lee picked me up in the Nuisance Wildlife truck and we drove to the woods where Aliza Bush's corpse had been found. From the tape recording I made, labeled "#2—Gabaree," comes the sound of swishing grass. We're walking the ditch. Our shoes make whippy noises in the dry grass until we duck through the hole in the forest wall. There's a steady crackling sound on the tape also, as if we were accompanied by a phantom campfire. I'm not sure exactly how many recording devices have traveled this route prior to mine.

We make our way through a creepy tangle of narrow black sapling trunks at the edge of the woods. Gordy's voice: "Now the thing is, if you came here at night and you looked around here, where the hell would you find the tree? You had no flashlight. Look at what you're looking at. She said she was in here in the dark, with no flashlight or nothing."

Lee: "Here's the creek." Then, "Oh, Gordy, look." A little fox skull lies among the stones. It's much smaller than a dog's skull, surprisingly small. Gordy explains that foxes are really just a lot of hair.

Crackling. After a minute, Gordy's voice sounds on tape again: "Now you see how close I was to her?"

We're standing under the pine tree. It has a massive, misshapen trunk. Lee holds my tape recorder while I climb the tree to look at the cut nubs Gordy had shown investigators. Gordy is up in the tree already, his work boots, big and stiff as wood, wedged against the bark; he points out saw marks. There aren't many branches left that we can try and fit back onto the trunk, since the best of them had been gathered and brought into court as evidence. Deputies piled them on the carpet near Christine Lane's feet. ("Burn the witch," I wrote in my pad.).

I climb down. Lee has placed my tape recorder on a broad root to free her hands. She reaches up and breaks off a fresh branch. But when it snaps that branch too looks as if it has been cut part-way by a flat saw. We discuss this discovery in subdued voices because I like Gordy, and Lee, I believe, loves Gordy. We pass around the branch and sniff it. "Smell this," Lee says.

Pine helps cut scent. "You use PineSol and all this kind of stuff to knock down odor," Gordy says. He climbs down from the tree.

Lee: "Now here's a branch, this one broke off and it looks very different than the ones that were sawed. Some of them she might have been able to break, but not the larger ones."

Gordy: "She had to case this place out prior. I felt that she had this all ready." And a while later: "Pouring rain, I'll never forget it."

We talk—about the Bush relatives, about pine branches. I say, "It's such a pretty place here, you know?"

Gordy: "I'm going to tell you something."

But he's interrupted. Lee and I are talking about the trial. Gordy comes back, "I'm going to tell you something that happened to me, that happens to me a lot. You've asked me the question and I've avoided it, avoided it, avoided it. How do I know?" Then, "I told Lee after you went from the interview because it bothered me real bad, and I have never really discussed this. Joe O'Brien was the only one I said anything to, and he says, 'How do you know?' and I says, 'I talked to the girl.'"

We're silent. On tape, silence makes a noise like distant falling water.

Gordy: "She died Saturday morning about 2:00 a.m. She was buried alive here." A raspy, small intake of breath. His voice changes. "And I know it. I don't know how the hell to explain it to you, but I know that little one was alive, because she asked me and I talked to her, and she quit talking about two that morning. And I felt like . . . I kept saying, 'Where are you,' and she's saying, 'I'm here.' I was up by the water tower when I heard the voice. I had *not* seen a picture of Aliza, all I knew was she had a pink jacket on and grey sweat suit pants, but I could have described that girl right to a T. Now, I don't want you to think I'm crazy, 'cause I think I am."

"This little one gets down like this." Gordy kneels. He gets down on all fours in the brown needles. "And she looked up and said, 'Help me.' And she talked like we're talking, it wasn't a baby talk. I says, 'Where are you sweetie? I'm here.' Then she says, 'Mommy? Mommy?' Half a dozen times. And she says, 'I'm so cold.' I'm thinking, 'Jesus Christ.' I'm going out of my noodle because I don't dare tell *anybody* what I'm experiencing out here and I keep coming here and coming here and coming here, and every time I got here, I was taken out of here. . . ."

"I started talking to her somewhere around ten o'clock, eleven o'clock, Friday night."

Lee gently: "And then she stopped talking at two."

Gordy: "About two in the morning."

Lee: "Which is why you felt she had died then."

Gordy: "That's when I felt she died."

Lee: "You had a vision of a pine tree."

"I saw the pine tree and she wasn't in the plastic bags, I didn't see that. I didn't see her covered. All I saw was her raise up and talk to me. I saw the tree, I could see the ground, you know, but I kept looking for a tree stand, you know, where guys hunt deer out of, because the branches were all cut off, and that's what I kept looking for."

We try to work it out. Gordy realizes this new angle damages his credibility. The awful dream, that for him caps this ghost story, is impossible for me to believe in the daylight.

Lee: "Now, I'm very skeptical of extrasensory perception and all that, but it's not that I don't believe that it's there, it's that I don't know that it is. There are people with heightened sensitivity."

We try to work it out because we like this man. Gordy says, "I know in my heart that it's true. . . .

"I went back a couple of times, but I still couldn't find this spot. I must have been within ten, fifteen feet of her a couple of times. . . .

"I know about the first three days, I kept being drawn here. After that, I really wasn't. It was like, I knew she was here but I couldn't figure out where." He tried to talk to Sheriff Howard about the phantom voice. "Sheriff says, 'Don't tell me you're one of them *Whoo-ooo-oo!*' So I shut up right after that."

We go over it all again. I'm grateful to Gordy and am convinced that he believes he heard the voice he describes. But I can't believe that the voice came from Aliza. I can't believe there's a chance she was buried alive. In fact there is no evidence at all that she was. Lee acts as mediator.

Lee: "You didn't want to find her dead."

"I didn't want to find her dead. I knew she was alive all Friday, I knew that."

Lee: "I remember when I saw you, you said, 'I can't find her, and if she's out there, I should be able to find her.'"

The reels keep turning as we stand by the tree. Lee and I are recorded asking dim questions about the garbage bags because we find it hard to believe a living child would not have torn the bags. ("Were the bags just tied with those little twisty ties?") We sound like students: bright, cautious, hoping for consensus. Eventually on tape there are new, magnified sounds of passage. We come back out of the woods politely.

My face feels sunburnt. Once we gain the field again, Gordy points to the cluster of white whirligigs in the back yard of a near, old frame house. A local psychic consulted during the search had told police that he felt the child was warm and that he saw windmills. "There they are," says Gordy. We say that we expected *big* windmills.

"Were they there before?"

"Oh yeah, been there for years."

The whirligigs keep still. They leave an impression. I wish I believed in psychics. And ghosts. In my imagination, the ghost of a child is not small. It is taller than a man. It walks with gigantic eyes closed. If a hunter stands in the forest after the sun has gone down, after his recording devices, compass and map have been lost in the bushes, he prays those gigantic eyes don't open. He prays the spirit can't feel his scent.

■ ■ ■

Diane and David LaBar live directly across the road from Chauncey Bush. They have been neighbors for years; they knew Greg Bush when he was a boy, "a little go-getter," and they've always liked Chauncey, whom they call "Chancy", saying he goes with the flow. The LaBars' youngest daughter Brenda got to be friends with Christine Lane when Greg came over to do some backhoe work and brought Chris with him. They all hit it off. Diane LaBar and Brenda agreed to stand up with Chris and Greg down at the county courthouse after Chris got pregnant and the two decided to marry ("she had a diamond and everything"). But that fell through, because when Greg announced this plan to his father and stepmother, "they went right over and told him no, so he didn't do it."

Greg and Chris were living together at the time in the side lot mobile home on the Bushes' property. There was tension. Once the daughter of Chauncey's second wife went over to Chris and Greg's trailer, drank a bottle of whiskey, stumbled back home and got sick all over everything. Chauncey's second wife blamed Chris. This incident would be described by the defense attorney during Christine Lane's trial in order to help establish the defendant's history of being misunderstood by authority figures.

Brenda LaBar was Christine's coach during labor, so Diane LaBar came along to the hospital and stayed in the waiting room with Greg and Chauncey. It was a difficult labor. Chris hadn't dilated, "and they had to give her shots to start the dilating. They gave her a shot or several shots, and then she dilated in like four hours and it's supposed to be a lot longer than that. That hurt. I could hear her *screaming*"—Diane LaBar looks up at the ceiling. "I was there before she had the baby and I could just hear her *screaming*. They finally shut the door. Probably that whole floor could hear her." When they finally wheeled Christine out after delivery, "I think she was a little shocky. Her blood pressure dropped way, way down. They brought her out and she looked like an Eskimo, cause they had blankets after blankets wrapped around her because she was freezing cold."

Greg couldn't take it: "He heard her scream once and that was it."

Diane LaBar often babysat for Aliza. "The child was very active, devilish. She liked to see what she could get into, if she could play with the TV and the knickknacks I had. And she liked to get into my pocketbook, so I got an old pocketbook and gave it to her, and she put all of her stuffed animals in it and carried them around. . . . And she liked to get into my pots and pans and under the sink, which I definitely wouldn't let her do. . . . She liked to chase the kitties." Aliza loved Trix cereal. She'd always go straight to the cereal cupboard. And she loved tickling: "Chris would play with her, she'd tickle her. She would get her down on the floor and crawl around like she was chasing her on all fours and make her giggle. . . .

"She had these two great big dimples. Big smile and all you'd see was dimples." Diane presses her own cheeks with her fingertips, but she can't quite smile.

The LaBars' house is ramshackle. At the same time, Diane LaBar herself gives an impression of contentment and frankness. She likes children. She likes living in this two-bath mobile home, among big fields near a quarter horse farm. Both she and her daughter have trained as nurses. Diane doesn't believe Chris could have hurt Aliza unless something was very wrong; unless some man slipped her drugs without her knowledge.

But even that crazy story doesn't make sense, because Chris was always "down on people who smoked marijuana." Chris didn't even like cigarettes. "She'd come in and she'd say, 'You still smoking?' And this was really cute, when she would come in and I was smoking, Chris would have the baby go, 'Ach ach ach,' like a cough. And soon as I'd put the cigarette down or out, she was fine, but I'd go to light another one and the baby'd 'Ach ach ach ach.' . . .

"I like Chris. She was always a very nice girl." Yes, Chris and Greg used to hunt together for deer, rabbit, squirrel, pheasant. Chris was a kind of tomboy. She played softball on the Rogue's Harbor team.

We go on talking. At one point, I ask about the search for Aliza. David LaBar, a large man who walks with difficulty, has been steadily patting the diapered backside of his infant grandson (Brenda's new baby) who rests on his chest. He tries to answer the question, but his voice breaks; he hands the baby to his wife and retreats to a back bedroom. In a few minutes, he returns. After Gordon Gabaree, David LaBar is the second man brought to tears by going over this story. His wife has been talking. David speaks: "In my mind, I knew something happened. But I've never seen Chris lose her temper or nothing like that, but you know things do happen. She's got a lot on her mind. Her and Greg had just separated."

Diane: "From what I heard, the guy that she was seeing did deal with drugs."

David: "I don't think she done it."

Diane: "No, I don't. I don't think she had a thing to do with it."

David: "If you could have seen her with that baby . . . "

Brenda LaBar has her new baby. Greg Bush has married since Chris Lane was jailed, and he and his wife have one baby, a son, and another on the way. Diane LaBar gave birth to five children in six years. Her only boy died of leukemia just before his second birthday twenty-four years ago. Aliza's death, at about the same age, was agony for Mrs. LaBar. It brought back memories.

But she continues to answer questions. I mention that one of the investigators said Christine Lane's apartment was bare of toys when he entered that morning, February 2. Diane LaBar is puzzled: "I can't believe that. That kid had toys in *our* house. The car she used was full of toys. I don't understand why there wasn't any toys." She looks at me. "That's really strange. She had all kinds of stuffed toys, rattles. All over the seat and tied to her car seat. That's really weird." She looks away.

Teachers at Lansing High School had a difficult time remembering Christine Lane, though her graduating class numbered fewer than a hundred students. She had transferred to Lansing from Ithaca High at some point, for some reason. Nobody knew, off the top of their heads, whether or not she graduated. It appears that she got through junior year and then dropped out. Lansing's biology instructor recalled a few discussions among her colleagues after the whole story came out: "The teachers who did have her in class had a very, very vague memory of her. It seemed like she was either there for a short time or she just was not a very noticeable person."

This silent girl emerged one February morning telling stories. Hundreds of people were convinced by her voice, her face, her pleas. A man who knew her well and asked to remain anonymous, spoke of her with resentment and awe: "I've never been skunked like that before and never will be again. I'll just set the clock earlier. Have to get up earlier than this old coon." He described her beauty off the record. But "it's like holding a snake. You don't know what that snake's going to do."

Christine Lane had power; she knew something about men. But her imagination seems to have been adolescent, hackneyed, and her judgment of the police investigators, naïve. It doesn't appear that she expected law enforcement agents—grown men—to don masks so that they could counter her mask and organize their own deceptions to thwart her deception. High school teachers didn't act that way. During Lane's trial, the prosecuting attorney would suggest that the defendant thought to use mittens for luring investigators down the wrong trail because she'd watched a made-for-TV movie called *Where are the Children?*, the story of an abduction. Her self-assurance was youthful, her command of source material elementary.

At some point, Christine Lane had to realize that the men trailing her around the apartment building with camcorders that Saturday morning were not so gently sheepish as they pretended. Nobody was telling the truth that day. The various actors walking in circles approached farce. In the right light, at the right time of day, those video tapes can be funny.

The tragedy of the video tape session is harder to see. Christine Lane, the young storyteller, stands queerly alone. We can't mourn with her because we don't trust her sorrow; she cried "*Wolf!*" once, and once is too much. When the investigators who arrived to videotape the re-enactment asked Christine Lane to walk outside and *pretend* to be the desperate mother she should have been on February 2, they were asking for a little payback. It was now Christine's turn to wander around calling "Aliza!" to the empty air. It was her turn to reach for the lively image of a child who was, in truth, already dead. Her turn to be teased and tricked. Give the lady a taste of her own medicine.

But this medicine is bitter, the lesson cold. Unfortunately, those who administer the punishment taste it too. Christine Lane and her pursuers could run in circles for years and never alter one plain fact: that an exposed human child is a pitiful animal, hairless, incompetent in its own defense. Stripped of family—stripped of its lovely furs—what a sad little bag of bones.

8

in the flesh

AND the only mode in which you can derive even a tolerable idea of his living contour, is by going a whaling yourself; but by so doing, you run no small risk of being eternally stove and sunk by him.

—Herman Melville, *Moby-Dick*

■ ■ ■

Indictment No. 90-023, Sentencing.
State of New York, County Court: County of Tompkins.
Before: Honorable Betty D. Friedlander:

. . . Now, the Court has considered every possible aspect of this case to determine the appropriate sentence. I've considered the nature of the events which led to Aliza's death, the defendant's behavior, and her mental and emotional state as reflected in her conduct and in the statements she has made.

I've given careful thought to the consideration which must be given to the interests of society. The information before the Court indicates that the defendant was not under any particular unusual stress at the time of those events.

Even acknowledging the stresses that a single person experiences under the best of circumstances, it is apparent in this case that the defendant was not without support. The sentencing report submitted by the Probation Department and the evidence in the case suggests that Aliza's grandparents and her father's family were eager to assist the defendant in caring for Aliza.

This family had, in fact, for a long period of time, assisted the defendant in Aliza's care, and she spent numerous nights in their home. Even on the night in question, Aliza's grandfather had come to visit the child.

Although on public assistance, the defendant was living in a comfortable home, with adequate food, with adequate furnishings, and clothing. And she had the help and company of family and friends, so that the tremendous stresses experienced by families without support, with no one to relieve them of child-caring burdens and the undermining burden of real poverty were not factors in the defendant's life.

The defendant's behavior after Aliza's death, in failing to seek medical help or any other kind of assistance, in placing the child's body in a plastic bag and secreting it, and standing by for days while hundreds of concerned citizens combed the area for Aliza in freezing weather conditions, is not adequately accounted for by her asserted concern that she would be blamed for Aliza's death because some years previously she had been wrongfully blamed for taking some money from her parents.

In the defendant's statements following Aliza's death and in her behavior, she has failed to demonstrate any sincere remorse or questioning of her own responsibility to Aliza which such a sudden loss might ordinarily occasion; the defendant's exclamation at the funeral home, her shifting of responsibilities to others, including Aliza, for the catastrophic events which engulfed her.

A jury has determined that Aliza's death was not caused by accident or illness. The jury has concluded that Aliza's death was caused by human agency, and that the defendant was the cause. Aliza was the most innocent of victims for whom there can be no question of complicity, provocation, or the possibility of fighting back.

The outpouring of concern expressed by the community at Aliza's disappearance is indicative of the despair that society feels about the loss of a child's life. The despair is even more overwhelming when that loss is the result of violence, particularly when committed by the very adult who should be most responsible for the child's nurturance and well-being, and it is compounded in this case by the defendant's calculating response to the child's death.

Society's abhorrence of the terrible dynamics and tragic consequences of violence against a child has been the most significant factor in determining the appropriateness of a sentence in this case.

Therefore, upon your conviction of the crime of manslaughter in the second degree, in violation of Penal Law Section 125.15, subdivision one, the Court sentences you to a term of imprisonment in the state correctional facility, the minimum of which shall be 5 years, the maximum of which shall be 15.

Upon your conviction of obstructing governmental administration in the second degree, in violation of Penal Law Section 195.05, the sentence of the Court is one year.

Upon your conviction of falsely reporting an incident in the third degree, in violation of Penal Law Section 240.50, the sentence of the Court is three months.

All of said sentences are to run concurrently with each other. You have thirty days to appeal from this sentence and judgment of conviction. If you are unable to afford a lawyer, the Court will assign one to represent you. We will be adjourned.

■ ■ ■

The Tompkins County trial of Christine Lane was conducted simultaneously with the trial of Shirley Kinge. The Lane case was less complicated. It began more than two months after the Kinge trial and ended one week earlier. It did not cross racial boundaries or neighborhood boundaries, and only one person died, not five. Because the Kinge proceedings were being conducted in the new courthouse, the Lane trial had to be scheduled in the old courthouse, in a paneled, cavernous room where Gothic windows and polished wooden arches do little to dispel an aura of barn, and where the judge's bench resembles an old radio cabinet cut down and monstrously elongated.

To get to the old courthouse from her office on the second floor of the new courthouse, Judge Betty Friedlander, in her running shoes, found it necessary to pick her way around the weary young reporters assigned to cover the Kinge case, reporters who congregated daily in the hallway to view those proceedings on a shared monitor screen (courtroom pews are slippery and hard). From there, Judge Friedlander descended a staircase, exited through the back doors and sailed along a narrow passageway between the rear walls of the old, defunct county jail and the First Baptist Church. Courthouses and big stone churches and their various parking lots entangle here on the north side of DeWitt Park, a venerable downtown green space. The old courthouse itself so exactly resembles a Gothic, grey stone church that even Ithacans are confused by it. Obviously, city fathers once equated civic judgments with Christian judgment. They don't any more.

In fact, it is illuminating to observe how little the atmosphere in a modern courtroom resembles the atmosphere in a church. Though both rely on ritual, costume and congregation, and both address questions about human behavior, guilt, judgment and penance, they differ very much in their *reach*. Even the most staid Protestant congregations sing and pray; thus, they imagine their celebrations partially unroofed—open to the sky. Modern courtroom dramas, on the other hand, function as strictly indoor games. Instead of trying to raise the roof, legal professionals seem eager to lower it, to enclose and contain public speech. A contemporary American trial works by manipulating series of questions and answers that have been *limited*, narrowed, in an attempt to decontaminate evidence presented to the jury or judge for consideration. By implication, this method reassures participants—notably jurors, the uninitiated volunteers—that the fierce questions they will be asked to consider, the awful stories they will be asked to hear, have also been decontaminated, made safe for consumption. Tamed. Judges essentially promise jurors that they will be able to walk out of the courtroom after proceedings have concluded with their clothes perfectly dry, because the monsters who tunnel in the waters below their feet are *not* allowed to breach or gape near the jury box. There will be no swimming allowed in bloody waters.

These proper assurances and constraints were all in place for the Christine Lane trial. Hundreds of men and women had crawled outdoors in the cold to search for Aliza Bush. Now, a smaller number of men and women would sit indoors and embark on a drier expedition concerning that lost child. They would be instructed to deal with evidence rationally, not emotionally. To this end, evidence would be formatted so that it prompted rational, not visceral, responses. A child had died. The jury would examine photographs picturing slices of that child's brain, lungs and heart. The child's face would not appear as part of the evidence.

Jurors adapt themselves to these restrained conditions with little apparent trouble. This was true even in the Christine Lane case, which might have been expected to stir up deep, visceral passions for two reasons: because the crime concerned the death of a young child and because so many of the participants involved in the trial happened to be female. The judge was female and so was the defendant and so was the victim and so was the most successful medical witness, who testified for the prosecution, and so were half the jury members, including the foreperson.

"Madame Foreperson, have you reached a verdict?" Judge Betty Friedlander called at the conclusion of the trial.

"Yes, Your Honor," replied Madame Foreperson. The verdict for manslaughter in the second degree was guilty.

In this case, women adjudicated, concluded and testified cooly. They did not shy away from making sharp, masculine judgments; they did not plead for some gentle, maternal verdict that would result in small rewards for all parties involved. They sentenced one another without apology and exacted vengeance when directed by law.

Females are not the usual defendants in New York criminal cases; the New York State prison system holds twenty-one male convicts for each single female convict. They are not the usual judges either, of course. Judge Betty Friedlander, a sharp-boned woman with a Bronx accent and unruly hair, is due to retire sometime quite soon. She runs her courtroom confidently, sweeping down the aisles in a long black robe for criminal cases, a shorter black robe for arraignments involving parole violations. She has gained a reputation as a thorough, delicate investigator in family court cases and a tough manager of criminal cases. Jurors trust her. She treats her jurors as capable, serious adult students, which in fact they are.

Local defense attorneys are more reserved in praising Her Honor, not because she's too feminine in some way, but, indeed, for the opposite reason. One of Ithaca's mildest defense attorneys, who asked to remain anonymous, referred to Judge Friedlander as a "hanging judge" and said it wasn't surprising, because Friedlander herself had spent years working as a topnotch local defense attorney before she was elected to the bench. He went on to explain that, ironically, excellent defense lawyers who rise to become judges often emerge as tough-skinned courtroom overlords. Possibly they grow weary of their own former ploys, the standard batch of pleas and objections used by any defense attorney. Possibly they have grown weary of institutional sympathy and the lawyers who specialize in pleading for it.

Christine Lane's court-appointed lawyer was a man, as was the prosecuting attorney. Wesley McDermott, defense counsel, stalked the queer stage marked off between judge, jury and audience for three weeks during the Lane trial. The back of his head, pink-pated and divided in halves by converging waves of reddish hair, became familiar to journalists, many of whom sat up in a high, sound-proofed loft where they eyed their monitors and traded comments about the activities below. McDermott is gifted with a fine voice and acknowledged as one of the county's most experienced trial lawyers, but he is not a man who appears graceful or privileged under the yellow lights in a cavernous courtroom. Interviewed, he described himself as a "country boy who likes to fight, okay?"

But it's hard to fight a judge. The counselor said he had trouble with Judge Betty Friedlander throughout the Lane case. She strictly limited his *voir dire*, for starters, forbidding him to use a number of the questions he customarily employs to weed out potentially unsympathetic jurors. She didn't authorize the money he had requested to hire a neuropathologist as an expert witness for the defense until "two days before the prosecution rested," and then she authorized only $2,000, an insufficient sum, according to McDermott. As for the judge's statement at time of sentencing, especially the paragraph about Chris Lane's failure to show "remorse" for the death of Aliza, it incensed him: "I don't see any basis for suggesting that you have to display remorse about having done something that *you continue to say you haven't done.*" In his opinion, Judge Friedlander had written her sentencing indictment to "bootstrap" a justification for doing what she planned to do anyway: max out Chris Lane with five to fifteen years.

"My body aches after a day of trial," Wesley McDermott said at one point, describing his work as a defense attorney. He was seated in his office, a brown, paneled room decorated with eagles and newspaper cartoons pressed under glass on the desk. "Anybody can prosecute a case, okay?"

Why is that?

"Because the prosecutor has available to him in Tompkins County probably no less than three hundred, four hundred bodies to do his legwork, his investigation. He has a staff of, what, there must be ten, twelve people on the third floor of the courthouse now."

And the defense attorney? Stands alone, works alone. He doesn't know what witness, what argument the prosecutor will introduce next during the proceedings, yet he must be prepared to stand and cross-examine each witness publicly, to counter each argument with his own legal or medical research.

The Lane case had been particularly difficult to defend. Complex medical questions were involved. The community had already been shocked by the Harris murders, and passions agitated by Shirley Kinge's trial may have heightened publicity of Lane's simultaneous trial. And there were "those thirteen days in February" when Christine Lane posed as the heartbroken mother of an abducted child. Said McDermott, "That was a very large part of my efforts, to try and deal with those thirteen days . . . to make the jury understand how someone could do something like this, how an innocent person could make these bad choices and be trapped."

Wesley McDermott did not think that the gender of his client or of the judge had anything to do with the special challenges of this trial. In fact, he had welcomed women on the jury, especially "liberal, well-educated" ones. (To prepare for his *voir dire*, he got the names of the four or five hundred potential jurors and checked out their voting and property records, looking for registered Democrats who owned their own homes.) "Who was more apt to identify with Christine Lane, a woman?" he asked rhetorically, though then he added, "I *was* getting people saying, 'Wes, watch out,' because there's nothing harder on a woman than another woman."

But the counselor may have underestimated the extreme difficulty of his main challenge, which was to establish *mother love* on the one hand and argue about *cause of death* on the other. To accomplish this divided task, he had to speak two languages, one to call up the spirit of a beloved little girl, the other to analyze the corpse of a discarded human being. The prosecuting attorney, Jim Church, a big, personable lawyer with a Prince Valiant haircut, didn't need to prove love, but only attack. That job was not so sticky.

How does a lawyer prove that his accused client loved her baby? First, he must be able to speak about baby things in front of a judge and jury. It's not easy. Since this case involved a single mother and her daughter—a female defendant and a littler female victim—courtroom dialogue bristled with words and objects associated with a traditionally feminine world, and Mr. McDermott was required to handle them all without embarrassment. Tike Bikes and wet diapers, hot dogs, Spaghetti-O's and little spankings were mentioned (McDermott: "Did you ever have to pat her on the bottom?" Lane: "Yes . . . but it was always on the diaper"). Exhibits presented as evidence during the trial included a dismantled, slightly rusted crib which police screwed back together near Lane's seat, bagged crib sheets, a pillowcase decorated with orange and green swirls, a crib mattress with big blue checked flowers printed on it, and a baby book Christine maintained to record Aliza's growth. The Xeroxed print of this baby book made available to journalists was sadly blurred.

Wesley McDermott put the baby book into evidence to prove that Christine Lane loved her daughter. He also submitted the defendant's letters to her family (including the letter full of woeful falsehoods she wrote to Andy Bush, Aliza's uncle), believing that those letters would help substantiate Christine's love. He called babysitters to the stand to say that Chris played with Aliza. He called Christine's best friend, Brenda LaBar, to speak about Chris, but her testimony was instantly neutralized by the prosecutor, who had discovered that Ms. LaBar had been charged with embezzlement by her former employers, owners of Klein's All-Sports store. Though the charges hadn't been proven, the prosecutor's barb thoroughly discredited Brenda. Brenda's high, frazzled red hair and clothes didn't help matters. One juror—she will be called Kate—would say later, "I question the character witnesses that McDermott put up. I thought, 'Is this the best he could come up with, or is this really reflecting his competence, or is it because Christine Lane just didn't have any friends?'"

Mr. McDermott did establish that no medical proof existed to show that Aliza had ever been physically abused by her mother, and that a number of people considered Christine Lane to have been a very decent young mother. The counselor was absolutely sincere when he spoke about his client's affection for Aliza. During the interview, he said, "Personally for me, in over twenty years doing this I have honestly never had a client that I believed in more than I do Chris, all right?" This was a credible statement. Other lawyers had noticed that Wes was deeply involved in the case. Even his family had been affected. The McDermotts are Lansing residents; they live among people who participated in the search for Aliza Bush, people who were shocked when the news broke that Lane herself was under arrest, accused of having killed and hidden the baby. One teacher at Lansing High School said she'd heard that Wesley McDermott's son told an instructor the high-publicity trial had been a grueling ordeal for his entire family, and when it was finished, they were all "going to take some time off to relax."

But the strict, dry acoustics of a courtroom diminished the counselor's arguments; they hollowed words like "love" and made them sound sentimental. McDermott repeatedly lost momentum. He appeared to be struggling, exaggerating: "If you want heart-wrenching proof of a mother's love, read the letters to the Bush family, where she pleads for the privilege of being able to lie down in death beside her daughter, to lay down for eternity with her," he argued during his summation. And "I think about my own children, how often with good intentions we tried to maintain their baby books, but we had trouble keeping up with it." And "Chris

Lane was a good and loving mother. There was no evidence of abuse, no one ever saw her abuse the child. In fact, the worst thing Chauncey Bush had to say was that she let Aliza get down on the floor and play with the puppies. . . ." After this, the attorney trailed off into a comment about "fostering a relationship with young animals."

McDermott believed Christine Lane when she spoke. He believed that the horror of discovering her daughter dead had unsettled her completely, causing her to act in a way that was wild, disjoint and weirdly deliberate. It made sense to him that because the young woman felt everybody hated *her*, nobody loved *her* and *nobody* in authority ever believed her, she started dialing the phone for help after attempts to resuscitate Aliza failed, but then . . . stopped. Replaced the receiver. Dressed her daughter and slid her into garbage bags and started walking straight out into the cold dark. If she could carry this one bag of garbage—this mistake—far from the apartment without opening her mouth, without begging for help from anybody, she would be in the clear. Nobody ever helped her much with Aliza anyway; they meddled, they dropped by for a visit at their convenience. Begging for help was garbage. She would finish this job alone, outdoors. She was capable outdoors. Then she would return to the new apartment. Once back home, everything would settle. At daybreak, she would begin again.

McDermott believed his client when she spoke to him. (Why? "I don't know. I've been doing this for over twenty years. Part of it is your gut.") What's surprising is that Wesley McDermott, an experienced lawyer, even believed Chris when she *wrote*, though her letters were obviously perforated with lies and juvenile threats. And, even more surprising, he expected that the jury would be favorably impressed by reading his client's changeable—girlish and manly, calculating and helpless—voice on paper. Therefore, he submitted these letters as evidence:

To Chauncey, Sandy, Andy and Kyle,

. . . It's very hard to be in here because I hate being locked up like some animal. But what I miss most is getting a hug. You see they have me in secluded visits to protect me from the public. I realize you all probably feel that I'll never be punished enough, but believe me, having to say my goodbye to Aliza that Thursday afternoon was punishment enough. Telling the authorities what really happened meant having to let Aliza rest. But also, it's hard when Mom comes to visit because she puts her hands on the glass and I can't touch her. And Kevin puts his head on the glass, but I can't do anything to help comfort them. . . .

There is no evidence in the DA's office that Aliza died because of me. He hasn't even charged me, that's why my attorney is upset with him. Please try to forgive me and in some ways I'm glad that she'll lye [sic] next to your Mom, Chauncey!

Love,
Chris

And the one to Greg:

. . . I've also been told that someone was seen messing around my apartment. So, see, I may be in here, but I still hear about what's going on.

Now, I love you and your family. I realize that's hard to believe at this point, but I do. Also, I'm not going to sign the release form for the funeral services. I want very much for Aliza to rest in the Lansingville Cemetery, it's her being next to Jenny that I can't agree to.

These documents did influence the jury, but not in the way the defense attorney hoped. The juror, Kate, recalled, "Some of the things that really affected us were the letters she wrote from jail. She was still perpetuating the lie."

There is something fearless in Chris Lane's voice. And something untouched. Do her letters represent her fairly? It is impossible to tell from them whether she knows *nothing* about suffering, or whether she simply never learned to write well about her own. But the voice does have flesh. When it goes on the offensive, it's youthfully offensive. Apparently, Counselor McDermott listened to this changeable voice with a parent's ear, and hoped that liberal, empathetic jurors would do the same. But even liberals can be strict. And women can be downright patriarchal.

McDermott and his client faced a number of professional women during the course of the trial. These included two female physicians, Dr. Mary Anne Kiernan, Aliza's pediatrician, and Dr. Lucy Rorke, a regally emotionless, mechanical neuropathologist. Both these doctors testified for the prosecution. Dr. Rorke easily overwhelmed the testimony of McDermott's own medical expert, a pediatric pathologist who theorized that Sudden Infant Death Syndrome (SIDS) results from massive allergic reactions, and that the unusual size of the victim's thymus indicated Aliza had suffered from allergies and was probably a victim of SIDS. His argument marked him, for the jury, as a quack.

Kate reported that jurors considered McDermott's medical witness "off the wall." She judged Dr. Lucy Rorke to have been the most influential medical witness, "even though people did not like her, because she was so cold, she came across very cold." The chill of the one woman did *not* alienate the other woman, though. Kate went on to say: "I just like people who are very direct and easy to listen to and present everything in a clear order to me."

It was Dr. Rorke who testified that her examination of relevant autopsy slides showed definite signs that the victim had died of asphyxiation. She noted the peachy color of the brain and necrotic neurons in the brain, as well as hemorrhages in connecting tissue around the trachea and signs of hemorrhaging in one of the sixteen slides cut from the victim's heart. A bruise on Aliza's forehead which Dr. Germaniuk, the medical examiner, had described as a "slight contusion," she called an "acute hemorrhage." There was some question about the bruise inside the right anterior of the victim's mouth. The neuropathologist found it significant. When the defense attorney challenged Dr. Rorke by asking her if she ever bit her cheek, she said "No." McDermott would later refer to the doctor as the "lady who never bit her cheek."

Since the body of the victim showed few and indeterminate external signs of abuse resulting from events that took place before her death, it was necessary to dissect her for signs of abuse, and then dissect testimony about the results. Both lawyers therefore found themselves required to gargle mouthfuls of medical terminology gracefully before the jury. Sometimes they managed, sometimes they failed. The task seemed especially difficult for the defense attorney, who had trouble finding a tone of address that could embrace both love and autopsy.

At one point, McDermott described Dr. Germaniuk as the one physician who, in his dealings with the little girl's corpse, "had his hands in there. He was the only one who examined the body grossly, the only one who examined the organs grossly." He went on to compare Dr. Germaniuk with a garage mechanic and Dr. Lucy Rorke with the "service manager" (he favored Dr. Germaniuk's report because the medical examiner had not concluded with certainty that the victim was asphyxiated).

There were arguments about "dumping time"—the time it takes for a child's stomach to rid itself of food. The victim's stomach contained "60 cubic centimeters of tan material consistent with apples," according to the autopsy report. There were arguments about the bruises and the patterns of lividity, marks that indicate how the victim's blood pooled after death. McDermott and Church both haggled over the color of the victim's brain. At one point, McDermott shook his own set of pictures in a little fan towards the jury and spectators caught a glimpse of them. The brain looked like a small cauliflower dished out onto a poker table.

Counselor McDermott was still working at the medical puzzle weeks after the trial had concluded. Doctors testifying for the prosecution stated that the material in Aliza's stomach proved she died soon after she ate supper, not early the next morning, as Christine Lane's testimony would have it. But the defense lawyer said, "I could show you a number of articles that say don't try and pin time of death on the basis of stomach dumping time."

Doctors testifying for the prosecution had argued that the lividity patterns indicated the child could not have died face down in bed with her arms straight along her sides and been found "stiff and cold" in that position as Lane described. But the defense lawyer said, "You missed part of the evidence if you think that the patterns of lividity, that there was anything to that." The prosecutor had argued that Lane could not have dressed Aliza, as she described, if the child were already stiff in death, as she claimed. The defense lawyer responded, "Rigor in a child is easily broken, okay?"

McDermott continued, "And some of Church's questions about that, I thought were—under those circumstances, under that stress, who the hell remembers where the child's hands were, whatever, got her hands on her shirt, whatever, and under any circumstances, even if she had done it, the adrenaline, the fear. . . . I don't believe she did it, but I mean, what I'm saying is, that kind of detail isn't something that becomes significant to someone under those circumstances."

The counselor imagines a young woman in a hideously dark, lighted room. Under her hands is her own daughter. The child is not alive any more. The discovery rends the mother. She acts in a way that only makes sense from a dark angle. She was *young* and *scared*. He can't quite explain it, but he honestly thinks it happened. He has children of his own.

It is ironic that Mr. McDermott, the self-proclaimed country boy, "one of the grunts of the world," as he calls himself, may have been one of the most motherly people in that courtroom.

■ ■ ■

Christine Lane attended the funeral of her daughter in handcuffs and a restraining belt. Services were held on the first of March—approximately one month after the victim's death—at

Shurtleff's, in Genoa, a dank little town pinched by the intersection of a few broad hills. Just inside the door of the shadowy funeral home, guards allowed Christine to remove her arms from her coat sleeves one at a time, then they immediately locked her wrists to her waist again. The restraints hobbled her; the guards therefore appeared solicitous as nurses. Family members were present, and Kevin Dexter, Lane's recent companion, and the Tompkins County guards, the corrections officers. Family friends were not notified about the services. Gordon Gabaree and the FBI's Joe O'Brien had already come and gone. They viewed the casket at a time when they knew Christine Lane would not be present.

Linda Edwards, corrections officer, stood near Christine Lane in the carpeted room where the coffin had been placed. She remembers, "It was very quiet. You could almost cut the air with a knife. You could feel the emotion building." The child's casket was embossed, pastel and small; the few people who saw it tended to describe its size later by measuring off the brief length with their hands. The coffin concealed a girl's body that had been frozen and thawed in garbage bags outdoors, then submitted to a thorough autopsy.

Christine Lane knelt at the casket. She couldn't put her hands on it because her hands were locked to her waist. She didn't try to touch it with her forehead. Edwards moved alongside the prisoner. Edwards is a rather short woman, brown-haired, handsomely brown-eyed, a working mother, with the manners and voice of a trustworthy grade school teacher. She had worked as a corrections officer for less than a year before Lane was arrested.

Kevin Dexter stood next to Lane at the casket. When Lane began crying, she spoke to him. Linda Edwards overheard them:

"She began crying . . . she was kneeling in front of the casket, crying. She was kneeling alone, then after five minutes her mother came up. After her, her boyfriend came up. . . . I heard her say to her boyfriend, 'Why couldn't she just lay down and go to sleep that night? But she had to fool around like she always did. Damn it, why couldn't she lay down and go to sleep?'"

All guards present at the funeral were required to fill out official reports when they got back to the jail, but Edwards kept this memory to herself. It did not go into her report.

But then, "It stuck in my mind," she testified. "I thought about it every day. I couldn't sleep thinking about it." Two weeks after the funeral she confided in a fellow guard who advised her to talk to the sheriff. She had been worried that her story would be classified as inadmissible, "hearsay" evidence; her colleague advised her to let the sheriff decide that. Months later, Linda Edwards took the stand as a prosecution witness. Her testimony was elicited to prove that Lane had lost her temper and done violence to Aliza when the child refused to fall asleep.

When Judge Friedlander eventually sentenced Christine Lane, she would note testimony about "the defendant's exclamation at the funeral home" which indicated that Christine Lane shifted "responsibilities to others, including Aliza, for the catastrophic events which engulfed her." The judge used testimony of this last professional woman, Linda Edwards, as proof that the defendant "failed to demonstrate any sincere remorse or questioning of her own responsibility to Aliza which such a sudden loss might ordinarily occasion." It is evident that Judge Friedlander, taking her cue from the jury, was not moved to pity by imagining Chris Lane, a single mother on welfare, captured, handcuffed and ringed by eavesdropping guards, crying on her knees beside her daughter's coffin.

In her sentencing statement, Judge Friedlander portrays Society as a kind of alternative mother, a civic Mother Mary figure capable of despairing when a child has been hurt and abhorring all acts of violence against children. Since Christine Lane happened to be the one adult who accepted most of the responsibility for Aliza's care, she is therefore held most responsible for Aliza and judged strictly. Yes, Lane was a single mother responsible for earning enough money to support her child, but she wasn't quite single enough (family members offered babysitting) nor poor enough (the furniture looked okay) to earn a lighter sentence. The band of citizens who never knew Aliza, but who spent four days searching for her, are credited with feeling more pity for the child than the defendant, a "calculating" woman. In fact, they are credited as members of a civic body that feels "despair."

The process concludes by taking the child from the arms of her irresponsible, convicted mother and giving her imaginatively over to us, good citizens who have delegated representatives to investigate people accused of crimes. But the unspoken, dramatic irony of a criminal trial involving a woman accused of killing her own child is that we must suspect that the child, revived in fantasy and given a choice, would run to the arms of her accused mother rather than to the many arms of the jurors, the sheriff's department investigators, the FBI agent and the black-robed lady judge who have all been assigned to defend the small victim's rights and, if necessary, seek retribution against her assailant.

This ironic vision relies on a fantasy. So does Judge Friedlander's reassuring vision of a despairing civic Madonna. We require fantasy to comprehend tragedy. Jurors depend on it despite themselves.

Kate, a mother herself, analyzed her experiences as a juror in the Lane trial: "I would say that the legal structure definitely was helpful for me. It took away a sense of personal blame. I was very grateful that I was not the judge." And "I think because they were so formal, and the whole court system is so formal, that it helped us to be more objective. And of course, one of the questions they asked when they were screening jurors was, 'How would you react to seeing photographs of the dead body and photos of the autopsy?' Actually, they were not emotional images when we saw the photographs and my response was not emotional." She reacted this way because, "In the pictures of the brain, the brain had been removed from the body. It didn't have this element of realness to it. Even seeing photographs of Aliza's body in the garbage bags. I think it was really hard to sense that was real." She did *not* believe there would have been any profit in trying to make the death more real: "No, I don't think that affected our decision-making process at all."

However, "I will say that I found myself dreaming things, so it did affect me on some level and that was something I didn't anticipate. I thought I was being calm and rational and that it wasn't affecting my personal life, but it did come out in my dreams."

She dreamed, then returned to the intellectual task at hand. At last she concluded that if the child's stomach contained food, it meant Aliza had to die around ten or eleven o'clock at night, which in turn meant that the defendant, Christine Lane, "had the whole night to think about what had happened, to plan, to do, to undo. . . . It wasn't impulsive." Therefore: "Actually, I was advocating for murder 2."

But the jury's vote was split, with seven voting for murder in the second degree and five voting to convict Lane of the lesser charge of manslaughter. The two sides deliberated the questions for hours without reaching a conclusion. They did not want to come out as a hung jury. Someone mentioned the great cost of the trial. At last, "we finally said, 'Well, can the people who wanted to go with murder 2 live with the manslaughter?'" They could.

Kate went on: "For me, to arrive at a verdict, I had to focus on the actual moment of death. Some people didn't want to look at that. They did not want to think about the fact that death was not instantaneous, that it took several minutes. We did ask people to think about it. We tried to re-enact it. We had the pillow and we used something to represent Aliza. And we timed it and we all sat there and waited for that time. . . ."

That time. A short time becomes an ocean of time, easily deep enough to harbor monsters.

∎ ∎ ∎

Early in February, Christine Lane left her apartment for a brief, awful journey. The back roads from Lane's apartment intersect with Etna Road. When Lane walked out that night carrying a weight in three plastic bags, she was keeping company, unwittingly, with Investigator Donald Vredenburgh, who had been assigned surveillance duty in preparation for the February 7 raid on the Kinges' apartment building. Don Vredenburgh drank coffee and read newspapers with a little flashlight to keep awake in his automobile in the dark. He had battery-powered night binoculars. Some animals came near the car. Now and then a vehicle would drive by him and park in the woods and stay about forty minutes. It was cold out.

Gordon Gabaree remembers that early during the search for Aliza, somebody reported noticing a car parked back near the water tower. The sheriff's department ran the license plates, and quickly received word to *back off*. The car was an unmarked, state police vehicle, part of the hidden web surrounding the Kinges' home.

What Shirley Kinge and Christine Lane were thinking, what they were doing in late December and early February cannot be perfectly retrieved. If we think of a trial as a kind of net, in fact, it seems to be a net deliberately slashed. The narrative progress of a trial is interrupted so frequently by objections, exclusions and indirection that, after a time, a person begins to think trials are *made* out of interruptions and exclusions, as a net is made of holes. In a similar way, if we think of a trial as drama, we notice how often the actors in a trial strive to appear undramatic. The action is done; the action happened on the night in question. It is time now to flip backwards in the program and examine a neat, disordered list of names—the cast of characters. It should not surprise us, then, that a good number of men and women who settle into the witness chair appear to be auditioning to play roles that in fact they have already played. They each look so startlingly real sitting there in the flesh. And they don't.

Greg Bush took the stand early in the trial. He wore a turquoise T-shirt, with a plaid flannel shirt over that. He kept his arms folded across his chest, and his head stayed down, his eyes were lowered, as if this were a divorce case. Asked by McDermott whether he remembered the winter when Aliza caught pneumonia because the family was living in a trailer warmed only by a space heater, he said, "Don't remember." Once Greg had struck Chris in the nose. McDermott asked if that was the only time he struck her: "I guess so." Greg Bush remembered that once he noticed Aliza had a mark on her face; Chris told him that the doctor had instructed her to slap Aliza to get her breath back. Asked by the prosecuting attorney whether he recalled the name of the doctor, Bush said he didn't.

Chauncey Bush took the stand next. He wore jeans and a blue plaid shirt. His hair was straight, fragmented. "Do you recall when Aliza was born?" McDermott asked. Bush answered, "Not really."

When Chauncey Bush was asked to identify the defendant, he had to wipe his face. His hand shook. He pointed and said, "There, in the brown coat," and his voice shook.

"Yes," he testified, on the evening of February 1 he went to Chris Lane's apartment to visit his granddaughter. Aliza was in bed. Chris said Aliza wasn't feeling well. But Aliza rattled the crib, so Chris went in to get her. Chauncey read books to his granddaughter in the living room. "I got on my hands and knees and she got on my back."

He had never seen Chris hit Aliza, but "the dogs and stuff, I didn't like the dogs. I thought she was abusing her by letting her run with the dogs and the pups on the floor all the time." Chris had stayed in the trailer next to his house after Greg had left. There were a number of dogs at various times in the trailer, but only one dog with Chris in the apartment at Warren Road. Chris used to have two dogs. She told him that one had gotten sick and died: "So then she only had the little dog." Chauncey Bush stepped down.

On October 18, Investigator Edward Hall took the stand. He was a short man, plump, who wore wire-rimmed glasses. He described how his department received information from the behavioral science unit of the FBI lab to help them organize Chris Lane's first press conference. They didn't want Chris to say anything that would frighten or anger the abductor. The press conference took place February 8. "She was calm. She was calmer than I would be in those circumstances," Hall remembered. He was trying to help Chris *and* trying to find the baby. He and the other officers, including Joe O'Brien, began the list of Christine Lane's "Inconsistencies" on February 9 or thereabouts. Nobody suggested to Chris that she ought to get a lawyer.

Roland Manley of the sheriff's department took the stand after Ed Hall. Officer Manley had been assigned to go into Christine Lane's apartment with the search warrant on February 16, after her arraignment. It was his job in court to open a number of stuffed paper bags and describe their contents to the jury. Exhibit 44, a pillow. Exhibit 45, pink blanket. Exhibit 46, Mickey Mouse sheet. Exhibit 47, white woven blanket. Exhibit 48, pink striped blanket. Exhibit 49, small striped blanket. Exhibit 50, the crib. (During recess that day, Christine and her mother were standing near the windows when a policeman carried a flat, dismantled crib past them. "Ohhhh," moaned an alert journalist in the loft, "the Death Crib!")

Thomas Donlan, FBI special agent, testified on the morning of October 26. Grey-haired, dapper and compact, he spoke with a lisp and so described himself as a "polygraph examinuh." Agent Donlan recalled that on February 15, at about 10:30 in the morning, he received a call from Joe O'Brien. O'Brien said he would bring Chris Lane to the hotel room in the Sheraton. At 1:00 p.m., they met. Chris Lane's father accompanied her.

Donlan explained that he furnished Christine Lane with forms FD328 and FD395. FD395 is the "advice of rights" form. FD328 is the "consent to take the polygraph" form. He then conducted the pre-test interview by going over Lane's biographical data, reading aloud to her the testimony she had given earlier and explaining the questions that would be asked. He asked her some "control" questions and measured her responses to use for a baseline. Then they started the "in-test" phase. The machine was on. Lane told her story again while attached to the machine. Donlan evaluated the charts. The third phase was the confrontational interview.

"As a part of that, did you tell her she was lying?"

"When I first confronted her with the fact that she was lying, she was vehement in her denial," answered Dolan.

"You offered a hypothesis of what might have happened, to Chris?"

"I offered her what we call a face-saving explanation. . . . I spoke about the fact that the child's father had left her, that she hadn't had a lot of support from her parents. She was living alone. I offered her a chance to put the blame on someone else."

After Christine Lane broke down and confessed, the law enforcement agents had to figure out what to do about her father. Somebody steered him away into another part of the motel.

Special Agent Joe O'Brien took the stand next. He was tall, gangly, a bit oily, moustached. His face can be examined on the dust jacket of his best-selling book, *Boss of Bosses*, which he authored with FBI agent Andris Kurins. The book describes the undercover investigation O'Brien and Kurins engineered to trap Paul Castellano, Mafia godfather, who unfortunately never got to trial because he ended up "whacked. Gangland style. Neat." The book describes how O'Brien and Kurins managed to bug Castellano's mansion (the job required a helicopter to drop doped meat to the Dobermans inside the fence) and what they learned from the bug: that Castellano had a penis implant in order to please his maid, saucy, ambitious, ridiculous Gloria Olarte, a lucky immigrant from Bogotá. O'Brien writes about himself: "O'Brien measured the moment. He did not believe that Castellano's mistress would clam up now; she was having too good a time showing off. So he dealt with her as one would with a cat. Make demands, it runs away; ignore it, and it rubs against your leg."

O'Brien was a key figure in the investigation of Christine Lane. He had spoken to Christine many times during the week as the search for her child continued. He helped with roadblocks and he helped by contacting the behavioral sciences unit to get advice for the press conference. He was present and held one of the three camcorders during the staged re-enactment. He tricked Kevin Dexter one night by asking to have a quick conference in Kevin's truck. O'Brien thought that the ballpoint pen Lane had used to address the envelope with the mitten in it was probably stowed in the glove compartment of the truck. O'Brien showed the jury how he pocketed the pen Dexter took from the glove compartment.

He was present the day Christine took her second polygraph exam. When O'Brien entered the room after learning that Chris was ready to confess, he "went over and sat on the edge of the bed next to Christine and asked her to tell me what had happened." Not much later, he accompanied Christine Lane, ringed by officers, to the dark grave site off Hillcrest Road. "We walked directly there. . . . I tore the garbage bag and I think we attempted to turn the body over so she could be photographed."

Christine Lane took the stand on October 30. Her bangs had grown and they fell down into her eyes, which looked tired. She began telling her story, piece by piece, in response to solicitous questions asked by Wesley McDermott, her own attorney.

"I don't really remember. I just kept walking. I didn't know where I was going," she said.

After she returned to the apartment, "I kept thinking about Aliza and I knew after taking her out in the woods that I'd made a mistake. I couldn't call the authorities or anything. I decided to report her missing."

The search began: "Well, I wanted her to be found, but I didn't want to be accused of her death." Was she frightened? "All the time." When she took her first polygraph exam, "I was kind of hoping they'd find out."

She mailed the mitten to herself because "when the rangers decided to call off the search, they said they wouldn't resume searching unless there was evidence of an abduction. . . .

"I did want her found, but then I didn't. I was scared. I had mixed feelings. I didn't know what to do. I did want her found. I didn't want her out there anymore. . . .

"I wanted them to find out that I wasn't telling the truth because I didn't want Aliza out in the woods any more. But I didn't want to be blamed for her death."

("She's on the stand" . . . "She's *on!*" Ladies lucky enough to arrive in court at this moment whispered to one another and took their seats.)

Lane's voice continued, fluty and uncertain, rich and plain. At her lawyer's urging, she described the time she tried to move back in with her parents, but "they were real distant. We'd sit in the house and nobody'd even talk to anybody. My dad wouldn't hardly stay in the same room with me." Apparently the defendant's mother had been warned about this line of questioning; she was absent from the courtroom. (The defendant's father had died during the months when his daughter was in jail awaiting trial.)

It was about 12:15 when Jim Church, the prosecutor, stood up to face Christine Lane. "Good morning, Miss Lane," he said, and began his questions. Church used a direct, businesslike voice for his examination. It was important that he not appear to browbeat this young woman. It was also important that he show her no fear, deference or pity.

Questioned, the defendant denied that she tried to hide the body to keep it from being examined by doctors. She repeated that Aliza was tangled in her blankets, lying face down.

"What position were her arms in?"

"I don't recall."

"How about her legs?"

"She was lying flat."

"Were her arms stiff like her legs were?"

"They couldn't have been very stiff, or I would have had difficulty getting her shirt on."

Later, "How could you take your little girl, who you were

worried about being cold, and put her in garbage bags and put her out in February?"

"I have no reason to lie now," replied Christine Lane, though she obviously had many reasons to lie at this time.

Jim Church asked about the sawed tree branches and about Christine's ability to find a hiding place without light in a woods where she had never been before. He asked about Aliza's medical history and sleep habits. The sound of the defendant's voice did not alter even when the prosecutor apparently struck home with his barbs. There was always a milky mildness and sadness in her tone.

One of the jurors, who will be called Susan, would recall, "There were times when she spoke of the child as if the child were still living, and it didn't sound connected with any deep feeling, but it was just as if she were running on. There were times when she described—I'm afraid of being inaccurate with this—but there were moments when her grief over the child seemed really true. And there were times when the prosecution attorney would ask her, 'Well, why didn't you let people know, why didn't you call?' And she would say she was afraid and there was something very palpably false about that whole line of what she said. . . .

"I wanted desperately to find her innocent. I was so hoping that there would be something to show this had been an awful accident. . . .

"It was my job to listen and I really worked very hard at it. But at night, you know, I would wonder. I felt like I wanted so much for her to be acquitted, and it seemed like the basis for this got eroded away little by little, and as this happened I realized that she probably was going to have to go to jail. But not usually during trial hours, working hours, did I think about that."

The jury began deliberation on the afternoon of November 8. Later that same day, there were just a few people left in the pews: three sheriff's officers, Christine Lane and her mother, two bailiffs, three journalists, two photographers and Judge Betty Friedlander in her jogging shoes. The judge looked tired, informal, as if she were a doctor come to attend a birth.

But nothing happened that evening. At 6:10 the door to the jury room opened and everybody sat up tight, but it was a false alarm. The jurors only wished to ask for a copy of Dr. Rorke's testimony, certain information on the brain and on Aliza's last meal, and for Dr. Germaniuk's autopsy report. Then it was dinner time. Jurors were treated to a dinner at Manos Diner, as usual, and then assigned rooms in the Ramada Inn. They were not allowed to watch television. They were not allowed to talk to one another.

I spent most of the next day waiting in the courtroom. We were asked to sit in the far pews, away from the corner room where the jury was sequestered, so that we couldn't eavesdrop. I wound up speaking with Almina, a writer, who has attended Tompkins County trials for many years. Almina wears magnificent pounds of silver and turquoise jewelry; the metal detector over at the Kinge trial caused her great inconvenience. But today we were at the Lane trial. We had time. She told me about her house on Bundy Road. It attracts lightning. Blue balls of lightning have fallen down through the chimney and run sizzling along the television wires. She told me about reading tea leaves. Ruth, one of the bailiffs, had joined us by this time. Ruth also knew about tea leaves. The person who wishes to have a fortune read must drink a cup of loose leaf tea till there is just a teaspoonful of liquid left in the bottom of the cup, then turn the cup upside down quickly. The same person then takes the cup and spins it on the saucer three times. Look in the cup. One leaf up high near the rim means a letter is coming. Leaves that resemble a bird's wings mean travel.

There was a noisy, rattling knock on the jury room door. We all sat up tight again. The judge put on her robe. Jim Church and Wesley McDermott arrived from somewhere. But it was nothing. Bags of blankets were carried into the jury room. We could see that the room was alight; its tall churchy windows face an open street. The bailiff emerged from the room carrying a menu and announced,

"This is lunch." Release. Everybody chuckled. Wesley McDermott threw his tie back over his shoulder. Christine laughed.

It is impossible to maintain solemnity over the course of three weeks. Even the defendant found times to chat and smile. A camerawoman took pictures of her friends, two other photographers, and Christine Lane, noticing, was amused. Evelyn Lane, Chris's mother, spoke with some of the female jail guards. She was a trim woman, dressed for the trial like a Midwestern Methodist, with round earrings and matching narrow shoes. Her features were clean, sharp, tired. Obviously, she knew the female guards from visits at the jail. They had become acquaintances. Apparently, people in a big room need a little talk more than they need enemies.

It was snowing outside. We could watch the snow falling outside the windowpanes.

There were noises—like sounds from a curtained radio—that seemed to be coming from the jury room. It took a while before I realized that the sounds actually issued from the loft upstairs. Two women journalists stood up suddenly and trotted giggling across the courtroom, right behind Chris Lane, to join their friends, who had a party going on in the loft. Lane turned to look. She appeared bemused, but not scared. She gave the impression that the dignified impersonality of the legal proceedings had impressed her, that she trusted the sequestered jury members in the shut room to her left were obeying instructions and discussing the *evidence*, not discussing her.

Another knock. This was it. A juror stuck her head out and whispered to the attendant who took his news to the judge. Messengers departed from the courtroom. Soon secretaries and assistants began to arrive. Wesley McDermott's family arrived. Twelve jurors emerged at last from their small light room into the larger, darker room. The judge had donned her long black robe and black patent heels. She took her place. The lawyers were in place. Wesley McDermott held Chris Lane's hand.

"Madame Foreperson, have you reached your verdict?"

"We have, Your Honor."

Guilty and guilty and guilty. Evelyn Lane, Christine's mother, was crying into her hands. The journalists' expensive cameras made rich sounds—"chrick, chrick." A picture of Chris Lane, her lawyer and her shadowy mother would appear next day on the front page of *The Ithaca Journal*. The judge thanked the jurors and called them meticulous, attentive. Those who had lost the fight embraced one another.

I noticed Evelyn Lane, a quiet figure throughout the trial, shoulder past a journalist who had come down from the loft to get this last piece of the story. Following, I looked out the window into DeWitt Park and saw her retreat down a concrete path, away from the churches and courthouses. She listed to one side. Her granddaughter and husband were dead, her daughter sentenced to prison after a trial that had portrayed Mrs. Lane, herself, as a mother whose frigid treatment of her child, Christine, was partly to blame for the tragedy. This woman had taken it in the flesh. Calamity had come upon her as a wide breaking-in of waters.

Nobody followed her through the park. Nobody had followed Gordon Gabaree, either, the night he wandered so deep into the woods that he heard the ghostly voice of a child. These two people, one in league with the defense, the other with the prosecution, had both found wilderness. Are there many citizens ready to follow them out into that abysmal territory for the sake of understanding? To go, one must leave behind the compass and the radio, and the jury trial, which is compass and radio. This immense territory is cold and quiet. Whispering, it shuts behind you.

■■■

PART 3　Debra

9

the last little room

EARLY AUGUST 1991, and we were back in court. A familiar stenographer and her partner, the court clerk, entered carrying stacks of folders and took their seats on the platform just below the bench in Tompkins County's main courtroom. They looked relaxed, collegiate, as women experienced in handling paperwork often do. Sunlight shone into the room. In this same bright chamber, with its tall, radiant windows and brass eagles affixed to the chandeliers, Shirley Kinge had been tried and convicted of armed burglary. Tom and Russ, dark-haired young reporters, spent weeks hunched in the front pew during that trial, and here they were, back again, first row center. And here was the bailiff, a loyal, snappish old man, leaning through the doorway near the jury box. Jury members remained offstage. The judge too was out of sight. Once everyone had settled into place, Judge Friedlander would emerge, her bailiff would command the audience to stand up, then sit down, and the new day would begin.

It would *not* be a completely new day. Judges, reporters, jurors and attorneys had played out this ritual thousands of times before. The studded leather doors leading into the Tompkins County courtroom are darkened from repeated blows in the spot one would expect: at chest level on the right-hand side.

The defense attorney now pushed through the doors and slipped into the courtroom quietly with his client, a trim, pink-cheeked woman named Debra—or Debbie—Dennett, who wore a tan dress so broadly padded in the shoulders she resembled a '40s actress. Her head hung forward. She had short, reddish-brown hair. The knife scars on her face were hidden by cosmetics. Dennett had been rushed to Binghamton General from Tompkins Community Hospital the evening of September 28, 1990 for emergency plastic surgery on cuts received to her face, arms and back. That reconstructive surgery made it difficult for the medical examiner, Dr. Humphrey Germaniuk, to read the depth and nature of the original wounds. Germaniuk inspected hospital documents before testifying in court that he did not believe all the gashes had resulted from a violent knife attack; his testimony suggested the cuts were self-inflicted.

Dennett settled at the table this morning with her hands folded and faced the empty judge's bench in an attitude that suggested both modesty and exhaustion. She had endured only two days in the defendant's chair so far, but already she appeared more burdened, more distressed than Shirley Kinge or Christine Lane had after weeks in the spotlight. Her attorney, Robert Clune, was solicitous. Clune is an established figure in the Ithaca legal community. White-haired, he resembles a successful pediatrician.

District attorney George Dentes entered the courtroom soon after the defendant and her lawyer took their seats. Dentes was accompanied by New York State Police Investigator Robert Lishansky, who helped him carry in a load of brown paper sacks and a roll of tan carpet that matched the defendant's dress. Both men wore good grey suits and they looked solemn, but also casual, even *domestic* as they laid out their stuff on the table. Police had sliced the tan carpet remnant from a closet in the defendant's lakeside home. In that home on the night of September 28, spots, smears and sprays of blood marked the kitchen floor, the kitchen phone, the stairway carpet, the bedclothes in the master bedroom and its doorframe, and the floor near the full-length mirror in the master bathroom. But this particular carpet remnant was significant because it had not been stained with blood.

George Dentes began his term as district attorney in early 1990, just as the Harris murder investigation was gaining momentum. During the autumn of 1990, when Shirley Kinge was being tried for her participation in crimes against the Harris family, it happened that Debra Dennett and her husband, Nathaniel Knappen, got into a fight. Debra shot and killed her husband. So, as one trial moved forward, private violence continued to erupt in other houses in the county and new litigation was conceived. Dentes took a few hours off from his job as prosecuting attorney in the Kinge trial to attend a memorial service for the deceased Knappen, who had been a successful Ithaca lawyer. The D.A. would eventually choose to prosecute this new case himself. He had succeeded in convicting Shirley and his assistant had succeeded in convicting Christine Lane, but he would not be so successful with Debbie.

A square-shouldered, organized, energetic man, Dentes fills his collars and calls hello loudly to people he distrusts. His desk up in a third-floor office of the courthouse is backed by the U.S. and New York State flags and flanked by a high-quality computer with a keyboard that must be generously salted with the D.A.'s fingerprints—he types rapidly. A conservative Republican in a predominantly Democratic college town, Dentes is wary, but also secure, unapologetic when questioned about his work as a prosecutor: "Crime and punishment is really what this job comes down to." Standing to challenge a defense attorney, he wraps his arms tight across his chest and keeps to the point. A whispery backdrop in the prosecutor's voice can spook defense witnesses; they don't believe he's as mild as he sounds. One woman who testified in defense of Shirley Kinge found the district attorney's smile chilling as a crocodile's and wished that he had the good taste to appear less friendly. But many other people approve of George Dentes. The state police like him just fine; Robert Lishansky considers Dentes "one of the best" district attorneys in seven counties.

The jury—eight women, four men—emerged now in their assigned order; since this was an August trial, jury members were informally dressed. The judge came out and the audience rose in a group, then sat down again as Her Honor rolled up her sleeves. Bob Clune, the defense attorney, left his chair beside Debra and stepped up to the court clerk. Relaxed, he took a folder from her and slipped out a batch of photographs that had been put into evidence the day before. He checked them over, then handed them back properly, easily.

Dentes asked to put some physical objects into evidence. People's Exhibits 1 and 2, broken pieces of a plate, were offered in two paper bags. "No objection," from the defense attorney. People's Exhibit 3, a frying pan, was offered. "No objection." The roll of unstained tan carpet was Exhibit 18. The box of shotgun shells was Exhibit 20. The single expended shotgun shell was Exhibit 22. The long Pardner shotgun purchased from Woolworth's by Debra Dennett on September 27, 1990 was Exhibit 27.

From a cardboard box, Dentes lifted Exhibit 24, "a" and "b": the male victim's black wing tip shoes. The toes were slightly upturned from use. The prosecutor put them on the table and the morning commenced.

Investigator Lishansky, who was questioned for five days when he took the stand as a prosecution witness during Shirley Kinge's trial, sat up in the witness chair with his hands folded over his belt and his back straight. Lishansky is a thin man whose head and neck stretch up very high when a cross-examination gets rough. It was time now for the "cross," time for him to face the defense attorney. Waiting for Bob Clune, the witness appeared politely at ease; it is possible that Robert Lishansky wears the same frank, alert expression in a dentist's office. It was Lishansky who had received the severed fingers of the Harris family victims in tubes and attempted to take prints from them using cotton, clay and rubber gloves. He also photographed many of the blackened rooms and an assortment of sad objects inside the Harris house. Less than a year later, he was called to bring his camera to another big house in Ithaca. He walked through Debra Dennett's home snapping pictures of a frying pan, a closet, a gun. Now it was time to answer for that investigation. Mr. Clune, a deliberately slow lawyer, rose to do a little work on Mr. Lishansky.

In response to specific questions, Investigator Lishansky explained that he had arrived at the Knappen/Dennett residence at approximately 11:00 in the evening, September 28. He stayed until 5:30 the next morning. He bagged and piled evidence in the front foyer of the house and made his list of the evidence the next afternoon, on Saturday. How did he do it? He picked up each item and put it in a bag, then labeled the bag. Did he consolidate any pieces of evidence? Some fragments of broken plate. Where did he get the paper bags? He always kept a supply of paper bags in his squad car.

Clune walked to a collection of blue-lined diagrams propped on a stand, pulled out the diagram of the Knappen/Dennett kitchen, and began to ask the investigator questions about it. Lishansky answered that the blueprint had been drawn by an artist using measurements provided by the state policemen who processed the crime scene. No, the artist did not personally visit the house. No, the diagram did not show every piece of kitchen furniture and its exact situation the night of September 28, 1990.

Clune replaced the map of the kitchen, then stepped up to the court clerk and took from her the stack of photographs he had been examining earlier. Photographs 203, 204, 205, 206 and 207 showed the kitchen: white walls, brown wood trim, frying pan on the floor, vinyl floor speckled with red blood. Handing this little pile to the witness, the defense attorney asked if Investigator Lishansky had any photographs of the *whole* kitchen where this domestic battle was alleged to have begun.

The witness paged through the available photographs as the court waited in silence. He was sitting very straight and his skin was slightly flushed. So was George Dentes, the prosecutor, sitting straight. At last, the witness offered to go upstairs to the D.A.'s office and get the contact prints to check whether he had any photographs of the *whole* kitchen. Clune said that would be helpful, so the judge called a brief recess. George Dentes and Investigator Lishansky rose to their feet simultaneously. By managing to lever the policeman out of his chair, the defense attorney had scored a physical coup.

Months later, Robert Lishansky would describe this as the most painful moment of the trial. He had not forgotten how Clune questioned him about those photographs of the kitchen: "That's what sticks with me about this case, because as I said, the next time, I'm going to make sure I've got them." He added that he actually liked testifying in court—"To me, that's a challenge"—but it could be extremely frustrating. "Many times we're talking about what might have been a split-second decision on my part, and now these people [defense attorneys] have had six months to turn around, and that one decision, they get to look that thing over with a great big microscope and say, 'Why did you do that?'"

Though during his career, Lishansky had fingerprinted a number of dead victims and photographed relevant Vaseline jars and blood specks in order to "process" crime scenes, he disliked feeling *himself* the object of a microscopic investigation. His complaint does point up a myopic quality in most of our legal games; it seems we organize a search for justice by handing out magnifying glasses to players on both teams, then instructing everybody to bend down and tail each other. This rather demeaning exercise doesn't seem so bad if, at the end of the game, you win. The investigator understood that. An experienced prosecution witness, he had testified in upwards of a hundred trials and won nearly every case.

Still, if at last a man loses, a cross-examination can feel humiliating, unfair and unjust. Next time out, for certain, the investigator would cover his rear with a heavier blanket of photographs. A sensible man, Robert Lishansky understands the game. The prosecution teams he has assisted failed to win conviction in just two cases: a DWAI and this one.

■ ■ ■

Lishansky had received the call from the dispatcher Friday evening, September 28. Since he hadn't gone to bed yet, he was ready—not particularly happy, but ready—for work. He climbed into the car with his equipment. Shut the door.

The drive over narrow rural highways took about an hour. It was easy, dark and quiet. Lishansky had lived in Ithaca for years before moving east to be nearer the Troop C barracks, so the final downhill sweep into the college town looked familiar. Stopping and starting with the lights, he wove through downtown, swept up Route 13, then swung off, under the bridge, to gain the two-lane road that ran along the eastern shore of Cayuga Lake. He found the address without difficulty; his headlights illuminated the big numbers—1510—painted on a low utility shed at the top of the private lane. He steered down the long, sloping drive. The house, partially lit, came into view. It was broad and isolated, surrounded on two sides by thick woods, its entranceway pressured by the slope. It had no garage (the construction of such a big house left no room for a garage on this difficult lot). Cars belonging to the husband and wife were parked in the driveway.

The open yard behind the house slipped down to a cliff's edge. Lishansky knew that the property backed onto Cayuga Lake, but this time of night he couldn't see the water. He parked his squad car near a few sheriff's department vehicles and entered the residence through the side door.

Investigator Emery Guest was inside the quiet house with a few deputies. He explained the situation. The distraught woman had called the sheriff's dispatcher at approximately 6:43 p.m. to announce that she'd shot her husband. Sergeant Brown and another deputy were the first to arrive at the scene. When they entered, the woman was still on the phone with the dispatcher. She was bleeding from knife cuts; she said her husband had come to the house to pick up their son for the weekend—she and her husband had been living separately for months—and they argued, then he attacked her with a knife in the kitchen. Trying to escape, she had run upstairs to her bedroom, locked the door, fled back into the dressing room, then into the closet. He followed. He worked open the door to the master bedroom with a punch tool. She had a shotgun in the closet. The body was upstairs. It was the body of Nathaniel Knappen, Ithaca attorney.

Investigator Lishansky listened and then began his tour of the house. Checking the kitchen first, he noticed the blood, the stained towels near the phone, the cold frying pan on the floor, and the shards of a broken plate, some lying on the counter, some on the floor. The kitchen furniture had not been much disturbed. He proceeded down the hall and glanced into the formal dining room; it was in perfect order: "So we moved on." A few of the throw rugs in the hallway showed drops of blood. He had seen worse.

To his left, now, was the living room, located directly under the master bedroom. He walked in. The TV was on. A wall of large windows overlooked a wooden deck and provided a view of the lake in daytime; now it faced a dark expanse of invisible water. The room seemed comfortable. It had been outfitted with big furniture, overstuffed pillows and a scattering of child's toys. He continued forward. There was a study full of books, undisturbed. Lishansky turned back, ducked through an archway and emerged into a grand entrance foyer. His shoes rang on a greenish marble floor.

This entrance hall was impressive, huge and high, with a big chandelier centering it. Above the policeman on two sides, French doors opened from second-floor guest bedrooms; the French doors were railed, suggesting that guests could step out onto diminutive balconies and view the proceedings in the lobby below. The investigator stood still and looked around. A pair of semi-circular stairways curved over the passage he had just come through and met in an open hall above his head. A trail of blood drops ran through the passage and up the southern arm of the carpeted stairs. Or maybe it ran down. He would not draw conclusions yet.

He had climbed stairs to reach the open hall that led to the Harris bedrooms. Here was another set of stairs in another elaborate dream house.

The investigator walked up the northern steps to avoid disturbing the blood trail and went straight into the master bedroom.

Deputies had been here before him, he wasn't the first; few surprises lurked in this house and even fewer dangers. He was standing in a bedroom that was large—approximately thirty feet long—but sparsely furnished, with a stationary exercise bike, a bookcase, a small TV and telephone, some toys and a wide bed with no headboard or footboard. From the door to the dressing room was a distance of about fifteen feet. It would be measured later.

The dead man lay slouched at an angle against the doorway that opened between the master bedroom and the dressing room. The dressing room with the double lavatory was attached by one door to a walk-in clothes closet and by a second door to the private bathroom area, which contained toilet, shower, tub (journalists trying to explain this lay-out to one another used the common motel bathroom as a reference point). The dead man had a big hole blown through his left eye. Near his right hand lay a wooden-handled filet knife. Lishansky walked over and looked down at him.

There wasn't any need to cover the body—"It wasn't going to be open to any public view; we didn't have to worry about scaring anybody or offending anyone"—so the corpse would stay in place, arms outspread, until about 3:00 a.m., when the small family of policemen that now occupied this house invited the coroner upstairs.

One year later, that same corpse would be transformed into a flat, immaculate image on clean white paper. Jurors would be invited to look over the blueprint of a 9'9" by 8'5" dressing room adjacent to a walk-in closet and bathroom. In this picture, the walls of the dressing room framed the outline of a crumpled man tucked against the doorway with his legs stretched out. A perfect shotgun drawn in blue, wedged between the closet and the dressing room, pointed towards this man's left foot, and a little knife was outlined near his right hand. A diminutive bathroom stool was drawn nicely inside the closet. In fact, all the objects in the diagram—knife, gun, stool—looked so neat that one suspected the police artist had lifted them from a specialized page of contact stickers. They were as perfect as the miniscule rope, gun and knife in a *Clue* game.

Lishansky took his time near the corpse. It was a grisly tableau, but not shocking to him. "I looked at it and thought that it was interesting," he explained later. "There was a petal pattern on his forehead. . . . Like a flower. From the wadding of the shotgun bullet. . . . What happened was, because of the close proximity from where the gun went off to where Nat's head was, very common, when there is such close proximity, for the wadding in the case to do some damage also. It acts as a projectile also. And that's why I say, to me, it was interesting to be able to see that petal pattern. It had to have been a relatively close shot." The investigator is no longer scared by dead bodies, though "now and then you get a little something in the back of your mind that just kind of says— it's a defense mechanism, just rationalizing to yourself or something—that says, I wonder if he really is dead?" It is often his responsibility to fingerprint decedents: "To be holding the hand of a dead person, it's obviously not a normal situation. It's just a weird feeling. I'm not sure how to describe it, but it's something that doesn't happen in the normal course of events." The bodies are not always cold, he says. "In this case, the Knappen case, by the time I got there, he was not that cold."

Robert Lishansky stepped around the victim, entered the dressing room with its mirrors, and then turned into the closet full of Debra Dennett's clothes. The woman had come here to hide. Or to load her shotgun. The rooms were getting smaller. He looked up and down.

Most of what he saw was consistent with the story Guest had told him. The shotgun lay on the floor pointing outward towards the body. He saw a shotgun shell near it: "There was a box of shells up on the shelf. A little footstool was there inside the closet." But no blood showed up on the hanging clothes or on the tan carpet inside this last little room. Lishansky knew from Guest that the woman claimed her husband had attacked her in the kitchen with a knife before she escaped upstairs.

Here was an inconsistency. Debra Dennett should have been bleeding as she stood in the closet and that blood should have stained the dresses or the carpet. Months later, he would say, "If I was covered with paint and somebody said that I have to go into that closet and they're going to close the door, and then I have to consciously make an effort not to get any paint on any of the clothing, I still think I'd have a tough time doing it."

The investigator made a note about the absence of blood in the closet, then stepped out of there and walked into the private bathroom area. This was a functional space: fiberglass tub and tub surround, vinyl flooring. He had reached the end of a path, and *there* was blood: "There were some blood droplets on the floor, some on the toilet bowl and more of it, as I remember, was in front of this full-length mirror." He must have glanced in the mirror. Mirror: an unexpected camera that luckily contains no film.

On Saturday, September 29, the police would get a blade to slice out a big square of unstained tan carpet from inside the closet where Debra Dennett kept her sweaters and dresses. Robert

Lishansky returned with his camera that Saturday and walked through the house again, snapping photographs in various rooms. One year later, after Lishansky helped bring the carpet square into court, he was on the stand to answer questions about his photographs of kitchen furniture, door frames and blood.

In fact, blood would be so minutely discussed with Lishansky that its color, red, became awfully clear. Listening, we understood that this was very familiar, household blood, the kind that shows up on pale, ceramic bathroom surfaces and white cotton towels. It could stain paper diagrams permanently. The court tried to hold it in check. The blood came in drops and the drops even had different shapes, so they could be mapped. Police witnesses had testified that most of the blood spots on the kitchen floor were circular, not elliptical. Elliptical blood spots "indicate directionality;" they suggest the wounded person was in motion. Circular ones do not. The prosecutor expected jurors to understand that if most of the blood spots in the kitchen were round, this cast doubt on Dennett's allegation that she had been attacked by her husband with a knife in the kitchen and had immediately fled upstairs. But Bob Clune challenged the police to prove that they could interpret blood spots with certainty, and Investigator Lishansky conceded it was true that "many imprecise variables go into judging patterns of blood."

As the court focus moved nearer the dead man, patterns of blood changed. They became finer, but not elusive. Investigator Lishansky had mentioned "high-velocity splatter" many times in response to questions from the prosecutor. What exactly did he mean by this phrase and where had he noticed splatter in the house?, the defense attorney asked. "High-velocity splatter" is a "misting type of pattern," the witness replied; it describes a fine mist of blood that sprays from a victim who has been shot at very close range. "High-velocity splatter" showed up on the painted door frame behind the victim's head. And what did the investigator mean by the phrase "blow back"?, the defense attorney asked.

"When a person has been shot at close range, a 'blow back' of the victim's blood and tissue will return to spray the barrel of the weapon," the witness replied. Did that happen in this case? Investigator Lishansky said yes, he did notice traces of blood or tissue on the end of the shotgun barrel, but he did not request to have it analyzed in the lab.

The blast caught the decedent on the left side of his head. He twisted counter-clockwise as if he had been struck with a massive fist. The filet knife which the defendant said he'd used to attack her in the kitchen, the knife which he'd apparently kept in his hand as he chased her upstairs, dropped from his grasp and landed on the bedroom carpet. No useful fingerprints were found on the knife; wooden handles don't retain prints well.

Did Debra Dennett pick up the knife, take it into the very last little room, the bathroom, look into a full-length mirror and slice herself on the face and arms, then replace the knife on the carpet near her husband's outstretched hand for the police to find? Did she complete on herself a job her husband had started? It's not clear.

Were some of the knife wounds on her face and arms self-inflicted? The answer to this question is "yes," but ironically, the fact would not be established as a certainty until the defendant took the stand to testify in her own defense.

Even before the trial began, however, newspapers reported that the prosecutor's office thought Dennett might have cut herself. As the district attorney would explain later, "She cut herself precisely because she knew she hadn't had enough justification to shoot him." Journalists picked up on this debate early thanks to Dr. Humphrey Germaniuk's public medical reports. The medical examiner would testify that Dennett's sutured cuts did not appear to be the results of a knife attack. They were too regular and shallow, more like incisions than gouged stab wounds. What's more, Germaniuk reported, there had been little blood on the tip of the knife; again, this was evidence inconsistent with an attack.

Dr. Humphrey Germaniuk had testified in both Shirley Kinge's and Christine Lane's trials; he took the witness chair early the first week in the Dennett proceedings to speak about the defendant's and the victim's injuries. Jurors always remember Germaniuk. One of the Dennett jurors described a scene that took place when the pathologist was being cross-examined. As she remembers it, Bob Clune, the defense attorney, reached into a bag and pulled out an immaculate white styrofoam model head on a stick. The weightless, blank head had a wooden bar driven through its eye down to its styrofoam jaw. It was an icon, clean, modern and primitive. Clune showed this head to the medical examiner.

In the juror's words, "Germaniuk said, 'No, that's not quite right,' and pulled out the bar and re-inserted it. You know what that sounds like, the wood going through styrofoam, the squeak of that into the proper location. There was something so bizarre about the entire testimony. . . . I found that scene like one of *Saturday Night Live*'s worst-taste scenes. There was Debra at the defense table, collapsing, collapsing, from the agony of it, while the witness is with a certain amount of zest and interest in his work describing this information. . . . And really, I had *Saturday Night Live* running through my head. Debra was finally let go from the courtroom because she was in a state of collapse. The doctor was followed by Lishansky. Wasn't he testifying about the rug and splatter?"

A shrieking styrofoam head. High-velocity splatter. Two empty black shoes, toes upturned, set out on a table near a brown plastic water jug. We were back in court.

■ ■ ■

George Dentes entered the courtroom Thursday morning, August 1, unaccompanied by any policemen—Investigator Lishansky had completed his testimony the day before—and unburdened by paper bags. Seeing me in the small audience, he said hello loudly and asked about my project. I told him I had been thinking about the children and grandchildren of Kinge, Lane and Dennett. It seemed to me that the presence of small children woven into a tragedy affected the impact and complexity of trials involving female defendants, though generally these faceless children did nothing to influence the verdicts. I had seen a photograph of only one of these children—Aliza Bush. Shirley Kinge's grandson, Ronan, who was asleep in the adjacent apartment when the police raided 520 Etna Road and shot Michael Kinge, his father, remained invisible to me. Debra Dennett and Nathaniel Knappen's son, Duncan, not quite three years old the night his mother shot his father, also remained invisible.

Duncan had been the only other person in the huge, secluded lakeside house the evening of September 28, 1990. He'd had a cold, so his mother gave him Dimetapp and put him to bed a short time before her estranged husband was due to arrive and pick up his son for the weekend visitation. The boy's door was closed when the fight erupted. Later, a member of the Lansing ambulance squad would see this child cradled in the arms of a uniformed deputy who stood outside the front door of the house while the mother, bleeding from knife cuts, sat dazed and crying on the front sidewalk. The ambulance crew would apply plain gauze bandages to the mother's cuts before speeding her to the nearest emergency room. A family friend would arrive to get Duncan.

This child could not act as a legally "competent" witness (to be deemed "competent" in New York State, an individual must be capable of taking and understanding an oath and must understand that legal consequences can result if he lies), so Duncan would never be questioned or videotaped by law enforcement agents. The small corner of privacy granted this child was a blessing and even a surprise: surprisingly decent. Jury trials rarely impress a layman as *decent*. Trials involving domestic disputes, especially, alternate between merciless exposure of intimate details about defendants or victims and then scrupulous displays of legal reticence, as other, disparate bits of information are kept from the jurors in order to protect the rights of these same defendants and victims. Juicy gossip does not mix well into legal proceedings that define themselves as objective, controlled inquiries, but in jury trials focusing on domestic disputes, gossip figures as a key ingredient. Trials that pit a husband against a wife and provide each spouse with an attorney trained in controlled antagonism will be dirty. In fact, a layman watching trials often suspects that our own legal establishment's halting procedural style and impenetrable rhetoric develop out of the profession's need to camouflage the sordidness of the work. It is wonderful to see how clients and attorneys manage to protect one another from the shock of lifting up their hands and finding them stained with a "blow back" of gore. A client feels himself shielded from the dirty battle by the intercession of a professional, while an attorney feels himself distanced from even the bloodiest feud thanks to the fact that he *is* a professional, a representative merely. It's a Teflon trick.

But what about the children? They listen from behind the walls. When I mentioned children to George Dentes, he said, "You writers are so romantic," off the cuff, before passing through the little gate into the arena marked off for legal professionals and their clients.

His response interested me. The district attorney assumed that I would perceive these three accused mothers—Shirley, Chris, Debbie—through a pink haze of feminine sympathies, liberal assumptions. This may be true. Still, there's another kind of haze, more masculine than feminine, more grey than pink, that frustrates me more. A jury trial is so convincing, so reassuring, minute by minute. It appears logical, dignified, masculine, dispassionate, tedious, difficult and fair. But some of this is adult make-believe.

Pretense makes the rigid courtroom theatre function. There are a lot of performers in any courtroom—competitive lawyers who appear detached, interested witnesses who appear disinterested. When these actors testify, they give the impression that they are doing their level best to speak rationally, to speak facts. And they are, to a point. But they are also trying to keep secrets, camouflage anger, follow the script. A capable witness or attorney must know how to dodge, exclude and suggest to function in a courtroom. Thus, ironically, the ritual clarity of a jury trial itself constitutes a sort of fog. The entire performance has been designed to measure guilt and punishment; it has also been designed to reassure the public that certain dangerous past events have been strictly comprehended, tamed and concluded. Yet they can't be.

Watching particular trials with full attention, trying to appreciate both the activity on stage and the pretense of the activity on stage, a spectator is tempted to look back, through the walls of the courtroom, to the obscure, vanished events that these legal proceedings manipulate and, sometimes, avoid. The trials I attended focused on three dark events: the murder of a family just before Christmas, the death and disappearance of a child in February, the explosion of a man with a knife in his fist who approached a clothes closet. Unfortunately, after staring backwards for a long time into the veiled past, it often happens that we find ourselves staring forward as well, into the veiled future. Then we notice children placed too near the shadows, too near walls that drift. Two of those children are mine.

These were the obscurities that filled me with dread. Watching trials, I found myself temporarily reassured that questions about the past had been caged and threatening individuals jailed or quieted. But the more distance I put between myself and the courthouse, the less sure I became that each case was closed. Yesterday and tomorrow, here and there, me and them, were much more awfully entangled than the courts pretended. The mysteries of the past are related by blood to the mysteries of the future. They are impenetrable, indestructible, fertile and destructive—*familial*. Family relationships defy all rituals that hope to settle an argument once and for all.

Duncan's babysitter, Catherine Arthur, testified Thursday morning, August 1. She said that she never saw any signs that Mr.

Knappen abused the defendant, his wife. The defendant was not short of money. She had two cars, a Jeep and a small grey BMW. Yes, Mrs. Arthur believed Mr. Knappen entertained female company at the house when Debbie was absent. She based her conclusion on the fact that she discovered extra dishes in the sink next morning. Yes, Mr. Knappen had phoned her, Catherine Arthur, at approximately six o'clock the evening of September 28 to ask if she would babysit for Duncan if he eventually won full or partial custody of the child.

The next witness, Charles Cirulli, was manager of the Kentucky Fried Chicken on Meadow Street. He remembered that Knappen, a regular customer, dropped by around dinner time on September 28, 1990, a Friday, and ordered his usual. Since the restaurant was undergoing a review at the time, the witness could testify that Mr. Knappen probably received his meal *fast* and continued on his way in a matter of minutes—two, three minutes. The customer's usual order was a nine-piece full meal, including potatoes, gravy and cole slaw.

George Dentes stood up: "Your Honor, the People rest."

The district attorney had begun his case on Monday and rested his case against Debra Dennett, an unemployed Cornell University instructor in the College of Veterinary Medicine, on August 1, the Thursday of that same week, before noon. It probably surprised a few jurors that the district attorney chose to rest with potatoes and cole slaw, but the order of witnesses in a trial usually makes no sense, as if many attorneys choose to keep the jury guessing until the summation.

George Dentes is an organized man. He had constructed an organized, succinct case. Aware that the defense attorney would try to present his client, Debra, as a terrified victim rather than as aggressor, Dentes had labored for four days to provide the jury with a load of disparate facts he'd eventually restructure. His concluding argument would challenge the defendant's own story about what happened that Friday night, and also attempt to convince the jury that this woman sitting meekly before them, this woman who dis-integrated when a pathologist shoved a wooden rod through a styrofoam head, was a capable, active, responsible person who deserved punishment for killing a man.

The prosecutor had called in a salesman from Woolworth's to testify about the gun; it was clear that Debra Dennett purchased a Pardner shotgun at the variety store just one day before she shot her husband. He also introduced evidence about the Kentucky Fried Chicken restaurant and Knappen's brief stop there on Friday, September 28, to show jurors that Nathaniel Knappen would have needed to travel very, very fast from his law office to Kentucky Fried and then up to the house on East Shore Drive, in order to arrive and start a violent fight with his wife by 6:23 or 6:25. Timing was crucial. Catherine Arthur had received the phone call from Nat at about 6:00. A lawyer had seen Nat driving from the office at Thaler and Thaler around 6:10. The earliest Knappen could have left Kentucky Fried Chicken was probably 6:15. Then he had to sweep north on Route 13 in Friday traffic, curve under the bridge and drive up the narrow road along the east shore of Cayuga Lake, turn at the utility shed, go down the drive to the big house where he no longer lived, park his car, enter and start to fight, all by 6:23 or 6:25, because at 6:23 or 6:25 (two clocks in the Tompkins County Public Safety Building registered different times), the sheriff's dispatcher received an anonymous, hysterical phone call from a woman who screamed "Help me, help me, he's trying to kill me!" before hanging up.

The woman was Debra Dennett. The prosecutor introduced the tape of that first, anonymous call, as well as the tape of a second telephone call from the same desperate woman, into evidence. No one challenged the "reality" of the second call which the sheriff's dispatcher received at 6:40 or 6:42; this time the woman, Debra Dennett, gave her address and said that she had shot her husband. The prosecutor did want to suggest, however, that the first, anonymous call might have been placed before Nat Knappen even entered the house, that the call might have been staged or at least exaggerated.

Like the knife wounds. Testimony elicited by the prosecutor challenged Dennett's story about the knife attack and her situation in the closet. Investigator Lishansky spoke about the carpet and hanging clothes unstained by blood. Dr. Germaniuk gave his opinion that a number of the defendant's wounds were not the result of a violent knife attack. These were all key elements in the prosecution's case.

But they weren't the only elements. Again, the prosecutor wanted to challenge the defendant's story *and* to challenge the defendant's appearance: Debbie's meekness, her tears, her presentation of herself. To do that, he needed a good load of evidence that smelled a lot like gossip. Of course, his opponent, Bob Clune, would be out trash-collecting too, stockpiling the dirt on Nat in preparation for a good fight across the barricades. How often the rules to our courtroom games seem plainly boyish.

Months after the case had ended with an acquittal on all counts, the district attorney talked about Debra Dennett. He still did not find her helplessness convincing. He understood the Battered Woman Syndrome that Bob Clune had used to help mount his defense; in fact, attorneys in the prosecutor's own office had used "the syndrome" in their efforts to convict men accused of abusing their wives. (The Battered Woman Syndrome describes cycles of domestic violence to help explain why abused women so often hesitate before contacting authorities and why so many abused women return to their dangerous husbands repeatedly.)

But Dentes did not think Debra fit the profile very well. In fact, he judged her to have been a "provoking agent" in the struggle that took place September 28: "She knew that he was coming to pick up the child and that he loved the child, and that he was very insistent on having the child during the agreed time, which was Friday to Sunday. She knew that, yet she put the child to bed and gave it medicine, in other words, to make him sleep and to keep him asleep. She took no steps to get him up or to be ready to go when the father got there." The prosecutor referred again to Dennett's own testimony that the fight had erupted almost immediately after her husband entered the kitchen, because she herself yelled that she didn't want him taking Duncan to be in an apartment with his "whore" over the weekend. (Knappen was at the time living with another woman.) "So the inference I got and that I asked the jury to accept, and I don't know whether they accepted it or not, was that she never intended him to have the child and that she was the provoking agent in this blow-up that evening." Dentes went on to say, "If that's true, it would *not* have justified past abuse, of course, and wouldn't have justified him hitting her that evening. . . ." But.

The prosecutor had collected information about Debra Dennett in order to prepare for trial. Inevitably, the stories he attracted and collected did not compliment the defendant, and indeed, showed her to be not only provoking, feisty and deceptive, but also jealous, dramatic and spoiled. He had heard from his sources that Debra, a veterinarian, never liked to chloroform her own animals at the vet school because she considered the menial job beneath her. He'd heard that Debbie could have renewed her job at the vet school, but chose to give it up, though she must have known that her husband was under severe financial pressure since this house that they had built in 1988 required mortgage payments of $4,400 per month. He'd heard that Nat gave Debbie everything she asked for. He'd heard that Debra went snooping one day in the rain to check out the apartment Nat was sharing with Audrey Vrooman, his legal secretary and live-in companion; Debbie and Nat had a scuffle at the door. He'd heard that Debra Dennett threatened to take dog medicine if Nat ever left her (this bit of news was presented as evidence by a rebuttal witness). He'd heard that Debbie attempted suicide on her honeymoon. The separation proposal from Nat to Debbie that the prosecutor wanted to put into evidence mentioned, without fully explaining, "a disastrous trip" to a resort town; Dentes believed this referred to the suicide attempt.

The source for the suicide rumor was questionable. Georgianna (Polly) Barnes, Nat's sister, could not be called objective. Eventually the whole town would read a series of enraged letters Polly Barnes sent to *The Ithaca Journal* after her sister-in-law was acquitted, including one in which she insisted that her brother would never have cut his wife because he "certainly had too much respect for kitchen utensils to use them on that waste of skin."

Still, the prosecutor had done what he could with Polly's information: "Polly tells me that she heard from Nat that Debbie had attempted suicide on their honeymoon. Now, I don't know if that was true or not because I got it from hearsay, all right, and when I asked Debbie on the stand, 'Isn't it true you attempted suicide on your honeymoon?', she gave me a blank look, like this, and denied it; maybe because she didn't. But it's obvious that Nat had thought something 'disastrous' happened because he wrote it in that letter. Now because he said some things like that in the letter, which were not complimentary to her, the judge wouldn't allow it in as evidence, saying that casts her in a bad light. But I said, 'Look, Judge, after all of the evidence they've put in, all of this character assassination, all this history of the abusive relationship, they've opened the door, and that's a legal doctrine. You shape the issues according to what you put at issue, and she was going to put in *all* of this evidence about the relationship, then my gosh, she's going to have to get as good as she gives!'"

The prosecutor's dilemma is clear. Bob Clune, the white-haired defense attorney, had thrown open the door to the closet where trial lawyers keep stuff they need to do a good job of character assassination. He had plenty of projectiles stored in there, and all George Dentes wanted was an equal chance to use *his* stuff. But the prosecutor could not afford to give the impression that he had come to mess up Debra Dennett. Someone else had done that already.

On July 24, 1990, in the evening, approximately two months before the shooting, Debra Dennett and Nat Knappen had a fight about the separation proposal that Knappen had composed and left in the kitchen for his wife to find. A friend of Debbie's who happened to phone from New York City that night interrupted the first round of the altercation. Glenna Maldin, a veterinarian, would testify for the defense during the second half of this trial. She described hearing Debra scream wildly over the phone, "He's going to kill me!" Then Nat got on the line and informed Maldin that everything was settled down. He hung up. Maldin then called the sheriff's department in Ithaca and asked that the police go to the house and check on Debra. Deputies arrived at 1510 East Shore Drive minutes later. They confronted the husband, Knappen, who appeared calm and promised that he would leave the premises. The husband had not yet departed when the deputies drove away.

The next day, July 25, Debra Dennett visited the emergency room at Tompkins Community Hospital. Dr. Tove Matas, who would also testify for the defense, had the records describing bruises on the inside of the patient's wrists, a large bruise on her right buttock, multiple bruises over her body. . . . "We did not photograph every single injury. There were just too many injuries." A urine sample showed evidence of blood; the patient had been beaten so hard that one of her kidneys was damaged. Over the district attorney's objections, the doctor explained his conclusions: "I believe that she was brutally beaten and kicked, and thrown down a flight of stairs."

A man, the named victim in this trial, had already "given" Debra Dennett what for, apparently. George Dentes had to beware. He didn't want the jury to imagine *him* pacing the floor in those black wing tip shoes.

The prosecutor rested his case against Debra Dennett on August 1, a Thursday. That afternoon, the defense attorney, Robert Clune, would begin *his* case against Nathaniel Knappen, the dead man.

■ ■ ■

I was able to use a recess before lunch on this particular day to go down and look at some photographs that had been placed into evidence. In the warren of offices where journalists gather to check out evidence files, the court clerk handed me a folder across her desk. The Dennett trial was moving along more quickly than the Kinge or Lane proceedings had, and the evidence folder accumulated in this case was slimmer than the others. It contained:

A picture of the two-story entrance foyer in the Knappen/ Dennett house. Curved stairways mount from the foyer up to a balcony hall lined with a wooden railing. The big yellow chandelier that hangs in the center of the hall suggests "Marriott Hotel." The walls are strikingly bare.

A picture of a red shotgun shell on tan carpet.

A close-up of a shotgun lying on carpet next to a clean, rubber-topped bathroom stool.

Picture of the exterior of the house. A mock Tudor residence, it has been faced in white stucco and dark wood trim. In the corner of the photograph is a child's play gym made of plump, colorful plastic rods.

Picture of an organized closet full of women's clothes.

Close-up of a woman's rounded back marred by black, sutured cuts.

A close-up of the male victim's head. It rests on white towels. The forehead has a white tag stuck to it. The top of the head is collapsed, oddly sunken; the skull cannot be intact. The dead man has a moustache, a slightly open mouth and wet, scraggly hair. A rod has been slipped through this head to show the trajectory of the fatal shot. It goes into the left eye and down, behind the jaw. It stays. The other eye is shut. The towels under the head are thickly stained.

A photograph of Nathaniel Knappen alive. His face looks perennially boyish, even with the moustache. He smiles confidently, mouth shut. One of his eyebrows cocks up higher than the other.

A photograph of blood specks on a very white wall.

The territory looked familiar. This should have been no surprise. I had checked through a number of Investigator Lishansky's photographs of the Harris crime scene. In that earlier collection, close-up pictures of lonesome, detached objects alternated with foggy images of dead bodies. Here was the same camera fitting new violence inside the right angles required by the courts. The blood specks on view in the Dennett file looked *new*, fresh and awful. The odd thing was they didn't move me to pity. That's the danger of this particular case, and why it's unlike the Harris case. It feels as if nothing much got lost when this man, Nat the lawyer, was killed and his exaggerated, empty home collapsed to become photographs. After all, the household was falling apart long before the night in question, long before the police arrived with their carpet cutters and paper bags.

A construction worker who helped finish the Knappen/Dennett house remembered the artificial balconies and marble-tiled floor in the entrance foyer, and the fact that there was no room for a garage. He remembered that one day Debra Dennett came by the job site and reportedly asked the foreman, "How many bathrooms are we having here now?" And he remembered the swimming pool in the basement: "It was like a huge Jacuzzi. It was probably thirty feet long by about fifteen feet wide. Took up an entire room in the basement." There were no windows in the room, and the pool was raised, so that swimmers would churn along just a few feet below the ceiling: "It seemed like a singularly inhospitable place to swim."

Debra Dennett had told friends she was afraid of prowlers. (The grand house where she resided alone was isolated. It didn't protect her. In fact, it scared and endangered her. The cost of the house had added strain to her marriage. She might have felt better protected in a barn.) She said that her dogs acted strangely one night, growling and running down to the basement. That was on September 20. Just a few days later, she and a friend entered the house and found that a door was unlocked and the mail had been disturbed. An acquaintance advised Dennett to get a shotgun to protect herself from intruders; she had already borrowed a high-powered rifle, but he warned her that a bullet from such a gun could cut through walls and might injure Duncan. She bought the shotgun.

When her husband pursued her upstairs the next evening, she passed through more than five doorways into progressively smaller rooms. Locked doors were no protection; that was why she had the gun. She must have known it was a paper house. A child could be hurt in it. A husband and wife could shred it.

10 home

DEBRA DENNETT's money shielded her from certain indignities after her arraignment. Able to remain free on $20,000 bail, she was not detained in a Tompkins County Public Safety Building cellblock for months prior to her trial, as Shirley Kinge and Christine Lane were, nor did she enter the courtroom each day of the trial chaperoned tightly by a pair of guards, with her hands cuffed to a broad leather belt cinched around her waist, as Kinge and Lane had. The influence of appearances in a jury trial even jurors themselves can't measure, but it was at least true that Dennett, in her low-toned, wide-shouldered dresses and button-down sweaters, resembled more an exhausted grade school principal than an inmate. Debra Dennett's financial resources also enabled her to select and hire her own attorney, who contacted a nationally recognized medical expert, Dr. Lenore Walker, experienced in testifying as a defense witness for battered women. Dennett had a wide freedom of movement. Before the trial began, she flew to Dr. Walker's offices in Denver, Colorado, and underwent a series of tests to determine whether she fit the clinical definition of a psychologically battered woman. Two months later, Dr. Walker in turn flew to Ithaca to testify that Dennett indeed showed classic symptoms, including schizophrenia, anger, depression, paranoia and the "learned helplessness" common among females who have suffered prolonged domestic abuse. The jury would learn that this expert testimony cost the defense $1,600 a day, plus expenses.

The jury also learned that Nat Knappen had a $350,000 life insurance policy, that Debra Dennett had received $125,000 as an inheritance from her uncle, that this inheritance was used to purchase the land on which the couple's house was built, and that in his proposed separation agreement, Nat Knappen gave the expensive house and land all to himself. Debbie got to keep the BMW. This separation agreement allegedly triggered the domestic battle that sent Dennett to the emergency room on July 25. The testimony of Dr. Matas, who examined her that day, was a key element in her legal defense and full acquittal a year later on charges ranging from criminally negligent homicide to second-degree murder.

In short, money was both a vehicle and a topic in the Dennett trial, part of the machinery and part of the story, as would have been true if this were a divorce case—and in a way it was. No one can exactly measure the effects of money. Access to cash empowered Debra Dennett when she faced trial, but it endangered her too. She could not afford to impress jurors as a *resourceful* woman, otherwise they might conclude that she should have found other, legal ways to avoid this dangerous husband earlier, or that she should have been able to stop him that night without resorting to lethal gunfire. The case developed by her attorney would present Dennett as a trapped woman whose resources did her no good at all. The one moment when she claimed power—when she loaded and fired the shotgun—would therefore be defined as the wild, sad culmination of prolonged helplessness, "learned helplessness."

And this was ironic. In fact, examined closely, the whole case proves to be knitted together with irony, with unexpected, unlikely conclusions that *fit*. To start, Debra, the established victim in the story, turned attacker at the last minute, killing her husband Nat, the more likely attacker, who suddenly tumbled into death and thus became the designated victim; the fact that this victim had been a lawyer, a tough guy accustomed to manipulating a system that would turn now and discard him, trash him, in this, his final trial, tightened the loop. And both these twists in the plot happened against a backdrop so awfully American, displaced and oversized, that the whole picture tends to repel our sympathy and invite us, instead, to shrug when we hear that this bubble house burst and two well-dressed people found themselves wrestling horribly in the slick. From an elevated perspective (the perspective of gods and cynics), violent human shenanigans look more farcical than tragic.

Irony (and sarcasm, irony's rough cousin) tends to distance us from pity. Only the noblest characters can stumble through a series of booby traps set out by the gods and still manage to win our sympathy and grave respect. A *tragic* hero, helplessly entangled, somehow gains the power to rock the landscape. But contemporary criminal trials do not accommodate tragedy very well; they are too corrosive and even too childish. Oedipus, the fugitive whose repeated attempts to elude prophecy ultimately fulfilled every single count of the indictment, would be fresh meat to a smart district attorney. Watching the jury trial of this old king on TV, listening for news about the semen samples, no doubt many of us would notice how the stature of the accused man had been reduced; fewer would realize that we ourselves, the members of the audience, were endangered by a civic spectacle that insulated us from sadness, legitimized drowsy voyeurism and solemnly promised, at last, to be forgettable.

Very few individuals emerge from a modern courtroom fight looking heroic or even presentable. Some of the most painful, demeaning courtroom feuds involve a husband and wife who have both been instructed to testify about their spouse's worst qualities while emphasizing their own best (or most convenient) traits. This sort of half-speak gets called fair because the other team's doing it too. The ethical principle at work here—*HE did it so I can too!*—is so plainly elementary that most children know better than to cite it. Thus, it's not surprising that few defendants or plaintiffs emerge from a courtroom with heightened stature; they have, after all, been advised to grab and gripe like children. They have been advised against reaching for generosity or insight. They've been coached to face the enemy with dirty missiles ready, but not coached to face themselves.

Debra Dennett would testify that she once discovered her husband masturbating as he watched a porno film on TV. Enraged, he turned and threw some toys at her, then chased her into the kitchen. According to a newspaper account, she said he often grabbed her during arguments and called her names—"stupid, ugly, fat, repulsive, a whore, a bitch, lazy, incompetent, a bad mother." They had been married thirteen years. The abuse started early in the marriage, when they were still living in New York City; she remembered the first time Nat struck her, how she had wandered away, dazed, to a movie theatre. In 1980, Debra moved to Ithaca and enrolled in the Cornell vet school. Nat joined her the following year. She said that as early as 1985 she discovered her husband in his law office with his secretary's bare feet resting in his lap, and that in 1987, when she was pregnant with Duncan, he moved out on her after she refused to get an abortion. Though her inheritance money financed purchase of the extensive lakeside property off East Shore Drive, Nat, her husband the lawyer, fixed things so only his name was on the land deed; Dennett might never have discovered that fix if research for the construction loan on their new house hadn't revealed it. And she said that during their worst fight, on July 24, approximately two months before the shooting, he not only threw her downstairs, he also held her upside down from a bed and smashed her head on the floor. When she grabbed for him with her fingernails, "he threw me on the ground and started laughing. He said, 'Now I've got you, you bitch,'" because she had marked him and he could display those marks in court as evidence of abuse.

Thus Nathaniel Knappen, described by his estranged wife, became a monster, a beast pieced together of selected parts. It is not surprising that a ritual so apt to chop up personal narratives would be perfectly capable of chopping up people too. This monster attorney masturbated in the family room and used his knowledge of the law to try and steal land his wife had acquired with money inherited from a beloved uncle. After brutally beating his wife, this same man threatened to drag her to court, drop his trousers, expose some little scratch and have *her* thrown into jail. This reads like unholy caricature. Of course we understand that Dennett needed to offer a strategically unbalanced account of her marriage in order to defend herself against the district attorney's own biased, strategic attack. But what were the ultimate results of this battle? Did it cost Debra Dennett something to offer this testimony as a final public statement about her husband?

It is ironic that our trial system, invented to thresh out and separate heavy loads of self-interested testimony, so often *generates* exaggerated, one-sided testimony, as if to provide more fodder for its choppers. But maybe that's not irony, maybe it's business.

Other defense witnesses also testified, describing Nathaniel Knappen as a vindictive, rigid, quarrelsome, violent man. One of Debra's friends recalled hiding in the house and listening to Nat yell about his son's dirty laundry. A guy who lived next door to the apartment Nat occupied in late summer 1990 with Audrey Vrooman testified that he sometimes heard thuds through the walls. Nat had broken up dinner parties with his tirades.

It is a reasonable human exercise to try and reach fair judgment by suspending two one-sided arguments across from one another to see how they balance, and we expect to do that here before we judge Nat Knappen monstrous, before we conclude that he was, as one juror described him off-handedly after the verdict, "scum." Unfortunately, in litigation that follows up an intimate domestic dispute, the odor of the stuff being measured on the scales can grow so pungent that it becomes obvious why Justice would hold her chains and dishes pinched between her fingertips, an arm's length from her face. Spectators could watch the scales move in the Dennett trial; as defense testimony accumulated, the victim's side descended, bearing its dirty load.

George Dentes, the prosecutor, in an effort to even things out, would finally call in a rebuttal witness, a lawyer named Amanda Cowley, to describe a few of Debra Dennett's worst moments. In other words, the prosecutor tried to balance accounts not so much by providing the court with evidence of Nat's good qualities (that proved to be difficult), but by offering evidence of Debra's bad ones. He would argue, in effect, that Dennett, a provoking, jealous woman, had demons in her too. Cowley flew in from the West Coast to testify that she'd heard Debra in the parking lot outside the Thaler and Thaler law office screaming she'd "kill that bastard," Nat, if he stayed with Audrey. She was also the witness who recalled Debra's threat about taking "dog medication" if Nat ever left her.

We generally trust compromise, and expect to discover the real Nathaniel and Debra by rearranging, recalculating the pieces of information offered by the two opposing attorneys. Unhappily our scales, well-designed to measure gold or bacon, have trouble weighing violence. Courts are always trying to calibrate and measure violence, but it's a slippery, hot compound that may have no weight at all. It can make smart people stupid. It can produce convincing nonsense and trigger dumb, unbelievable responses from highly intelligent women and men. There's a good chance that Debra Dennett had lived inside an actual, intimate nightmare for so long that it made sense to her. Maybe Nat Knappen *was* a monster. Maybe the court, by pulverizing him, discovered him. That would be the darkest irony of all.

Nat Knappen, the lawyer, got processed by the court; dead, he fell into the machinery and went through the buffeting commonly endured by legal clients. This sounds like old-time justice or something out of a Dickens novel, and maybe it's both (Dickens was a vengeful man). In any case, now we will find it very difficult to mourn Knappen, but easy to poke around and analyze what's left of him. Judging from such evidence, he appears to have been compounded of the most villainous elements in our legal system—he was aggressive, vindictive, unsympathetic, a bully without a conscience who played every game to win. It was *very* interesting to watch other legal professionals examine this rogue lawyer closely. Lawyers said Knappen's tactics had dismayed them. No one appeared bemused by a situation that called on professional combatants to challenge a fellow, deceased combatant by inviting him to one last game and then protesting that he had always played too rough.

Two of the lawyers who testified against Knappen on Friday, August 2, the first full day of defense testimony, had spoken with Debra Dennett in late July, only days after she was kicked and pummeled by her husband; she was just beginning her search for an attorney to represent her in divorce proceedings. These men remembered the woman's bruises. They also remembered her reports that Nat had warned her he was invincible in an Ithaca courtroom—he knew how to handle the judges and outsmart his colleagues—so that she could never expect to win a legal dispute. If she even tried to contest his proposed separation agreement, he would plow her case straight into the ground. As these lawyers testified about what Debra told them her husband had said, it was safe to conclude that they spoke truly, since neither one had a personal stake in this trial, but also that they spoke with some feeling—subjectively. The merest scent of revenge was in the air. Even Judge Betty Friedlander looked increasingly stern as she listened to third-hand reports of how the dead man had boasted he could hog-tie any judge in town.

Attorneys sworn in as defense witnesses described Knappen as uncompromising, aggressive. The prosecutor challenged this by asking if it wasn't true that attorneys were supposed to be aggressive; that was part of the job. Lawyers were everywhere in the room. For a while they were filling every position: defense, offense, witness, victim, judge (a former defense attorney). It was a dizzying performance to watch, but things grew clear if one simply concluded that a few of these professionals, each trained to fight hot while appearing cool, secretly disliked one another. And that a fair portion had always disliked Nat. George Dentes, the prosecutor in this case, would say later that Bob Clune, Dennett's defense attorney, had "never liked Nat Knappen. There was an enmity there. They were competitors and Clune did not like Knappen, and the Clune law firm and the Thaler law firm were real competitors, and there was a lot of stuff going on. . . . You really don't need much fictionalization to make a soap opera out of this case."

It would be Bob Clune, consulting with Debra Dennett, who rounded up other local lawyers as witnesses. One of those men, Frank Smithson, testified that he had been visited at his law office by Debra Dennett in late July, 1990. Smithson recalled Debra Dennett's wrists were "puffy, red and raw-looking" when she entered his office. She had brought along the separation proposal drawn up by her husband. Smithson looked it over, then assured this potential client that Knappen "couldn't get what he's saying he can get" as a divorce settlement. He did not think Dennett finally believed him, however; she seemed befuddled and resistant, genuinely terrified of her husband's self-proclaimed powers as a lawyer.

On August 2, L. Richard Stumbar, another Ithaca attorney, also took the stand as a defense witness to testify about the visit he had from Debra Dennett in late July, 1990. He recalled that Dennett was distraught and bruised when she came into his office—"big ugly bruises, very much discolored. Something that isn't received by bumping a piece of furniture." He recalled that one of the first things she said to him was, "Nat hates you, you know." She spoke about her marriage and her husband's increased drinking and hostility. She handed Stumbar the proposed separation agreement her husband had drawn up. It was *not* good, but she obviously feared that Nat could make it stick, because "he told her many times he knew the legal system and knew how to manipulate the legal system," Stumbar said. Nat told her he would get the child and the house: "He told her he always won his cases. . . .

"In the legal community," Stumbar testified, "Mr. Knappen had a reputation for being quarrelsome and vindictive."

Interviewed months later, Richard Stumbar would explain frankly that he had never liked Nat, and that his primary objective as he testified that Friday was to defend and support Debbie: "I was certainly open to her perception of Nat because I had a similar perception and, to be candid, I really didn't like him at all." He found Knappen "sneaky" . . . "mean-spirited" . . . "tremendously arrogant." The two attorneys had faced one another in a few matrimonial cases. Stumbar usually represented the wife and "Nat would accuse the wife of not being a very good person for stupid reasons, reasons that had nothing to do with the case." He remembered one particular civil case that involved a middle-aged couple: Ithaca professional met a younger woman, decided to divorce his wife of many years and marry the younger woman; wife had spent her life raising the kids, so was ill-equipped to support herself . . . the old story. Knappen, who represented the professional, kept "adding a lot of fuel to the fire by telling this guy that if he could prove this or that accusation, he could pay less in support. If he could show that his wife was a bitch, basically, that she nagged him, that she didn't really go out and try to get a job when she could have, it would help their case." Knappen pressed to have Stumbar's client sell her house so the proceeds from that sale could be divided. But Stumbar fought and won that point.

The particulars of this story (husband, lover, wife, house, court) of course sound familiar; Knappen appears to have been defending his own shadow when he hired on to represent the unnamed professional. The moral of this story told by one lawyer about another is also interesting. Richard Stumbar implies Nat Knappen was a dangerous man to be working as an attorney because ritualized antagonism pleased him all too much. The work fit him too well. "Nat was not sensitive at all," Stumbar concluded. "That's not exactly his job, to be sensitive to my client's problems, but it seems to me that he really was insensitive to them. It wasn't just lawyer posturing. He didn't see a life in the other client."

Stumbar had represented a variety of women in difficult divorce cases. Asked if he believed that Debra, who knew enough to shop around for her attorney, was actually as cowed by her husband as she appeared to be, he replied yes: "So many of the matrimonial clients that I deal with, particularly women, have been beaten down psychologically by their husbands, and he had a perfect personality for that." He found it credible that Debra Dennett, this lawyer's wife, might be professionally competent, intelligent *and* incapable of comprehending that her husband's reports of his own legal powers were ridiculously exaggerated. Stumbar understood how frightening a husband, especially a lawyer, could be to a woman facing divorce, and was even willing to imagine that Dennett's dread of her husband prompted her to take the knife and cut her own face immediately after she shot him: "It's somewhat consistent with her feeling that he's a powerful guy and perhaps that power comes from the grave as well. Perhaps it will follow him from the grave."

Nathaniel Knappen, described by Richard Stumbar, emerges looking drawn and even furtive. "I would see him around the side of the office there, you know, dragging on his cigarette. . . . His body language was very tense. Almost kind of an addictive need to have a cigarette. You see it sometimes, how they drag like it's their savior." Stumbar's own workplace, which contains a special room for his daughter to play in after school, is liberally posted with signs requesting that clients not smoke. Stumbar arrived at his office the morning of our interview wearing a purple and green tie and carrying a Minnie Mouse backpack, which he dropped off in his daughter's play room. Married to a politically active college professor, he displays the friendly markings of an Ithaca leftist. When he's interested by a topic—the legal defense of women, for example—he plows his hands through his hair until it stands up, shocked and informal. It is clear that his style would clash with Nat Knappen's; one cannot help wondering how Knappen would have testified if he were called before a jury to describe Stumbar.

Richard Stumbar agreed it was ironic that Knappen, a highly successful lawyer, came up for this last trial and got shredded: "Yeah, he was trashed. There's no question about it."

And he perceived an additional irony; he thought Knappen's ultimate weakness resulted, in part, from earlier, exaggerated shows of strength: "This whole situation, telling her about his power—it contributed. If she weren't so afraid of him and there had been some real ongoing negotiations, whatever, perhaps all of this would not have happened. Obviously that's pure speculation. But in a way he did make too strong a case for himself."

The prosecuting attorney had difficulty countering the defense portrayal of Nathaniel Knappen as a manipulative, bullying attorney who tested out a couple of his favorite strong-arm maneuvers at home, on his wife. Witnesses who showed up in the courtroom to testify for the prosecution seemed to have little feeling for Knappen. Police investigators had photographed his body and it was clear they wanted Dennett convicted, but that was all. One attorney who turned up to act as a character witness was lukewarm in his praises. George Dentes could not find friends of Nat's to offset the witnesses who spoke for Debra. He was surprised to discover, in fact, how little Knappen's own law partners knew of his activities.

"When I first heard about the case," he said, "I wanted to find out about where he was living and they didn't know. A lot of things. They just did not know about his private life. They didn't know about his relationship with Audrey and a lot of them didn't know he had moved out of the house on East Shore Drive. They were in the dark about his private affairs and that's the way Nat kept his private life. And I don't think he had a lot of close friends."

The person who emerged as Knappen's most passionate defender never took the stand. A juror I interviewed did keep expecting to see Georgianna (Polly) Barnes, Nathaniel Knappen's sister, rise and testify during the trial, since members of the jury knew from other witnesses that Barnes had been present in the Knappen/Dennett house immediately following the key incident in the case. Jurors were aware that Polly Barnes arrived with her husband Randy at 1510 East Shore Drive for a visit on July 25, the same day Dennett, accompanied by her friend Bethany Hannon, checked into a local emergency room with terrible bruises and a damaged kidney. This juror had also been made aware that Barnes continued "living with them, Nat and Debra, for the better part of a month, going off and coming back." The juror, then, was mildly surprised that Barnes was never sworn in: "I kept saying to myself, 'Well, surely if she was there for the critical month of July to August, surely one or the other side will call her to give some evidence.'"

After the trial concluded and the juror was free to open newspapers again, she read Polly Barnes's smoking letters to the editor of *The Ithaca Journal* and saw why Barnes would not have been chosen as a safe witness by either attorney. Another cloudy piece of evidence concerned the controversial anti-depressant, Prozac. A prescription bottle of Prozac was found and confiscated by police in Dennett's house immediately after the shooting. Newspaper reports implied the prescription was made out to Debra Dennett; jurors would never know about it, though, because Judge Betty Friedlander ruled the medicine had been seized improperly and so could not be presented as evidence in court. In its reports, *The Ithaca Journal* paraphrased a *New York Times* article which said that lawsuits filed against Prozac's manufacturers contended the drug could cause "side effects such as suicidal tendencies, self-mutilation and homicidal tendencies. . . ."

It is impossible to sort out for certain what forces were at work in 1510 East Shore Drive during July, August and finally September of 1990. Jurors were excused from trying to figure out the entire domestic tale, because legal decisions removed Polly and Prozac from the equation the jury was given to solve.

When the trial ended with acquittal, the whole equation was erased, Dennett legally freed and the files sealed. But the family passions, the family story was *not* concluded by the jury's decision (nor, in fact, were civil disputes relating to the Knappen estate). Polly Barnes continued to defend her brother Nat, proclaiming that he was a gentle man wrongfully murdered, and that his wife was unworthy of being cut by a good kitchen knife. Months after the verdict, Barnes would write the *Journal* again to tell all of Ithaca that Debbie was trying to get her shotgun back from the prosecutor's office. (George Dentes would neither confirm nor deny that report; he suggested I contact Bob Clune, but Clune never returned the call.) The voice of Georgianna Cross Barnes is vehement:

> . . . Thanks to Judge Friedlander for her obvious bias in favor of the defendant. Impartiality be damned, I say. Thanks to the people of Ithaca for being duped so easily. It was inspiring to see lies and slander work so well to manipulate public opinion.
>
> "Thanks also to the defendant, Debra Leigh Dennett, DVM, for her fine performance as the poor abused wife. Her Actors Equity card is in the mail. She certainly accomplished what she set out to do: Murder my brother, ruin the reputation of a fine and gentle man, and hoodwink a town for which she had utter contempt.
>
> Finally, to all the husbands in Ithaca, watch out!
>
> It's obviously open season.
>
> Nice going, everyone. In disgust and horror.
>
> > Georgianna Cross Barnes
> > *The Ithaca Journal*
> > August 15, 1991

Barnes calls her brother a fine, gentle man. It seems only fair
that we should make an effort to believe her. There is evidence
available to highlight the good qualities of Nathaniel Knappen.
His letter to Debra, the letter that accompanied the separation proposal, explains that he had not been happy in a long time. The
prosecutor thought the tone of this important letter was actually
rather civil, tired and sad, and he attempted to get it submitted to
the jury, but the judge didn't allow it. She said "it cast Dennett in a
bad light," according to the prosecutor, who remains irritated with
that judicial decision. There is evidence to show that Nat Knappen
loved his son Duncan; Catherine Arthur testified that he regularly
came home to have lunch with the boy. There is evidence to show,
in fact, that Knappen was himself loved by Debra Dennett; the
letter she wrote him in the summer of 1990 asking for a reconcilia-
tion was passionate. Dennett's own statements show that
Knappen sustained a relationship with Audrey Vrooman that
lasted many years; he was entangled with two women a long time
before he finally asked for a divorce. In short, there is evidence
suggesting that Nathaniel Knappen understood sadness and de-
serves sympathy. There's even evidence to suggest that he was
chained in loneliness and emotional confusions, like his wife, and
that he suffered from his own brand of helplessness.

Still, it is very difficult to reconstruct this victim and *very* difficult to mourn him, because all the voices that surround him sound
wrong and people cannot mourn a stranger unless some convincing voice or picture leads them. But Knappen's wife defended herself by speaking against her husband. Knappen's sister sounds
more ferocious than sad. Knappen's colleagues dismissed him. His
partners, apparently, did not choose to ally themselves in public
with an accused wife-beater. The little eulogies presented at the Bar
Association memorial service soon after Knappen's death sound
pretty flimsy in retrospect; everybody called Nat a "competitor."

Did Nat Knappen's professional and personal loneliness influence the final verdict in a trial called to judge the woman who shot

him? Do jurors subconsciously figure up the value of a man's life by listening for reports that other members of the community felt great loss when he died? One juror thinks yes, such considerations do come into play: " . . . If Knappen had been a revered figure, a loss to the community, to his son, or if not revered, at least hail-fellow-well-met, yes, it might have tipped the discussion." This juror remembered that at one point during deliberations somebody muttered, "It's astounding no one killed him sooner."

A person said to me about this case, "But even if he was a jerk, he deserved to live. It doesn't mean anything if you prove he was a jerk." And "One day she got a friend to show her how to use the gun, the next day she bought the gun and then the next day she shot him. That doesn't sound helpless to me."

Other people I spoke with were skeptical about the Dennett defense. Obviously the Battered Woman Syndrome is sex-based; one cannot imagine a man using it to explain why he raised a gun and shot his wife. Skeptics accuse liberals of being inconsistent when they shift from defending equal rights to arguing that certain women must be given special consideration in the courts because they suffer from a feminine "syndrome" which renders them so helpless, so incapable of making logical, pragmatic decisions about their situation, that they cannot be held fully responsible for their own desperate actions. These same skeptics notice the irony when this relatively new, politically correct defense prompts a Republican district attorney to argue in opposition that no, Debra Dennett was capable, resourceful, and ought to be judged just like a man.

Even jurors can find the territory baffling and irritating. One politically liberal juror, who eventually voted to acquit Dennett, nevertheless sympathized with the prosecuting attorney when he tried to press Dr. Lenore Walker, the expert called as a defense witness to explain the Battered Woman Syndrome, into acknowledging various inconsistencies. This juror, who will be called Nancy, saw how difficult it could be to make legal sense of medical testimony that uses such a wide range of human responses—inertia, helplessness and violence—as symptoms to identify a battered woman. She recalled, "Dentes began to press Dr. Walker. He said, 'Let me get this straight. If a woman does not react, that is predictable because she's afraid. If she *does* react, that is predictable because she's afraid. Where is it, Dr. Walker? Can we judge anything as predictable?' To which she smiled sweetly and said, 'Human beings are not scientific objects, Mr. Dentes.' And this was minutes after she herself had been presenting these clinical charts of hers! That was infuriating."

Nancy interrupted her own critique of Dr. Walker by affirming, "I want to tell you that I am totally sympathetic with her work; I am totally sympathetic with an effort to relax the laws on convictions in cases that involve spouse abuse." Still, she remained skeptical about many of the claims both Dr. Walker and Bob Clune, the defense attorney, made to establish Dennett's helplessness and paranoia in the months before and after the shooting. This juror recognized that Dennett failed to match up with the standard profile of a battered woman in some ways. In a classic situation, a battered woman will endure cycles of abuse repeatedly, passing through phases when tension builds in the house, violence erupts and then loving contrition follows for a time before the tension escalates again. Typically, battered women who finally retaliate after years of abuse, women who wound or kill their husbands because they can imagine no other way to escape the nightmare, don't turn on their abusers during a violent episode, but instead attack when they themselves are in no immediate danger—when a husband is asleep, for instance. This pattern makes these women difficult to defend in court, obviously, and those difficulties prompt efforts like Dr. Walker's.

But, as the juror recognized, Debra Dennett did not appear to have been a person attempting to escape an intolerable, "obsessive, domineering lover." In fact, the juror said, judging from Debra's own undated letter to Nat, which was put into evidence, Dennett "wanted this marriage to continue" and was in distress because "he was indifferent to her and that was what hurt." This juror, Nancy, said she found it odd that a woman who lived in paralyzing fear of a violent husband would write such a sweet letter, saying only "it hurts when you ignore me" and not also "it hurts when you hurt me."

Thus, when Dr. Lenore Walker, a nationally recognized expert on the Battered Woman Syndrome, declared under oath that her own psychological tests of Dennett revealed this patient to be "one of the most abused cases she'd ever seen," Nancy thought that statement an "extraordinary exaggeration." Skepticism sharpened her recollections of this medical witness and certain evidence relating to her. She remembered, for example, hearing that Dennett had read Dr. Walker's own books about the Battered Woman Syndrome before going out to be psychologically tested at the doctor's clinic. When Dr. Walker rose to speak, armed with those test results and a wealth of charts, the juror hoped for objective, medical testimony, but didn't think it was forthcoming. In her opinion, Lenore Walker "absolutely oversold the case. . . . Whenever she was giving a specific example of the generic syndrome, the example always applied to Debbie Dennett."

As a result of all this, Nancy recalled the cross-examination of Dr. Lenore Walker by George Dentes with some satisfaction, as if she would have liked to stand and rap out a few questions herself. "At one point, while cross-examining her, Dentes read from one of her own books in which she said, 'When you're talking to a jury, be persuasive, make eye contact, roll your eyes when the lawyers are over talking in sidebar conversations with the judges to suggest that you together with the jury are just cogs in this system that none of you quite understand.' And Dentes said, 'Have you used any of these techniques in this case?' And she said, 'No, not since some other district attorney read that passage in court.' But I'm telling you, she had used *every* technique. One of the things that bothered me about her was the amount of eye contact she was making with the jurors! . . .

"Dr. Walker, she's been on every talk show but, she told us, *Geraldo*. She will not do *Geraldo*."

This juror noticed, of course, that Bob Clune worked at all times to reinforce the medical expert's portrait of Dennett as a helpless, muddled victim: "One of the things that bothered me about the case and bothered me about Clune a lot was that he painted Debra as a hopeless, helpless wreck from the beginning of the trial and claimed she had been no help to him whatever."

And then there was Debbie herself.

Describing her own chronological responses to the trial, Nancy recalled that she did not think the case against Debra Dennett had been proven "beyond a reasonable doubt" after the prosecution rested on Thursday, August 1. She mulled over the issues for a long time in a hot bath that evening—this was her cure for the aches that resulted after hours sitting motionless in a juror's chair. The string of defense witnesses who began testifying the very next morning, on Friday, generally reassured her. The two emergency room doctors, the lawyers, and Bethany Hannon, Dennett's best friend, were all credible, forceful speakers, many of whom testified that they had been convinced Debra Dennett was terrified of her violent husband, Nat, in the late summer of 1990. It was no act.

"And then Debbie took the stand"—on Tuesday, August 6, after a weekend recess. This juror recalled, "And not the morning of her testimony, but in the afternoon, I began to get uncomfortable."

Robert Clune spent the first part of that day asking his client questions about the early years of her marriage with Knappen. Then, "as he brought her up toward the two days in July and then September 28, she broke down. But she broke down," the juror said, "in ways that I didn't believe after a year of living with the events, so that I felt that I was seeing a performance. . . . It was too much, it was too much. The trembling and the shaking. At some point, Clune approached her and said, 'It will be almost over,' and she said, 'It won't get any better.' She was in tears, and I found her increasingly, as the day went on, less authentic. I was disturbed.

And then the last thing she said that day was that, as she emerged from the closet and saw him—you know, she's breaking down as she's saying this, but she said it was the most awful thing she'd ever seen—and then, 'What did you do then, Debbie?' Clune asked. And she replied, 'I felt no one would believe me. I didn't know that I had been hurt so badly, that I had been badly cut, *and so I cut myself.*' And that was the end of that testimony."

It was a shock, this abrupt little confession followed by nothing, no questions, no protests, only proper courtroom silence. The direct examination of Debra Dennett was over. The plainest description of her actions just prior to and after the shooting did not look good: September 26, she went out with a friend to learn how to use a shotgun; September 27, she purchased a shotgun at Woolworth's; September 28, she shot her husband with the gun, then cut herself cruelly and told police her husband had done it. Nancy recalls, "And I went home. . . . I went home feeling suddenly immensely uncomfortable."

The following day did nothing to reassure her. During the cross-examination, she found Debra Dennett "ridiculously cagey." When the defendant tried to sidestep relatively minor questions posed by the prosecutor, claiming that she couldn't remember if she'd ever spanked her child and that she couldn't remember the route she had taken back from New York City on the night when she surprised Nat and Audrey Vrooman in their Ithaca apartment by arriving at the door unexpectedly to pick up Duncan, the juror was put out. Dennett's "incredible carefulness" during the cross-exam contrasted too oddly with her distraught performance of the day before. Nancy essentially approved of the way George Dentes handled the "cross," controlling his litany to highlight this new Debbie. She was interested to see that the prosecutor strategically *avoided* questioning the defendant about her unsettling confession of the day before. And she noticed when Dennett's attorney stepped in at the last minute to put things right again:

"Dentes, in cross-examining Debbie, took her up to the 28th of

September and did not say a thing about it, for two reasons, I think. One was that testimony had ended the day before with her saying, 'And I cut myself,' nothing more specific. That was extremely useful testimony for him, with no clarification. Two, he didn't want to push her into the mode she'd been at the end of the day before, because she had been cagey all day in response to him. He didn't want to get her crying and seem to have badgered her into that state. But at this point, Clune got up and said he wanted to redirect, and he took her immediately to the 28th, and Dentes said, 'I object. You can't redirect on what I haven't crossed on,' and Friedlander overrode that. I think Dentes was *accurate*. But what Clune did was said, 'You cut yourself, where did you cut yourself?' 'On my arm and my face.' So it was clarified; she still asserted Nat had made the cuts on her back, but as she said the words, she became a basket case again."

Nancy did not care to be conned. She listened to three of the most important players in this trial—the chief medical expert for the defense, the defense attorney and the defendant herself—with skepticism, and found the prosecutor's challenges to them intellectually pleasing. She thought that the judge herself "bent over backwards" for the defense. It was not difficult for Nancy to imagine Dennett was in fact less passive, less wretchedly helpless, than she was portrayed by her attorney in court. In fact, this juror thinks it possible that Dennett bought her shotgun half-knowing, half-dreaming, she might one day turn the eye of it to face Nat:

"She'd had break-ins since living at the house alone. Bethany Hannon testified to that. But I do think they were done by Nat, and I think she probably thought they were done by Nat Knappen, so that the idea she was buying the gun to protect herself against a possible intruder becomes a little less strong. But she doesn't know, perhaps, how dangerous her husband is. She may be purchasing a gun to dissuade him. But do I think, as she is learning to shoot this gun the day before she actually uses it, do I think that it passes through her mind that she might shoot Nat Knappen? In an imaginative scenario, yes. Because I believe that feelings run so high when a relationship breaks up. I have a friend who got divorced and saw her husband within the next six months jogging along the road, and she said it was all she could do to keep the car in the lane. So I think it's almost inevitable this occurred to Debbie. . . . I didn't say that to the jury. *But* do I think she absolutely bought the gun with the intention to set this all up to kill him? That's what I don't know and that's what can't be proved."

Nancy ultimately voted to acquit Debra Dennett not because she trusted the woman absolutely, but because she concluded that the prosecutor had not proved beyond a reasonable doubt that Dennett did not pull the trigger in a moment when she was terrified for her own life.

This glinting, narrow strand of argument drawn from the phrase "reasonable doubt" was sufficient to save Debra Dennett. It ought to be. One suspects, however, that this lifeline might have snapped if empathy (and disgust with Knappen) hadn't already floated Dennett in towards shore. District attorneys despair when they are asked to prove guilt "beyond a reasonable doubt" in a case where only one interested witness survives. George Dentes protested: "If the truth be known, if a person's smart enough about it and he or she knows how to kill someone privately, you can almost always come up with the right version of facts to get yourself off. All you've got to do is, you shoot someone and you make sure the person's got a weapon, and then you don't say anything when the police come, you don't answer questions, and then you get to trial and for the first time you tell a story which the prosecution cannot rebut because it all relies on just what happened between you two."

Discussing this particular case at last brought Dentes up out of the chair in his office and set him pacing between his computer and the file cabinets, between the New York State flag and the U.S. flag, trying to figure how this particular battle could have been lost: "It is extremely hard to disprove things in a private context.

That is why the physical evidence was so important. *That* was why we harped so much on the fact that she had to have knifed herself. Frankly, when she admitted that she had cut herself and when I thought she was clearly lying in the peripheral things in her testimony, I really thought that she was going to be convicted of something. I always knew that there was a strong tug-at-the-heartstrings there, and obviously she was emotional and there weren't a lot of people who had a hell of a lot of nice things to say about Nat and he was a hard-driving guy and I knew him in private practice, he was an aggressive lawyer. There were a lot of people who didn't like him. But you know that's not a capital offense. And I would have just loved to have been a fly on the wall in the jury room to find out how they could have ignored it!"

But of course jurors didn't ignore it. They discussed whether the fight in the kitchen could have broken out within minutes after Nat arrived at the house, and a few men who'd witnessed barroom scuffles reported that fights like that turned on a dime. They measured out the phantom closet in the jury room. They discussed whether or not Debra's T-shirt could have kept in the blood, and whether her blood vessels were constricted in terror, which reduced the bleeding. At one point two *male* jurors said it was immaterial to them whether or not Dennett inflicted all the wounds on herself. And when one juror murmured, "I just think she was scared to death," a hum of assent went up around the table.

The lesser charges—manslaughter 2 and criminally negligent homicide—required jurors to decide whether Dennett acted "reasonably" when she loaded the shotgun and pulled the trigger. "Would a reasonable person operate in this way in these circumstances, and was the risk unjustified?" Nancy explained. In short, the jury needed to decide whether this defendant, who had been portrayed by defense witnesses as unreasonably terrified of her husband, then acted in a *reasonable* panic when she loaded and fired the gun to stop her husband.

They decided yes. They believed Knappen came upstairs to attack his wife with the knife and that Dennett's story was, essentially, true. They did not concern themselves with irony, paradox or oxymorons like "reasonable panic." They gave Debra Dennett leave to fire.

■ ■ ■

Men and women who have participated in a trial do not shake hands when it is over. The judge removes herself. The jurors each drive home. After scrambling with reporters, the prosecutor climbs back upstairs to mourn or celebrate with his staff, and the defense attorney heads to his office. The defendant steps out of the courthouse directly into a free, wide world or into the fenced back seat of the sheriff's car. That's it. There is good sense in the practice— one cannot imagine a line of jurors shuffling up to grasp the hand of a convicted woman without a shudder—and there's loneliness in it too and pride, and maybe a touch of shame. New juries will be selected tomorrow, and these same lawyers will appear beside other clients. A partially new set of chessmen will place themselves in order on the board.

Only later, after one has been out of the courtroom for a while, do certain hushed oddities in this game become clear. A jury trial is a talky ritual strictly divided by high silences. Thus, the prosecutor who had Nancy in the corner of his eye for days, who spoke *at* her for days, wishes he could know what she thought of his performance and how in the world she and her fellows hidden back in the jury room ever decided to acquit this particular woman who shot her husband in the head. George Dentes did not hear this juror's voice again once she had passed through the *voir dire* and was selected as one of twelve. And he will probably never hear it. His own office policy forbids him to phone jurors after the verdict's in: "We do not call jurors after verdicts of not-guilty. . . . You can't help having an edge in your voice and that makes them feel defensive, so we just don't do it. If they call me, I'm happy to talk to them."

These high silences in the courtroom are necessary. They keep order, quell chaos and protect citizens who have been drafted to make decisions about men and women accused of violent acts. They are haunting, too, however, because they do seem to imitate, in structure and height, the silences that isolate men and women trapped in a private, awful place. Private violence must be exposed and judged by the community. We should notice, however, that our courtrooms are really *not* communal. The game that gets played in a courtroom is shifty, rigid, frequently awkward, quarrelsome, regularly hypocritical and truly lonesome, because it has evolved to accommodate combat while disallowing touch.

I expected that the chief difficulty in understanding this trial would come when I tried to imagine myself living in a certain place: the home of a battered woman. The private landscape an abused woman comes to know is both narrow and limitless. It hobbles her because she feels partially responsible for constructing it and for colluding in all efforts to keep it secret from outsiders. The rooms where a female lives with her dangerous partner are foreign, illusory and everyday: even women who escape these rooms and look back at them with loathing can remember that many days they were able to make things look all right. This place was never home. And it was never outside of home.

Unfortunately, the problems involved in penetrating to the heart of the Debra Dennett trial only just begin here, with imaginative sympathy. Let us say that we do sympathize with Dennett for her own sake and because she stands as a representative of other abused women. Then we will be glad that she managed to *prove* her case to the courts by using documents, witnesses, a plane trip to Denver and Dr. Walker's charts, by using every single friendly resource available to her. We will cheer (as many people did when the jury announced that they had found Dennett not guilty) to learn that the horrible territory this woman, and other women, have been forced to inhabit is now at least partially exposed, partially conquered. We will stand and overlook the battlefield with satisfaction.

Unfortunately, the light dims here and the boundaries of this field waver. We recall that other, less wealthy women have tried to convince Ithaca juries that they too were helpless, desperate, pressed by circumstance, lost in a territory that ruined their judgment. Certainly, it's not hard to imagine that Shirley Kinge was half-paralyzed or disoriented by living in a household with her frightening son, or that Christine Lane was befuddled by the loneliness and economic hardships facing a single mother on welfare; in fact, from a certain perspective, the terrors and financial uncertainties that these two women faced look to be much more severe than those faced by Debra Dennett.

This challenge requires that we think in terms of imaginative, psychological space. But courts require a good number of solid markers before they will allow testimony about imaginative, psychological space, so we look for solid markers, for evidence that will distinguish Dennett, who was judged not guilty, from Kinge and Lane, who were convicted. And we find one very good one; we remember that Dennett was able to show proof of physical abuse with documents. Dr. Tove Matas, the emergency room physician called to witness in her defense, submitted his laboratory records, his labeled photographs, and told the jury firmly that in late July, 1990, he had recommended this patient use ice and elevation for her bruises *and* that she contact the police to report that she had been battered. This evidence, more than any other, tipped the trial towards acquittal. One juror even said, "I told myself before going to bed the night we were sequestered in the Ramada . . . thank God for the well-documented abuse attack back in July—thank God for that."

Neither Kinge nor Lane had papers to match Dennett's. They had no legal proof that they had ever been abused. When their attorneys attempted to establish that these women had been disoriented by stressful family situations, judges and juries were not particularly impressed; courts must set limits.

They must draw the line somewhere. But there seem to be so many lines painted onto this field, or fields. Clearly Kinge and

Lane were more socially isolated than Debra Dennett and much less likely to connect with a network of articulate professionals who would help them in the event that they ever had to appear in court. We have been told that isolation is a key factor in defining abuse. We recall Shirley Kinge and Christine Lane, their physical appearance in the courtroom. Stiff, unhappily familiar with the deputized guards, these two women almost never cried. It is possible they felt no grief; it is possible, too, that they found it necessary to resist hysterics in such alien company. Their friends, dressed in unpredictable ways, showed up poorly as witnesses. When the guilty verdicts were announced, only the defendants' mothers and their lawyers protested with much conviction.

Debra Dennett, on the other hand, broke down and lost control repeatedly; her lawyer would emphasize the fact that Debra had been of no help to him whatever as he tried to prepare for trial because she was so completely devastated by the events. This attorney succeeded in convincing the jury that his client was rendered helpless by the paranoia and isolation that result from prolonged domestic abuse. Yet Dennett appeared surrounded by capable allies. When her attorney snapped at the bailiff who had attempted to keep her friends behind the gate, the bailiff surrendered sheepishly. When Dennett's best friend, Bethany Hannon, testified as a defense witness on Friday, August 2, she impressed one juror as a "solid gold" witness: "You sort of figured the ethical center of the world might well rest on her story. . . . She was so clear, so intelligent, so smart and fair in her interpretation." And when Dennett's many other allies continued to show up in the courtroom, they worried the district attorney, who suspects even now that their presence influenced the verdict: "Of course she had a very large following, and as the jurors go into the wee hours of the night and are called back into the courtroom to reread testimony and this and that, they see who's watching."

In short, we are asking which of these three women was most abused, most helpless, most isolated. Now, this sort of comparison makes sympathetic people understandably impatient because it implies that Dennett was somehow guilty when she used all her social and financial resources to defend herself against the district attorney. After all, Debra Dennett was not literally competing with Kinge and Lane; her acquittal did not *cost* them. She might well be seen as their ally, in fact, if her trial strengthens precedents which help other abused women defend themselves in court.

But would Shirley Kinge and Christine Lane or their attorneys consider Debra Dennett to be an ally? The legal defense of Dennett as a representative abused woman invites us to analyze territories, many of which happen to be battlefields. Dennett's defense attorney asked jurors to think about the contemporary, national battleground where a secret army of violent men regularly face off against women—he called in a medical expert to chart how the cruel game is played there—but he did not speak much about the equally large field where the rich regularly gallop over the poor.

It is misleading to press too hard on these three cases. They do not prove that poor women are always convicted and rich women always acquitted; the sample is too ridiculously small. Three deliberate groups of citizens judged these cases and concluded that Shirley Kinge and Christine Lane were telling lies while Debra Dennett was essentially telling the truth. They chose verdicts accordingly and those verdicts finished the criminal trials of three local women who were all mothers to children, all Tompkins County residents, all citizens free of any prior criminal convictions, and all suspects arrested inside the space of a single year.

It is a narrow, local sampling. It doesn't tell us much about our national landscape, national battlegrounds. Yet there are certain things we can learn by investigating the stories of even this small group of contemporary jury trials and the trails that radiate from them. We can *see* hierarchy in the courtroom. We see how during a trial passionate speech gets fragmented and controlled by intermediaries, and how terrible objects, like a dead man's shoes, cool down when they are displayed next to pieces of broken crockery.

We can see how it is that both professionals and laymen who par-
ticipate in trials are reassured that they have taken part in a system
that's imperfect, yes, but also honorable and workable, and how
participants are made to understand that the burdensome responsibilities involved in sending a person to jail have been so well-
divided and distributed that they won't hurt anybody. They won't
haunt anybody. We can see how trials actually imitate both the
quarrels and the impassable silences that so often make litigation
necessary. And we can ask whether or not these antagonistic courtroom games, which are designed so beautifully to work revenge
and distribute property, can really be expected to help still American violence.

I had thought it would be relatively easy to figure out this last
trial because, from a distance, it looked so small. After the Harris
murders, many members of the community were terrified and efforts to track down the murderer involved hundreds of law enforcement officials. After the disappearance of Aliza Bush, crowds
of men and women volunteered to help search for the child. But it
wasn't necessary to go out looking for a perpetrator or a victim
after the September 28 shooting of Nat Knappen by Debra Dennett; both perpetrator and victim, along with one knife, one gun
and one child, were waiting in the house when the police arrived.
They were easily found, together alone.

And yet the truth about what happened to Dennett and
Knappen in private won't be found, and this is the last thing we
can see by watching even three defendants face their juries. Shirley
Kinge's memories are not accessible. Christine Lane's memories are
not accessible. Even Debra Dennett, who was judged a truth-teller,
has not made her thoughts accessible. We can never know for certain which of our conclusions about these women have been correct. We can never *see* what happened at the Harris house in that
late December, in Lane's apartment in early February, or in the
Knappen house seven months later. Though we must assign investigators to ferret out the facts and arrange for tribunals to decide

guilt, we can't undo the events themselves. We can't reach them. We can't run backwards in time and stop them. That is tragedy.

So many people tried following the trails left by these three women. Some turned lasers on doors, looking for fingerprints; others crawled through thickets of snow, others followed spilled blood drop by drop. Others heard days of testimony and then re-treated to discuss and weigh that testimony. Listening to these many people speak, it becomes clear that a good portion of them weren't only figuring their way through assigned legal equations in order to decide guilt or innocence, but were also trying to understand how violence arrives. They weren't only playing the *Clue* game, ready to close up the box after the solution was named, but they also hoped to reach through the game and catch the thing that makes victims. Catch it. Look at it. Tell it to stop.

Because it feels so close to home. The threat feels too close to home. This has always been true. Tragedy requires family.

Our own ineffective attempts to reach back into the past will not profit the victims of these particular events nor will they help the three accused women. But they may save us. They may make us truly citizens.

epilogue

THE TRIAL OF Shirley Kinge was undoubt-
edly one of the most complex and lengthy ever to take place in
Tompkins County. Now, thanks to the confessions of Investigator
David Harding, it has been emptied of its weight, its meaning, and
it's difficult to recall how we ever believed in it. But it did have
weight and meaning. It put a woman in prison. The questions it
raised were serious, and the crime it tried to examine was so violent that rational explanations could never reach all the way
around the events. Then, the fingerprints were real. Reinforced by
the testimony of professionals and experts they worked. They
held.

And, obviously, they weren't real. They were trick cards. David
Harding was playing the game to win. People in the courtroom
could see that Harding was a slick, determined player, but that
seemed only fair; he was up against a determined attorney. Even
now, it is difficult to feel sincerely outraged by him because no
policeman on the witness stand is himself. Harding was expected
to perform. He did. We watched.

In November 1992, Tompkins County dropped all charges against Shirley Kinge: she was completely cleared of arson and armed burglary. Confronted with felony forgery raps in two nearby counties, she bargained her crimes down to misdemeanors by agreeing to plead guilty to charges that she used the Ithaca victims' credit cards, the day after their deaths, to purchase $600 worth of merchandise in stores to the north. She was sentenced to pay the stores restitution, with no additional jail time. Although she conceded that her son had eventually told her he was the murderer, she insisted that she knew nothing of this when she took the VISA card to go shopping. She claimed to believe that her son had bought the gold cards off some guy in downtown Ithaca.

One district attorney prosecuting her forgery case said he would not have agreed to the relatively gentle, plea-bargained sentence if he hadn't received a separate, personal plea from the relatives of the Harrises, who asked that the matter be concluded as swiftly as possible. Don Lake Jr., Dolores Harris's brother, told the newspapers, "We were happy not to have to go through two more trials. We can kind of put it behind the closet door now and lock it."

Kinge's defense lawyer, William Sullivan, announced that his client would be suing the New York State Police for millions of dollars.

■ ■ ■

Also in the fall of 1992, a spokesman for the New York State Police announced that Senior Investigator Robert Lishansky, an eleven-year veteran, was suspended from the force. Lishansky testified at length as a prosecution witness in the case against Shirley Kinge, and corroborated Harding's statements about the damning fingerprints on the gas can. He also testified in the Debra Dennett case, and spoke with me at length about that case for this book. On November 23, 1992, Robert Lishansky was indicted for perjury, tampering with evidence, official misconduct and obstructing governmental administration.

I liked Robert Lishansky. When he talked about holding a dead man's hand, he spoke straight. But as I finish this book, we wait on the news, expecting to hear more of him.

In the November of these newest revelations, more than three hundred musicians crowded onto a stage at Ithaca College to per- form Verdi's *Requiem*, the mass for the dead. They trumpeted songs of wrath and supplication.

Judex ergo cum sedebit
Quidquid latet apparebit:
Nil inultum remanebit.

Tremens factus sum ergo, et
timeo, dum discussio venerit
atque ventura ira, quando
coeli movendi sunt et terra.

Libera me
lux perpetua luceat eis.

And therefore when the Judge shall sit,
whatsoever is hidden shall be manifest;
and naught shall remain unavenged.

I am seized with trembling, and
I fear the moment when the trial comes,
and the coming wrath, when
the heavens shall be moved, and the earth.

Deliver me
let perpetual light shine upon them.

Judgment: it fascinates me, it escapes me. Illumination: the word makes me thirsty. How handsome the phrase "perpetual light" sounds to residents of a cloudy neighborhood. *Lux perpetua.* Shine on the children, please.

But even handsomer than a vision of universal justice and per- fect revelation is the vision of a single cruel act erased, withheld, before it happens.

chronology

DECEMBER 22, 1989 — In the night, the four members of the Harris family are murdered in their Ellis Hollow home. Gasoline is poured on the bodies and various furnishings and the house is set on fire.

DECEMBER 23, 1989 — The alarm system in the Harris house goes off about dawn, bringing police and fire fighters who discover the bodies and extinguish the fire. Later that same day, Michael Kinge and his mother, Shirley Kinge, use the victims' credit cards to go shopping.

JANUARY 1990 — Forensic investigation in the Harris case is ongoing. State police investigators focus on the Kinges.

JANUARY 29-31, 1990 — Investigator David Harding, posing as "David Savage," meets Shirley Kinge at the Peregrine House and later at a Friendly's restaurant. In both places, he obtains objects she has touched.

FEBRUARY 2, 1990 — Christine Lane reports to the Tompkins County sheriff's office that her child, Aliza Bush, is missing. A widespread search for the child begins.

FEBRUARY 5, 1990 — Christine Lane and Aliza's father, Greg Bush, each take and pass a polygraph test. The search for Aliza is called off in the evening.

FEBRUARY 7, 1990 — Michael Kinge dies in a police raid on 520B Etna Road. Arrested in the adjoining apartment, Shirley Kinge is interrogated and later incarcerated in Tompkins County jail.

— Christine Lane reports that she received one of Aliza's mittens in the mail from an anonymous source.

FEBRUARY 10, 1990 — Law enforcement agents videotape Christine Lane's re-enactment of her own movements the morning of February 2.

FEBRUARY 15, 1990 — After failing a second polygraph test, Christine Lane confesses that she hid her child's body and leads investigators to the gravesite. She is arrested and incarcerated in the Tompkins County jail.

MARCH 1, 1990 — Funeral services are held for Aliza Bush.

JULY 24–25, 1990 — Following a severe beating by her husband, attorney Nathaniel Knappen, Debra Dennett visits the emergency room of Tompkins Community Hospital to seek treatment for extensive bruises and a damaged kidney.

— Polly Barnes, Knappen's sister, arrives with her husband for a visit at the Dennett/Knappen home.

AUGUST 3, 1990 — Shirley Kinge's trial begins.

SEPTEMBER 27, 1990 — Debra Dennett purchases a shotgun at Woolworth's.

SEPTEMBER 28, 1990 — Debra Dennett shoots and kills Nathaniel Knappen. Following a hospital visit for emergency plastic surgery on knife cuts to her face, arms and back, she is indicted and released on her own recognizance.

OCTOBER 1, 1990 — Judge William Barrett calls a recess in the Shirley Kinge trial so attorneys can attend a memorial service for their colleague, Nathaniel Knappen.

OCTOBER 16, 1990 — Christine Lane's trial begins.

OCTOBER 30, 1990 — Christine Lane takes the stand in her own defense.

NOVEMBER 7, 1990 — Jury in Lane case is sequestered. Deliberations begin.

NOVEMBER 8, 1990 — Christine Lane is convicted of second-degree manslaughter, obstructing governmental administration and falsely reporting an incident.

NOVEMBER 15, 1990 — Jury in Kinge case is sequestered. Deliberations begin.

NOVEMBER 16, 1990 — Shirley Kinge is convicted of burglary in the first degree, arson in the third degree, forgery, criminal possession of stolen property and hindering prosecution.

JANUARY 16, 1991 — Christine Lane is sentenced to 5–10 years in state prison.

JANUARY 30, 1991 — Shirley Kinge is sentenced to 15–30 years in state prison.

JULY 29, 1991 — Debra Dennett's trial begins.

AUGUST 6, 1991 — Debra Dennett takes the stand in her own defense.

AUGUST 13, 1991 — Debra Dennett is acquitted on all counts.

SEPTEMBER 11, 1992 — Shirley Kinge is released from prison on reduced bail, following news that State Police Investigator David Harding had tampered with evidence in a separate case.

NOVEMBER 4, 1992 — David Harding confesses he concocted the fingerprint evidence that convicted Shirley Kinge; he signs plea agreement.

NOVEMBER 9, 1992 — Shirley Kinge is cleared of all charges in Tompkins County.

NOVEMBER 23, 1992 — State Police Investigator Robert Lishansky is indicted for perjury, tampering with physical evidence, official misconduct and obstructing governmental administration.

DECEMBER 16, 1992 — Investigator David Harding is sentenced to 4–12 years in state prison.

index

about the
author

DEBORAH HOMSHER teaches English literature at Ithaca College in Ithaca, New York. She graduated magna cum laude, with honors, from Brown University and received an MFA in fiction writing from the Writer's Workshop at the University of Iowa. Homsher was a Wallace Stegner Fellow in fiction at Stanford University. She has won a number of writing awards, including a 1990 Fellowship in Nonfiction Literature from the New York Foundation for the Arts which allowed her to work on this book. She is married, with two children. Her short stories have appeared in *Ms.* and *Chicago Magazine. From Blood to Verdict: Three Women on Trial* is her first book.